CONFESSIONS OF A GAY PRIEST

CONFESSIONS OF A GAY PRIEST

A Memoir of Sex, Love, Abuse, and Scandal in the Catholic Seminary

TOM RASTRELLI

UNIVERSITY OF IOWA PRESS
IOWA CITY

University of Iowa Press, Iowa City 52242

www.uipress.uiowa.edu
Printed in the United States of America
Design by April Leidig

ISBN 978-1-60938-709-9 (pbk)
ISBN 978-1-60938-710-5 (ebk)

Printed on acid-free paper

Cataloging-in-Publication data is on file with the Library of Congress.

The names of many individuals and places in this work have been changed. A few individual characters are composites of multiple people.

For my nieces and nephews

CONTENTS

PART III

St. Mary, Mother of God, Patron Saint of Crusaders, Needle and Pin Makers, and Virgins, 1998–2002

PART IV

St. Jude, the Apostle, Patron Saint of Lost Causes, 2002–3

PART V

Resurrection, 2003–4

PART VI

Beautiful Child, 2019

CONFESSIONS OF A GAY PRIEST

PROLOGUE

A procession of one hundred men adorned in ankle-length white albs snaked through the rectory's rooms of antique furniture. Priests, deacons, and acolytes bantered about vacation plans and sexual abuse headlines. The stale scent of dry cleaning permeated the air. A few priests gave me thumbs-up. Others nodded solemnly. Just behind me at the end of the line, the archbishop stood. His mitre—an upside-down fang-shaped hat that climbed to a point fifteen inches above his forehead—lent him imposing height. His knuckles were wrapped around his crozier—a six-and-a-half-foot golden staff topped with a nautilus-shell swirl—the symbol of his office as shepherd of the people. In ancient times, shepherds used their staffs to protect wayward sheep by compassionately breaking their legs. In the coming two-and-a-half-hour ceremony, this shepherd would ordain me a priest.

I excused myself to the bathroom and looked in the mirror. The man staring back seemed a stranger: silvery blue eyes behind rimless, oval frames, cropped brown hair gelled into a side part, angular cheeks, and dimpled chin. A few church ladies claimed that I looked like Christopher Reeve. Father Clark Kent. Reverend Superman. No pressure.

"You can do this," I said to myself. "God come to my assistance, and Lord make haste to help me," I recited the opening line of the Liturgy of the Hours—the prayer that priests promise to pray multiple times a day. I put on a smile and straightened my diagonal deacon's stole, which ran from shoulder to hip. I looked like a newly crowned beauty queen.

An explosion rocked the building. The lights and air conditioning died. I rushed to the window, worried about my family and friends gathered in the cathedral. Over its roof, purple smoke swirled before treetops into cobalt sky.

I hurried back to my place in line with my two classmates.

"What exploded?" I said.

"I thought it was your irritable bowel syndrome," the younger one said.

"Hey," the older one said, "you won't joke about that when you're my age."

He was in his thirties. I was twenty-eight. We were about to become three of the youngest priests in Iowa.

The master of ceremonies announced that a squirrel met its demise at the intersection of a power wire and the cathedral's junction box. A priest with a rusty stain around his neckline said, "That's what happens to those who bridge the gap between heaven and earth." His stole hung in parallel lines like a choirboy's. He snapped his dentures. "Prepare to be zapped, boys."

No humans were injured. A severed power line had lashed a car, stripping it like Christ's back. The ordination would continue but without electricity. We quipped about God's portentous sense of humor.

As I followed the procession through the rectory's front door, the mid-June humidity engulfed me like a fever-drenched blanket. From the top of the stoop, I looked eastward over the oldest neighborhood in Dubuque. Beyond the rooftops, the brown waters of the Mississippi flowed south toward my hometown, my history. *That was then. This is now*, I thought. I followed the white-robed procession toward the towering cathedral named after St. Raphael, whose name means "God's remedy."

The building's red brick nave supported a bleached-white façade. A stained-glass lancet window rose into a single square steeple, topped with four marble trefoil crosses. Facing east, west, north and south, the crosses reminded me of the mission I shared with the men walking with me: take God's healing love to the world.

Seminarian-acolytes added incense to their dangling golden thuribles. A sweet spiciness replaced the burnt rubber and ozone scent of the electrical explosion. The master of ceremonies trotted past, shouting last-second orders: "Open your worship aids." "Maintain your spacing." "Don't rush the procession." I stepped into the cathedral. The pipe organ's sound crashed against my chest. I strode down the stained-glass-lit aisle, flanked by my classmates. The remains of the squirrel still smoldered in the parking lot.

An hour later, I knelt at the foot of the altar with my hands folded and eyes closed. My kneecaps ground into the thin carpeting. An endless succession of priests filed past, pressing their hands on my bowed head.

As they compressed my vertebrae, spasms shot down my spine and legs. I willed myself not to collapse. Sung Latin phrases echoed through the packed cathedral. My back twinged. No one had warned me that the rite was agonizing.

After the pressing stopped, I opened my eyes. One hundred priests with folded hands stood before the braided spires of the sanctuary screen. Some smiled. Others had the constipated gaze of piety. Under my sweaty alb, I shifted from knee to knee, trying to relieve my burning thighs without drawing attention. I closed my eyes and listened to the archbishop's frantic vibrato intoning the Prayer of Consecration. In this moment, the Holy Spirit would transform me into something new.

The Church needed something new. In January, the *Boston Globe* had exposed Cardinal Bernard Francis Law for covering up the sexual abuse of minors by priests. As the months before my ordination passed, a mounting number of bishops fell in shame. I doubted my calling. But the Church was different in Dubuque. My archbishop hadn't harbored pedophiles. He'd turned them over to the police. He'd offered their victims support and healing. I would do the same.

After the archbishop completed the prayer, a priest lifted the deacon's stole from my shoulder and replaced it with a priest's stole. Over my head, he lowered a chasuble with gold-and-blue embroidery matching the archbishop's. I crossed from the center of the sanctuary to the cathedra, the ornately carved oak throne where the archbishop sat. I knelt before him. From a crystal pitcher, he poured syrupy chrism—holy oil scented with balsam—over my upturned hands. Pressing his palms against mine, the archbishop smeared large crosses as he prayed: "The Father anointed Our Lord Jesus Christ through the power of the Holy Spirit. May Jesus preserve you to sanctify the Christian people and to offer sacrifice to God." He folded his glistening hands around mine. His dark eyes were absolution. I would sacrifice myself for him, for God.

Hands dripping with chrism, I stood, turned, and walked to my spot at the foot of the altar. I glanced at the front row into my parents' eyes. They were crying, grinning. I smiled through tears. I was a priest.

Less than two years later, I turned my back on the archbishop. This time, I held my tears. I rushed from his office into February's darkness. The frigid night air burned my cheeks. In the corner of the icy parking lot, my black pickup offered refuge. My only private space, it was where I retreated to sing, talk on my phone, and cry—all the things a young priest didn't want his pastor or cleaning lady to witness. I drove through blocks of Catholic neighborhoods, people who trusted the archbishop. Now, I had to obey his command by covering up sexual abuse.

Skirting the line of bluffs that edged the river flats, I approached the cathedral. I recalled the squirrel electrocuted minutes before my ordination. Who had buried it or mourned its passing? Illuminated by spotlights, the cathedral's façade sprouted from the night, an omnipresent watchman in the darkness. I passed like a blowing cinder.

On the north end of town, a boat ramp would provide easy access to the frozen Mississippi. My plan: drive until the ice buckled under the weight of the truck.

PART I

ST. STEPHEN, THE FIRST CHRISTIAN MARTYR

Patron Saint of
Stonemasons
1994–96

As they were stoning Stephen,
he called out, "Lord Jesus, receive my
spirit." Then he fell to his knees and
cried out in a loud voice, "Lord, do
not hold this sin against them"; and
when he said this, he fell asleep.
—Acts of the Apostles 7:59–60

AUDITION

Stuck between my parents, I knelt in a pew with my two sisters and brother. I hadn't been to Mass since transferring to the University of Northern Iowa in the fall. On an earlier campus visit, Mom and I had walked by the red brick building without realizing it was a Catholic church. It looked like a cross between a bank and a Pizza Hut. Now, students packed the nave. Some were dressed up. Others wore the usual college grunge. I stared at the neck of the guy in front of me, trying not to nick his collar with my folded hands. My parents made the sign of the cross and sat back into the pew. I crossed myself to appear as if I'd been praying and followed suit.

They were in town for Theatre UNI's spring run of Shaw's *Saint Joan*. I had the role of Brother Martin Ladvenu, Joan of Arc's Franciscan confessor. He had the honor of holding the cross before her eyes as her own Church incinerated her. Hoping to be the next Al Pacino, I'd followed my director's instructions for "method acting." He'd shown me a clip from the documentary *Faces of Death*, in which a Vietnam War protestor burned himself to death. I'd scoured the library for accounts of Joan's trial and execution. The only thing I hadn't done was interview a priest about his life. No need. Everything I'd researched convinced me priests were hypocrites.

A young woman smiled from the wooden lectern that matched the pew's wheat stain. "Welcome to St. Stephen the Witness Catholic Student Center. No matter where you're from, we're glad you're here." My dad nudged me. Below black wavy hair, brown eyes, and silver glasses resting on his self-proclaimed "Italian schnoz," he offered a satisfied grin. I smiled back. Whatever.

"Please rise and welcome one another, especially anyone who is new," the woman said. I shrunk into the rigid pew. Someone was bound to reveal I was new.

My parents knew I was frustrated with the Church. For years, our discussions about religion had ended with Dad's irritated surrender and Mom's silence. They didn't know I'd quit Catholicism. I'd tried the Lutheran, Methodist, and fundamentalist Christian churches. God was the same patriarchal bastard everywhere.

Dad tapped my shoulder. I stood and hunched to offer him a partial hug and tap on the back. He kissed me on the cheek. Italians. Now everyone would think we were gay.

"I love you," he said.

I didn't believe him. Throughout my childhood, he'd worked sixteen-hour days at our family's Italian restaurant. "The business" and the "good family name" came first. Now, he had his newfound sales career. He loved work, not me. I turned to Mom, but he grasped my shoulders. He forced me to meet his gaze. "I mean it, Tommy. I love you."

"I love you too," I lied.

The priest preached forever. I made use of the wasted time by silently running through my lines. At Communion, I did as Dad had taught: I stepped out of the pew into the aisle and extended my open palm, letting Mom and my sisters go first. I took the host by hand but skipped the flu-magnet chalice. After singing every verse of not one but two songs during Communion, the congregation sat waiting for the mustached priest to stand. I checked my watch. We were seventy-two minutes into the Mass. At home, the entire liturgy took forty-five minutes. But we weren't done. The priest stood and meandered about the aisles rattling off upcoming events at the student center. When he mentioned the choir, Mom, who was an elementary school music teacher, smiled at me. Interested parties were to sign up in the lobby on something the priest called "the ugly orange piece of furniture." Everyone laughed. I felt like I'd been transported into *The Bells of St. Mary's*.

My dad whispered, "He seems cool."

I wanted to say, *I'm sure the little boys he's screwing think so*. I nodded.

"Have you met him?" Mom added. I kept nodding.

I'd seen the priest once. My art history professor had taken my class into the newly erected St. Stephen's to view its "prize-winning minimalist design," lack of stained glass, and icons. I'd never seen icons in a church. At home, we had faded statues that shed paint chips the size of Communion wafers. Minutes into our visit, the short priest with glasses, puffy salt-and-pepper hair, and a mustache, had huffed across the chapel. "You need to go," he said to my professor. "Our daily Mass is in twenty-five minutes."

Throughout the announcements, the congregation and my parents laughed at the priest's jokes. After ten minutes, he concluded by introducing a visiting choir director. They'd met in the early seventies while studying music at Mount Saint Clare College in my hometown, Clinton, Iowa. Mom majored in music there in the late sixties. I'd gone to preschool there. Mom's cousin, a Franciscan nun, had lived there. Nuns, priests, and parishioners had frequented our house. My parents would want to meet the priest and his friend. They'd invite them to lunch. I wanted to choke myself to death on a missalette.

After the crowds dispersed, my parents cornered the priest in the back of the chapel and introduced themselves.

"Rastrelli?" his nasal baritone proclaimed. "I loved Rastrelli's Restaurant." He jabbed my arm, "You've been holding out on me, son."

I smiled through my guilt as they combed through shared acquaintances. Then it hit him: in 1974, a young Rastrelli mother with flowing blonde hair and a little girl had roamed the college showing off a newborn boy. He had held me in his arms.

His brown eyes scanned me. I silently pleaded, *Don't say, Where have you been all year?*

He could have humiliated me, but he didn't. He let my parents believe what they wanted: Father Scott Bell and I were buddies.

AN ACTOR PREPARES

From a futon across the smoky dorm room, some theatre and music majors cackled. They were drunk or high. I didn't know the difference. Outside of sipping Dad's traditional Chianti at family dinners, I'd had maybe ten drinks my entire life. I'd never been buzzed. I was frightened of what I'd do, what others might discover.

Jonathan swigged Boone's Farm while holding court from his ratty armchair. The others shared cigarettes and bottles as he outed the music majors he'd blown. I sipped Cherry Coke and watched the news, trying to appear uninterested.

On the TV, a boy with a Muppet-like voice spoke. "He's adorable," I said.

"Who knew?" Jonathan said. "Tom's a pedophile."

A pain like nothing I'd felt before shot through my gut. "Shut the fuck up," I yelled.

Jonathan jumped up. Booze splashed from his bottle. He had four inches and eighty pounds on me. He released a smoky laugh, "Whatever, pedophile." The others laughed.

I shoved him into a dresser and ran into the hallway. He pursued me shouting, "Pedophile." I slid into my room and bolted the door. He pounded on the wood.

"Shut up," I howled at the door.

"I fucking hate you, pedophile," he yelled and left.

The pain in my gut spread. My chest tightened, as if breathing might make my heart explode. I gasped for air and curled up on the cold linoleum.

The violence exploding from me made no sense. I needed my best friend and roommate Tobey. He'd understand. But he was on a drive with

Jonathan's boyfriend, Kent. I knew what happened on drives with Tobey. Blow jobs. Just like the ones he'd been giving me for the past two years.

Tobey and I played Sega in the basement of my house. Lying in our sleeping bags on maraschino red carpet, we chatted and took turns with the game. In two weeks, I'd leave for my first year of college; Tobey would remain for one more year of high school. With a short pudgy frame, he was my physical opposite. He had the face of a little boy and the tongue of an old letch. We'd conversed about everything from eternal life to what finger we used to wipe our asses. Of all my friends, I feared leaving him most.

He tossed his controller aside and ran his fingers through his feathered black hair, "Why do Catholics believe Mary's hymen didn't break during Jesus's birth?"

"We don't believe that."

"You do." His brown eyes flashed in the TV's light. "I read it in my dad's books."

He was a "PK," pastor's kid. His family belonged to the Evangelical Lutheran Church in America, the largest and most progressive Lutheran denomination, unlike the conservative Missouri and Wisconsin synods stippled across Iowa. Until Tobey, I'd thought all Lutherans were diet-Catholics.

Masked by the air conditioner's growl, our theological discussion deepened and then morphed into talk of sex. Tobey adjusted the bulge in his sleeping bag. I adjusted mine, making sure he noticed. Our voices quieted. "I think mine's small." "I bet it isn't." "I'll show you mine, if you show me yours." "How do you jack off?" "Let me show you." "That feels good." "Have you ever fanaticized about, you know, blow jobs?" "I'll do it if you do it."

We flipped his Swiss Army knife to determine who'd go down first. The side with the cross-encrusted shield on it he designated as heads; the blank side, tails. The knife landed tails mere feet from where I'd touched my first penis, during kindergarten.

His name had been Jimmy. A girl at school had asked me to play "Under the Covers," but I'd refused. A week later, I led Jimmy into the basement and played with him. My older sister, Jenny, caught us and tattled. Mom sat me down on the harvest green couch in the living room and explained that it was okay *only* for the doctor to touch me "down there." Mom didn't seem angry, but I heard something new in her soft voice: flatness, like disappointment or shame.

Tobey smelled of secondhand smoke, fabric softener, and a sweaty blanket. He tasted of salt and freedom. I didn't think or hesitate. He fit in my mouth perfectly. It was the most natural thing I'd done. Until he came, triggering my gag reflex. I barfed into an empty Big Gulp cup. He tried to weasel out of reciprocating. I begged. He gave in. Pleasure and bliss eradicated my lifelong shame. As I was about to cum, he pulled away, leaving me to finish myself. I wiped off with some tissues and retreated to the bathroom to flush the evidence. When I returned, the basement was dark. I felt my way into my sleeping bag.

"We can't do that again," he said.

"I know."

My parents had taught me to save myself for marriage. Dad told me to pray every night for a good wife. Staring into the darkness, I made the sign of the cross.

Lying on the floor of my dorm room, I couldn't move. I'd transferred to Northern Iowa to be with Tobey. We'd been blowing each other, but there'd been no kissing. He claimed to be straight. I'd waited, trusting that his bodily response proclaimed the unspoken, real presence of love in his heart, but the argument with Jonathan had exposed my illusions.

Tobey was screwing Jonathan's boyfriend. He'd probably given me AIDS. I lay there on our dusty floor, in the very spot where Tobey had topped me. When I'd tried to enter him, he'd spazzed out. He didn't want me inside of him. I was infected. Queer. Faggot. Sinner.

I pounded the linoleum. Why had God made me like this? Did God even care? God didn't defend my family after my parents withdrew us from the Catholic school because the male teacher had harassed my sister. The parish shunned us and old schoolmates threw rocks through our windows. When Alzheimer's was deleting Grandma Rastrelli's memories and she called the house, sobbing because she'd found another copy of Grandpa's twenty-five-year-old obituary, God didn't comfort her. I did. God didn't answer my family's prayers during the farm crisis that drained the restaurant of business. Dad declared bankruptcy a week before I graduated high school. God wasn't there when Dad's siblings parted ways. The family that prayed together didn't stay together.

Dad would cut me off if he knew about Tobey. Mom would mutely follow. I deserved it. I'd thought the boy on the news was cute. Was I destined to abuse children? According to the televangelists, that's what gay men did. My family couldn't know me. Tobey did, and he didn't love me. I was a transfer student from a community college that was a glorified high school with ashtrays. I couldn't even get a leading role at the University of Fucking Northern Iowa. I'd never make it on Broadway.

I searched the room. Everything reeked of Tobey: the movie posters we loved, the couch where we sucked, and his jar of Vaseline on the dresser. I dug through my toiletries. Tylenol? Too weak. I needed something serious. How many slices would a disposable razor take? I'd never contemplated suicide. It felt strangely exhilarating, powerful.

But I hated blood. And pain. As a kid, I feared shots. I hated that doctor, his oily mustache, rubber gloves, and nurse, who wiggled the needle.

What about the theatre? I could dive from the catwalk onto the main stage. But it was locked. Even in suicide, I was a failure.

I curled up on the floor again. Hours passed. I stared at the baseboards. Tobey didn't return.

In the milk crates under the TV, I noticed my *Aladdin* and *Beauty and the Beast* videotapes. I'd watched them with my little sister and brother, Maria and Jeff. What would committing suicide teach them? That it was okay to give up, to be a failure? But I was a failure at being Catholic, at being straight. Still, they loved me. Could God? I hadn't prayed in a year. I wanted to believe that Jeff's and Maria's love was real. I wanted to believe that God's love was constant. My lips opened in the only prayer I could muster.

"Help."

As the sun rose, I pulled my exhausted twenty-year-old body into my loft bed, my head at the foot of Tobey's mattress, and fell asleep.

Tobey returned late afternoon. I sat on the couch studying for finals.

"I had a breakdown last night," I said. "I needed you. But I guess Kent did more."

His boyish features contorted in scorn, "Jesus. I don't care." The door slammed behind him.

The semester's final days passed. He returned to the room to change clothes and pack. He didn't need me to suck his supposedly straight cock anymore. I convinced myself the pain in my gut meant nothing. I focused on my finals and got straight As.

ACTING IS BELIEVING

A week before the fall semester, I moved into my new apartment and rehearsed for auditions. My junior year: it was my time to shine, my chance to break into the upper echelon of the casting pool. My baritone range matched the leads in Sondheim's *Assassins*, while my looks were ideal for Chekov's young lover in *Wild Honey*. I was cast in the chorus and got a bit part in the play.

Tobey landed a large role in the musical. I'd seen him once over the summer. I'd given him a blow job. He'd given me crabs. He and my other friends hung out with the A-listers. I wandered dazed through my first week of fourteen-hour days—classes, work-study duties in the scene shop, and rehearsals. I'd loved the unrelenting rush of theatre life, but now it had lost its intoxicating bliss.

Each morning, when I opened my bedroom curtains, St. Stephen's loomed through the trees of the two backyards separating our lots. Over the summer in Clinton, I'd continued to pray, hoping to understand my breakdown. I'd gone to Mass with Mom and led the singing while she accompanied. I'd started reading the Bible, beginning with Revelation. Fundamentalist Christians were confident about these apocalyptic texts and the Catholic Church's being the Whore of Babylon. I wanted to be ready when Campus Crusade for Christ ambushed me in the quad with "Are you saved?"

My parents and I had discussed my questions about the Church. I'd always enjoyed the Church's music and social outreach, but its teachings about women and sex frustrated me. The Inquisition and Crusades, killing in God's name, angered me. This time, when my parents couldn't answer my challenging questions, I made a decision. If I were going to quit the Church, I needed to consult Catholics with religious degrees first. Then, if I left, no one could blame youthful ignorance.

Father Scott and the St. Stephen's staff were the obvious choice, but I hadn't been to Mass since the weekend of *Saint Joan*. I worried he'd smell the sin on me.

I walked down the alley and entered St. Stephen's through the back door. Mass had already started, so I didn't have to face Father Scott. During Communion, I avoided his line. A downpour pounded on the roof, as I joined the premature exodus of other "marginal" Catholics. I wasn't ready for the inevitable queries and implied judgments of the "real" Catholics who remained until Mass ended. Who are you? Why did you quit the Church? You're a theatre major? I fled through the back door. The muddy alley sucked my shoes. I was sick of being stuck.

The following weekend, I arrived at Mass on time. The front doors opened automatically. A greeter extended a handshake. Another distributed hymnals. A small waterfall cascaded into a waist-high font that looked like a holy hot tub. Its flowing waters promised blessing and cleanliness. The chapel's stark brick walls called my gaze upward. Rafters of caramel wood angled into a barrel vault of clear windows that summoned the sky. Earth-toned flowers accented the simple wooden altar and chairs. The pews smelled of lemon oil. Unlike those in my hometown, the padded kneelers were soft. The lector rose from the front pew, bowed to the altar, ascended the sanctuary's three stairs to the ambo, and welcomed all. Those nearby offered handshakes and warm words, as if I'd been joining them for years. Accompanied by piano and clarinet, cantors beckoned everyone to sing. And everyone did. Nothing between the peeling plaster walls of my childhood churches had prepared me for such liturgical bliss.

After the readings, Father Scott lifted the Scriptures and said, "The Gospel of the Lord." As he bowed to kiss the book, I responded with the others, "Praise to you, Lord Jesus Christ," and sat.

Bible in hand, Father stepped into the center aisle and preached on Mark 7:31–37, "The Healing of the Deaf Mute." His green vestments undulated as he ambled about the congregation. I listened from a pew off to the side near the three tall windows that framed the college campus.

"Through dusty streets, a crowd dragged a deaf mute to Jesus. They begged, 'Heal him, Lord.' Jesus recognized the fear and shame in the beleaguered man's face. Back in those days, people believed physical deformities were a punishment for sinfulness."

I thought of my attractions, what I'd done with Tobey.

Father strutted toward my side of the chapel. The sunlight flashed through his tuft of salt-and-pepper hair.

"Despite the man's resistance, Jesus pulled him into an alley. He put his fingers in the man's ears. He removed them and spit in his palm and touched the man's tongue. At this point, the deaf mute must have been thinking: Is this Jesus dude nuts?"

Everyone giggled. After holding for the laugh, Father extended his hand over the nearest person. "Jesus groaned and shouted *Ephphatha!* which means 'Be opened!' The healed man and the crowd proclaimed, 'He makes the deaf hear and the mute speak.'" Father opened his arms and heralded, "He still is today!"

I had never witnessed such joy and passion in a priest. He'd delivered a monologue more potent than any play.

"Be compassionate," he said. "Just as Jesus cured the deaf man out of compassion, he calls each of us to live lives of radical compassion."

I understood. The second of four children, I was the family's peacemaker. Growing up, I'd worried about Mom coming home from teaching to work the "second shift," while Dad remained at the restaurant. From age ten, I made sure she got seven hugs a day. As a teen, I tried to understand what other people needed so I could please them. I tried to walk in their shoes. As an actor, I brought characters to life by unmasking their motivations, fears, and dreams until I found a piece of myself in them. That was compassion. In my frustration with God, the theatre, and Tobey, had I buried my instinct to care for others?

"Be vulnerable," Father said.

I fidgeted in the pew. I didn't understand. I didn't want to. I'd begged for an increase in business at the restaurant, the healing of Grandma's Alzheimer's, and to like girls. I'd told God exactly what I needed. When my prayers went unanswered, I quit believing. But now, Father Scott claimed God wasn't a "cosmic vending machine" that gave us whatever we want. Being vulnerable wasn't about what I wanted but about listening for what God wants. I'd become so angry that I didn't know how to listen to God. But I knew how to act. The essence of acting was being vulnerable. In my professor's shorthand, it was saying "fuck it" to fear, resistance, and baggage. To have a genuine reaction onstage, I had to emotionally strip myself, listen, and be present to the other actors. This was called "surrendering to the moment." Was it the same with God?

From center aisle, Father said, "And finally, *Ephphatha*. That is: be open."

I closed my eyes and summoned the blame and wrath, all the shame, hurt, and fear I'd hoarded for years. My lungs emptied. I prayed: *Okay, God, here's your chance. Here I am. This is all of screwed up me. Come in. Tell me what you want me to do.*

When I inhaled, it felt as if I'd pried apart my sternum and peeled back my rib cage. Warmth flooded my chest. I'd never experienced anything like it: pure joy and peace without judgment. I wasn't alone. God was with me in my struggles. God loved me and had a plan for me, just as he did for the deaf mute. A thought bubbled into my consciousness: *Holy fuck. God wants me to be a priest.*

After Mass, I waited in the lobby for Father Scott. I scanned the signup sheets on "the ugly orange piece of furniture," which was a credenza the color of carrot baby food. The pianist introduced himself. He was a seminarian on an internship to learn about parish life under Father Scott. It seemed like a sign.

"Tom Rastrelli of Clinton," Father shouted from the chapel's doorway. He looked me up and down, "From the looks of it, you didn't break a leg in *Saint Joan*." I couldn't believe he remembered my name. His mustache rose over a smile. His handshake was strong. A silver band with etched words encircled his left ring finger. I didn't know priests wore wedding rings. I wondered what the inscription read.

"Do you have a minute?" I asked.

I explained my desire to talk to educated Catholics.

"It sounds like you need something more," he said, and suggested weekly spiritual direction sessions in which he'd help me navigate my relationship with God. He was a night owl, so my theatre schedule wasn't a problem. Anytime until he locked the church at midnight worked. We scheduled my first appointment.

"I feel like a hypocrite," I said from the black rocking chair at the edge of Father Scott's desk. It had taken me three meetings to admit this. In our previous sessions, I'd vented about my frustrations with the theatre, not feeling welcome in my home parish, and my anger with God. He'd probed with questions, but now he was mute.

He picked at his black cuffs. Joyful faces filled the numerous picture frames on his desk and cabinets. Potted ivy and African violets accented the windowsills. Scented candles smelled musky, masculine. Volumes of books about Catholic teachings packed his floor-to-ceiling bookshelves.

"I don't believe everything the Church teaches," I said.

"Who does?" His thick fingers tapped his desk. His nails were gnawed halfway to the cuticles. "The path to faith is through doubt, not denial."

I'd come to believe that skepticism was the opposite of faith, which was supposed to be blind. "But I have so many questions."

"Thank God. It's your Christian responsibility to ask hard questions. Use your noggin." He knocked on his head and made a hollow clicking with his tongue until I laughed. "See, don't be so serious. And, when those theatre folks give you a hard time, tell them to sit and spin."

He twirled in his chair. My concern faded.

"The greatest saints struggled to believe," he said. "The struggle opens us to God."

I recalled the deaf mute's fear and the rush of feeling I'd experienced during that homily. Fear had kept me from understanding my faith. From growing. I squeezed the arms of the chair. "I think God's calling me to be a priest."

Behind his round glasses, his brown eyes softened. He clenched his lips and nodded. "I suspected as much." I couldn't tell whether he was happy.

I recounted my *Ephphatha* moment. He acknowledged my feelings but told me not to rush. "We want to be sure that we're right about this." He said I needed to attend his vocational discernment group for men. I needed to keep a spiritual journal of my experiences, thoughts, and actions. Everything. I needed to take it all to prayer. I needed to contemplate whether it was God's will or my pride compelling me to be a priest. But I wasn't to worry. I was young. I had time. He scheduled my next late night appointment, gave me a hug, and sent me on my way.

I tore at the edges of my paper napkin. "My life is changing," I said to my parents and siblings during a post-Mass breakfast at Village Inn. They were in town for my performance in *Assassins*. "Theatre isn't number one anymore. I'm quitting *Wild Honey* to focus on church." I looked up. They leaned forward as if they already knew. "I think God's calling me to be a priest."

They didn't move. I'd hoped they'd be excited and proud, but Father Scott warned me not to expect anything. Celibacy and obedience were "countercultural" and "misunderstood," even by Catholics. Some Catholic parents didn't want their sons to be priests. They wanted them to have financial success or grandchildren.

Mom spoke first. "Tommy, I've had a feeling about this for months." Over the summer, she'd observed "something different" about me at Mass. Dad couldn't speak. He, Jenny, and Maria cried joyfully. My fourteen-year-old brother, Jeff, nodded and said, "That's kinda cool."

"It's not a hundred percent. I mean, there's a lot to consider, to discern," I tried to sound mature as Father advised. I didn't want to overinflate their expectations, but in my heart, I was sure. The rush of applause during curtain call paled in comparison to God's grace.

That night before curtain, I went through my usual routine. I applied my makeup, warmed up my voice, and put on my costume. The director congratulated the cast and wished us well on our last show. As the others embraced, I slipped out to the loading dock. I gazed at the October stars, white specks in a sky as black as the Iowa soil. The grainy scent of harvest whisked across my face. For the first time in my acting career, I made a precurtain sign of the cross and offered my final performance to God.

FREEING THE NATURAL VOICE

As autumn passed, everything rained priesthood. The world outside St. Stephen's blurred in the periphery. Instead of reading plays, belting Broadway scores, and rehearsing, I devoured the New Testament, sang hymns, and attended daily church events. I told my faith-sharing group that it felt like I was climbing higher and higher on the endless first hill of a roller coaster. Each day, I could see more of what had been just beyond the horizon. The view revealed how everything in God's world fit into place. I was going to be a priest.

There was one small problem.

Not that I ever used the word "gay" to describe myself. I couldn't even admit I was . . . homosexual. Those words described faraway effeminate men dying of AIDS in San Francisco or nearby married men blowing dudes in backroom booths at Danish Book World. Those labels were as foreign to me as Baptist or Buddhist. Sure, I had attractions to males, but my life was more complicated than the stereotype. Gay culture was dangerous. Priesthood would save me from that fate. But to start down that path, I needed confession.

The last time I'd gone was my freshman year of high school as preparation for confirmation, the sacrament with which, at fifteen, I took responsibility for my faith as an adult by confirming my baptismal promises. The symbol of this transformative commitment was taking the name of a saint. I chose St. Stephen, the first Christian martyr, because he got stoned.

As a kid, I had a book of saints. In one picture, rocks pelted Stephen. Moments before his death, stoned Stephen lifted a bloody rock to heaven as crimson dripped before his yearning eyes. I'd wanted to possess his aching desire for God.

To do so, I had to "Let go and let God." That's what the students who were leading Antioch, St. Stephen's Halloween weekend spiritual retreat, said. As we loaded our cars, they joked, "We'll scare the bejesus out of you." I laughed, hoping they couldn't see my fear, for Father Scott had told me confession was on the agenda.

After caravanning through black fields lined with sheared cornstalks, we arrived at an abandoned rural Catholic school and proceeded through the schedule at breakneck speed: prayers, meals, student talks, small group discussions, meditations, and late night conversations with little sleep. In their talks, students struggled to reconcile tragedy, anger, and loss within the contradictions of Catholicism. They asked probing questions and admitted doubt. They shared how they found peace in their faith.

During the discussions, I spun my tale: angry with God after Grandma's death and Dad's bankruptcy, I'd sold my soul to the theatre. That self-centered lifestyle led me toward suicide, but God was there in my despair. God led me to St. Stephen's, *Ephphatha*, and the priesthood. As the others listened, I realized I was formulating my Antioch talk and auditioning for coleader of the spring retreat.

Then Father gave his talk, expounding Catholic teachings on sin and the need for a priest-confessor—a Jesus proxy. It wasn't enough to confess alone to God. Our sins had damaged the entire community. We sinners needed a priest to embody the forgiveness of not only Jesus but the entire Church. I'd always thought confessing to a priest was lame. Priests were sinners, even hypocrites, but on the retreat, Father and the students were transparent. I longed to be free like them.

He led us into a darkened school gym. On the basketball court, a half-dozen votive candles spouted pools of light. Priests in white albs and purple stoles floated from the shadows into the brightness and sat in folding chairs. Under the aural camouflage of a mixtape of contemporary hymns, students stepped forward and slid into the empty seats that accompanied each confessor and named their sins.

My eyes monitored the flickering halo at half court, where Father Scott sat. Each time his chair emptied, I struggled to move. What would I say? At my last confession, I'd voiced menial sins: fighting with my siblings, swearing, not praying enough. I'd omitted how I fantasized about *G.I. Joe* characters, how I watched my male teachers' crotches, and how I learned to masturbate.

Nine months before my preconfirmation confession, in the summer of 1988, I'd finished eighth grade and worried about going to high school. Unlike the majority of boys in my class, I was still a seventy-five-pound weakling with rubber band biceps and hairless genitals. When it came to sex, I knew very little.

My dad attempted the sex talk, once, when I was in fifth or sixth grade, while we were on our way home from working at one of the family's satellite restaurants in Davenport. Going to work with him on school breaks and weekends was our one-on-one bonding time.

Dad shifted in the driver's seat. He clicked his silver wedding ring on the steering wheel. He was proud of his callused palms, thickened by rolling pins, sewer snakes, and scalding dishwater, whatever it took to run a restaurant. I knew this because he'd mentioned the soft handshakes of other boys that he'd received during the sign of peace. I slid my delicate palms under my thighs.

Without pulling over, he turned to me. "Tommy," he crinkled his black mustache and cleared his throat, "do you have any questions about sex?"

Not wanting him to drive into a ditch, I responded, "I learned all about it on TV."

He turned back to the road. Ten minutes later, we were home.

It's not that my parents didn't talk about sex. They took us kids to Chicago's Museum of Science and Industry to see a display of miscarried fetuses in formaldehyde, the miracle of God's forming a baby in the womb. They called sex God's holiest gift, to be shared only after marriage. They read us *Where Did I Come From?* This children's book provided a cartoon explanation of sex: a naked husband hugged his wife, lying on her, until something in his penis that felt like a sneeze sent a school of sperm equipped with eyes and smiles to fertilize her circular, lifeless egg.

At age fourteen, I understood sex to be a mysterious, God-given penile sneeze.

Then, after a day at the neighborhood pool, I experienced my first sneeze at home in the shower. As I washed myself, my penis grew hard. I'd had painful boners like this for months. They usually throbbed, but this time it itched. I rubbed it, and it exploded with a caramel-like substance that periodically dripped from my penis over the next few days. Frightened, I didn't tell my parents.

My ears felt infected from swimming, so I asked to see the pediatrician.

Alone. "I'm not a kid anymore." Mom dropped me off and went to run errands. Dr. Lauz was Catholic, often attended the same Mass as my family, did medical trips to his native Philippines to help homeless orphans, and wore too much musk. When I was ten and in the hospital, he'd saved my life after a strep infection invaded my kidneys. He would know what to do about the stains in my underwear.

I confessed something was wrong with my penis. He asked to see it and the spot on my underwear, which he called "the discharge." As I laid down and lowered my underwear, the examination bed's paper sheet crinkled. Dr. Lauz's dark eyes, magnified by thick glasses, blinked above his mustache. He inspected my scrotum and my penile shaft. His beige fingers squeezed gently, what he called "milking the urethra." My penis hardened. He asked whether it hurt when it got like that. I responded affirmatively. His hard-soled, shiny black shoes clapped against the linoleum as he stepped to a drawer. He returned wearing a rubber glove on his right hand and began stroking my penis with a jelly-like substance. An intense pressure filled my groin. Within seconds, it squirted more of the caramel-like fluid. He walked to the flip-top garbage can, disposed of the rubber glove, washed his hands in the sink, sat on his rolling stool, wrote a prescription for my ear infection, told me to schedule a recheck in two weeks, and exited the room. I lay there worrying about what the medical test he'd performed on my penis had revealed, hoping that he'd explain at the checkup.

He didn't explain, but he did ask to check "down there" to be sure everything was "OK," just as he did in a dozen or so office visits throughout the next year. The routine was always the same: check throat, ears, chest, and penis. Checkup after checkup, he failed to cure my recurrent ear infections that he said were related to sore throats. We didn't want an untreated strep infection landing me in the hospital again, so my parents thought nothing of the frequent visits. "That's why we have medical insurance," they said.

When I got sick, my older sister dropped me off at the doctor's office after school. Mom taught at a nearby school and picked me up on her way home. The doctor had me to himself. He asked me questions about my parents, my ears, my roles in school plays, my throat, my male friends, my breathing, my brother and boy cousins, and my penis.

"You have a nice one," he once said, but he'd also told me that I had nice tonsils and a nice heartbeat.

One time, he ordered me to stand naked in the middle of the examination room for a scoliosis check. He reached around and performed the usual penile test. Sometimes when I was lying on the examination bed and he was testing my penis, he placed his other hand over my palm and his thumb against my wrist, as if he were taking my pulse, only he would squeeze it as my penis exploded. I wondered if this was the test. What did it mean if I squeezed back?

One evening, I looked up his home phone number. I wanted to call, to ask what was wrong with my penis. I wanted to know what the test meant. Was it supposed to feel so good? Instead, I locked myself in the bathroom and performed my own test, using Vaseline, but it seemed like rubber cement compared to the gel he used, which evaporated.

Toward the end of my freshman year, Mom took me to an ear specialist who said I didn't have chronic infections. The monthly tightening of my braces was responsible for my ear pain. He didn't check my penis.

That summer, I sat on the examination table, inhaling the rubbing alcohol scent of the room. The sound of Dr. Lauz's heels clicking on the linoleum grew louder. He entered, closed the door, and greeted me with thickly accented questions. He checked my throat, ears, glands, breathing, and penis. He got the rubber glove and jelly stuff, performed his test, but then something changed. Rather than writing a prescription, he pulled the elastic of my underwear over the pool of wetness on my abdomen, tapped the bed for me to sit up, and moved his face so close to mine that his mustache prickled the end of my nose. His warm breath curled over my lips. He stared into my eyes as if he were checking for something. After a few seconds, he hugged me, resting his chin on my shoulder. I left confused. He'd never hugged me before. But what was a hug? My family, friends, and even some of my teachers hugged me.

Later in the summer, I got sick again. Mom dropped me off at the doctor's office and left to run errands. Dr. Lauz took me through the usual routine until the checking of my penis. While I was still sitting, feet dangling over the edge of the examination bed, he unzipped my shorts and tucked my underwear under my balls. He stroked my erection with his hand, without using the jelly and rubber glove. My skin buzzed with the touch of his skin.

"Do you like it?" He stroked me harder, faster. "Do you like it?"

He'd never asked me if I liked getting my ears or throat checked. I couldn't tell him the truth. I said nothing. He raised his nonstroking hand, grabbed the back of my head, and pulled it toward his face. His mustache needled my upper lip as he shoved his tongue through my lips, past my braces.

I couldn't move. His bumpy tongue twisted around my mouth. His bleached, musky scent suffocated me. His hand stroked my penis, testing it, but doctors didn't kiss boys. Perverts, sexual abusers, did.

The doctor was abusing the boy on the examination table. But that boy couldn't be, wasn't me. I was Tom Rastrelli, son of a restaurateur, straight-A student, class treasurer, thespian extraordinaire, and president of the foreign language club. I wasn't the pitiful nerd getting his first kiss from a pediatrician. I hated that boy. He had to disappear.

Voices echoed from the hallway: the nurse and the boy's mom. The tongue slid out of the boy. The doctor recoiled to his wheeled stool and the boy's chart. The boy zipped up his shorts. The door opened. His mother entered. The doctor handed her a prescription and left. The boy followed the mother out and went about his day.

A few weeks later, the boy told his parents that he was too old to see a pediatrician and asked to see a general practitioner, his friend's dad, instead. They agreed. He focused on school and building a resume of activities and accolades for college applications. He never returned to the trauma of that first kiss. Not until the summer of 1994. He was twenty and waiting tables at the Clinton Country Club, pouring waters double-fisted as wedding guests arrived, when he smelled a familiar musk. He glanced up over the water goblets. Two feet away, the doctor's dark eyes leered. While his body stood in the dining room, the young man's mind was back in the examination room, with the mustache, the jelly, the tongue.

The boy—no—*I* had been sexually abused.

I rushed from the dining room through the kitchen, out the back door, and collapsed against the building. I couldn't breathe. I couldn't stop shaking. The doctor had sexually molested me and no matter how hard I'd tried to believe that it hadn't affected me, it had. And it still did. I'd sinned with the doctor and needed help.

Four months later, I sat before Father Scott in the darkened gym and confessed my sins: I let Dr. Lauz kiss and stroke me. I was attracted to men. I masturbated to fantasies of men. I'd exchanged blow jobs with Tobey and let him have anal sex with me. I was going to hell.

Father took my palms and squeezed them. He assured me of God's love, forgave my sins, hugged me, and sent me off to do penance. To make up for my sexual sins with the doctor and Tobey, I was to make a list of good things about myself. Instead, I wandered through the shadowed gym, climbed onto the stage, and curled up behind the stage curtain. The boy who hadn't cried when the doctor's tongue invaded his mouth, the boy who never felt the sadness of losing his innocence, sobbed.

GENESIS

"You need therapy," Father Scott said during spiritual direction. "No buts."

I crossed the street and entered Student Mental Health, where I was assigned to a grad student.

Counselor Number One had cropped hair and wore pantsuits. She had a poster of crudely drawn circular faces labeled with the emotions they exhibited. After asking her help to "deal with the abuse," I spent a couple sessions explaining the evil theatre and salvific St. Stephen's. Her eyes narrowed whenever I mentioned my calling.

"Let's set aside the priesthood for now," she said, with the compassion of a wire hanger. "Is it possible that you're denying the anger you had—and still have—toward the Church?"

"But I love the Church," I said.

She urged me to "own" my anger at the priest pedophiles exposed by the press in the late 80s. She said my priestly calling was self-created, a way to avoid the shame surrounding the doctor's violation and my sexuality.

I fired her.

"Good for you," Father said. "Typical psychobabble. She's obviously an anti-Catholic with a feminist agenda. They strip God from the process, as if He weren't an intimate part of our lives."

I didn't need Number One's negativity. I didn't need theatre, where I'd been telling others' stories while neglecting my own. I'd focused on my pain and everything that was wrong in the world, where God was absent. When I spoke about my life in spiritual direction, Father asked, "Where's God in this?" He instructed me to discern God's presence and pray Psalm 139, "The All-Knowing and Ever-Present God," daily.

Probe me, O God, and know my heart;
 try me, and know my thoughts.
See if my way is crooked,
 and lead me in the ways of old.

Every night, I wrote about the day's events in my spiritual journal: where I saw God, where I didn't, and what God had called me to do in each moment. In my weekly spiritual direction sessions, I read these reflections to Father Scott.

He was unlike any priest I'd known. He wore blue jeans and sweatshirts, not the typical dandruff sprinkled "clerics"—the black uniform worn by priests, meant to symbolize death to self. He had a clip-on clerical collar that snapped around his neck like a giant black handcuff with a white, plastic tab in front—the white symbolized Christ's resurrection. He drove a sporty, black sedan-like KITT from *Knight Rider*. His special-issue University of Northern Iowa license plate proudly proclaimed "FR SCB"—Father Scott Christopher Bell. The eldest child of an alcoholic father, he knew how to protect himself. At five feet, six inches, he took down guys twice his size. Headlocks from behind. Ticklish jabs in the side. Titty twisters. He claimed to have stuck a fork into an inebriated seminarian's thigh under a dinner table to shut the guy up. Students called him "Padre." He nicknamed everyone. Parodying how people mutilated my name, he rechristened me "Dom Pastrone." He also called me "Baby Priest," which I hated. And loved.

During Mass, I sat at the front of the chapel. When the congregation left the pews and gathered around the altar for the eucharistic prayer, I stood by him. We all held hands during the Our Father, squeezing and raising them high during the doxology. Afterward, we exchanged hugs during the sign of peace. Standing with my peers and Father at the altar, I felt complete. God was present and always had been.

"God never abandoned me," I said from Father's rocking chair in our next session. "Not even when the doctor abused me. God was there with me on the examination bed, my cross. In my pain."

Everything that I wanted to communicate to God, I shared through Father Scott. He didn't reject me, so God didn't reject me. At times, he said I'd misinterpreted God's will. He explained that I didn't know who

I really was. I'd come to define myself by the theatre, my anger at the Church, my absent father, and my sexual desires. I had to bring these "urgent longings" to prayer.

"Only God knows the core of your being, Pastrone. He knows your darkest secrets and desires. He knows you better than you know yourself. Pray to know yourself as He does."

> Probe me, O God, and know my heart;
> try me, and know my thoughts.
> See if my way is crooked,
> and lead me in the ways of old.

Number One had been partly right. While I loved the Church, I was angry with the priests who'd abused children, the Catholics of history who'd killed in God's name, and the men in the Vatican denying women ordination.

"How can I be a priest when half my friends can't?" I asked Father Scott.

He stroked his mustache and leaned back in his chair. "Do you agree with 100 percent of what our country does? No, but you don't move to Scandinavia. So why condemn the Church? The guilt you have about becoming a priest while women can't is just the devil trying to submarine God's plan. The Church has its own timeline, Pastrone. Pray for patience with the Church."

God was calling me to renew the Church from within. Even if I didn't see the fruits of change in my lifetime, I had to have faith in the seeds I'd sow. Just as God sacrificed his son on the cross, I had to sacrifice my desire for the Church to change.

"Focus on your moral conversion," Father said.

If I offered up my desires, God would reward me with peace in celibacy and maybe take my nightly sexual fantasies away. But it was more than fantasies. When I closed my eyes in prayer and pictured God's face, I saw Father Scott.

I withheld my deepest desire. I didn't tell him that from my bedroom I could see his apartment windows. I knew when he did dishes, when his car rolled down the alley at night, and when his bedroom light flickered off. What I didn't know was whether he looked into my window and watched me undress. Did he offer every student bear hugs at the end of spiritual direction or just those planning to be priests?

"Take it to prayer," his voice echoed in my head.

> Probe me, O God, and know my heart;
>   try me, and know my thoughts.
> See if my way is crooked,
>   and lead me in the ways of old.

"I can't be a priest because of my attractions to men," I said.

"Celibacy is celibacy, even if your thing is goats," Father Scott said.

"What?"

He told me to watch *Mass Appeal*, a film about seminary, and loaned me his videotape. I screened it, alone.

An old priest played by Jack Lemmon cashed in his popularity to defend a progressive seminarian. The film's antagonist, a monsignor who alleged gay priests were pedophiles, expelled the seminarian who, though celibate, was honest about being bisexual. Jack Lemmon's character responded in a drunken rage: "Celibacy is celibacy, even if your thing is goats!"

Father said to bring questions the film stirred to spiritual direction. I presented five pages. "Is the Church still dismissing seminarians for their homosexual pasts? Should I hide mine?" I wanted to know how celibacy worked for someone like me. "Is celibacy easier after ordination? Do you get lonely? Is it possible to stop masturbating? Have you? Do you still have wet dreams? Fantasies? Are you attracted to men?"

"These sessions are about you, Tom." He turned to his desk and thumbed through his Rolodex. "It would be a boundary violation to speak to you about personal matters."

I slid to the back of the rocking chair and closed my notebook. "I'm sorry."

He picked up his phone. "It's time for you to meet someone."

A PLACE AT THE TABLE

I sat in an empty office at St. Stephen's with Father Jim Hunter, director of seminarians for the Archdiocese of Dubuque and chair of the board that would accept or deny my seminary application.

"Priesthood is a rewarding but difficult life," Father Hunter said. "You're talented, Mr. Rastrelli. Handsome. You could do anything; have a family." He straightened his tweed sports coat. "Why do you want to be a priest?"

"I want to help people find healing and peace."

"But there are many ways to help people. Why priesthood?"

I told him everything about my calling. Except for the doctor. And my attractions to men. Father Scott advised me to leave those for later.

Father Hunter's dark eyes were steady, refusing to betray his thoughts. He wanted more. I had to show I trusted him, to risk it like the seminarian in *Mass Appeal*.

"I have attractions to men."

He didn't look away. Neither did I.

"Have you acted on them?"

"Yes. But I want to be celibate."

He offered a sober smile and a slight nod. He reaffirmed what Father Scott had said about orientation not mattering for celibacy but without mentioning goats. He affirmed my honesty and stressed that our relationship should be based on trust. He invited me to his annual seminarians' Christmas party.

Father Hunter resided in the gumdrop hills west of Dubuque, the northern reaches of Grant Wood territory. His modest, low-pitched rectory nestled between a single-spire brick church and the crossing of two county roads. Not bad for a priest's gig: Mass on Saturday night, another

Sunday morning, a twenty-minute weekday drive to the office through *American Gothic*. Father Scott let me ring the doorbell.

"Merry Christmas!" Father Hunter burst forth. His towering frame engulfed Father Scott. With black wavy hair, he looked like a taller, chunkier version of my dad. His plush hand pulled me into a half hug. He smelled like a spiced candle and cigarette ashes. "Welcome to my humble abode, Mr. Rastrelli."

Father Scott ran his finger along the top of the doorframe, checking it for dust. "Impressive," he said.

"Don't mind Scott." Father Hunter scooped his amber drink from the vestibule's side table. "He's the most anal cleric west of the Mississippi."

"I don't know." Father Scott messed with the perfectly arranged pottery on a nearby bureau. "Your OCD has reached godliness proportions."

Father Hunter raised his drink. "Touché."

I'd never seen priests banter. There was a shared energy between them. They'd known each other since seminary, but I sensed it was something more.

Two seminarians rushed into the vestibule: a short hairy man and a skinny bald guy. Father Scott hugged them. I offered handshakes. The bald guy had a possible closed-up earring hole. Father Hunter led us into the dim living room.

The other guests looked normal. They ranged from undergraduates to borderline Social Security recipients. Some wore pants, others jeans. No one was in clerics. A young guy with blond hair and no lips, they called "Father," whereas gray-haired guys were not. "Gentlemen," Father Hunter pronounced. The room quieted. "I present Mr. Rastrelli of Clinton, a Scott Bell recruit." The crowd toasted. I felt at home.

A few guys reeled Father Scott into the kitchen. Father Hunter put his hand on my shoulder and steered me into the dining room. On the table, forty or so multicolored bottles stood erect, arranged like soldiers ready for battle. The only place I'd seen so much alcohol was behind the bar at Rastrelli's Restaurant. At home, my parents kept a modest, dust-coated collection of bottles in the cupboards over the refrigerator. I didn't know which liquors they preferred. Father Hunter drank Dewar's. Neat. I didn't know what Dewar's was or what "neat" meant. I didn't ask. He reached for what I later learned was a rocks tumbler.

"What will it be?" He double snapped the ice tongs.

My conscience spun. My twenty-first birthday was in three months. Father Hunter held an empty glass. His smile waned.

"Do you have any wine coolers?"

He guffawed. *Shit.* Wine coolers were apparently for wimps. I scanned the table for white zin but saw only bitter reds and liquors with names as foreign as Latin. I needed something I could stomach, something sweet. What would Mom drink?

"I could do a fuzzy navel."

He smirked, set my empty glass by the bottles, added more Dewar's to his, and led me into the kitchen. From an ice bucket, he snatched a fuzzy navel wine cooler, twisted it open, and handed it to me. "You'll have to meet Steve. Another seminarian who prefers froufrou drinks." The kitchen crowd laughed. I joined in, not knowing why, just hoping to survive, to be a seminarian.

The seminarians spun tales of crazy professors. Father Hunter topped each one with something more bizarre. He leaned against the range, his full lips blowing cigarette smoke into the fan's intake vent. Each tilt of his dark, calculating eyes and every imperious flick of his wrist over the ashtray solicited attention. I couldn't imagine myself so secure, so regal.

The fellows pitched me their schools and cities: St. Paul, Baltimore, DC, and Rome. They drank gin and tonics, Manhattans, and brandies. They seemed so cosmopolitan. I sipped my fruity drink.

As the evening passed, we nibbled at the homemade Italian appetizers, antipasti according to our host. I admitted never before having prosciutto-wrapped muskmelon. They called it cantaloupe. I mispronounced "bruschetta."

Father Hunter hollered at Father Scott: "Do you have any real proof that Mr. Rastrelli is Italian?"

Everyone chuckled. So I did too.

Father Scott snapped: "Do we have any real proof that you quit smoking?"

Everyone howled. Father Hunter lit another cigarette and exhaled in Father Scott's direction. He tossed me another wine cooler. I untwisted the cap.

"That's enough," Father Scott said.

"Really, Scott. Loosen up." Father Hunter clinked my bottle. We drank.

Father Scott's lips snarled. "Well, I have an early meeting." He leaned into me, pinched my bicep, and whispered, "Be good, Pastrone." He asked the short hairy seminarian lacking visible piercings to return me to the retreat house in Dubuque where we were bunking and scuttled off. I felt dazed. Should I stay or follow? Was it just the alcohol?

"Oh, don't mind Scott." Father Hunter inhaled. His cigarette flared. "He's just sensitive." He exhaled into the range. "His daddy was a drunk, so he has issues. When you're feeling brave, ask him about a certain drink called a Rusty Nail."

A staccato dinging rattled the kitchen. In the entryway, a seminarian with an auburn mustache and the build of an offensive lineman grinned. Thick lenses, one with a large chip in the lower corner, magnified his eyes. He held a mug with a bicycle bell on the handle. "I'm empty," he proclaimed in a wooly tenor. He rang again. I grabbed a beer from the cooler and filled him up while inspecting his earlobes. No piercings. I followed him into the living room, trying not to stumble. If I kept his glass full, maybe Father Hunter would quit handing me bottles.

Men filled the furniture before a stone fireplace. I slipped into the crowd standing behind the couch. From the large chair nearest the fire, a sixty-something seminarian, a beardless Santa, bellowed about his pre-seminary escapades: all the women he'd "sport fucked." He christened them bitches and whores. Leaping from his chair, he thrust like a satyr. Everyone howled. I joined in, hoping to mask my shock. Was this what priests really thought about women? I averted my gaze to the hodgepodge of crucifixes over the fireplace, but my eyes kept scrutinizing beardless Santa's bouncing package.

Across the room, I recognized a floppy-haired brunette who looked disgusted with the misogynistic rant. The previous summer, he'd played Jesus in *Godspell* at a community theatre. I'd seen the show because the guy who'd blown Tobey played John the Baptist. He'd bragged about screwing a seminarian. Apparently Jesus gave up his head for John the Baptist.

As I approached, the actor gave me a double take. "You look familiar," he said.

"I saw you in *Godspell*." I couldn't tell whether he had an earring hole. "I know Kent from UNI."

He chuckled. "I'm sorry you experienced that fiasco."

I wanted him to know I didn't think less of him. His secret was safe. Maybe we could be friends and support each other in our celibate commitments. "It wasn't that bad."

"Absolutely forgettable." He looked over my shoulder. "Excuse me."

He decamped to the priest with no lips and definitely no earring scar. Beardless Santa babbled on. I retreated to the kitchen and informed the short, hairy seminarian without holes that I was good to go. Whenever.

Father Hunter passed me another wine cooler.

BY WAY OF THE HEART

Nothing could remain unclean in Father Scott's presence. That's what my partner in grime, Josie, taught me. At Father's behest, I dumped my job in the theatre's shop to be St. Stephen's janitor and yardman. Josie, a speech pathology major, was the other cleaner. With blonde curls and a movie star smile, she accepted me as an acolyte and catechized me in the way of the dust mop.

"Why wouldn't you date Josie?" Father said in spiritual direction. "You need to date women before seminary. Take this to prayer. Find out what's really in your heart."

I left confused. As I scraped gum from the pews' underbellies, I wondered whether he meant Josie could release my God-given orientation and make me straight.

Father referred me to Counselor Number Two to address my "sexual issues." Unlike Number One, Two, who worked for Catholic charities, didn't think talking to God was a mental disorder. A soft-spoken, lanky priest, Two towered over me but looked as if the flutter of butterfly wings might cause him to crumble into dust. We met in the deacon's office. I divulged the sexual abuse and my attractions to men.

"It sounds like you need to forgive the doctor," Two said, with a painful grin.

He instructed me to pretend he was Dr. Lauz.

"I'm sorry I abused you." Two offered a gentle smile. His dimples blended into crow's feet. He looked nothing like the fat-faced doctor. "Is there anything you want to say to me?"

I looked at the office's drab carpeting. I recalled the gray floor of the doctor's office. The shoes clicking. The wheeled stool. His voice, his hands, his touch.

"Fuck you." My fingernails dug into my palms. "You ruined me. Made me hate myself. And God." My jaw clenched. The veins in my neck felt like they would explode. "I wish you were dead."

Two recoiled, as if he'd seen Satan. I focused on the carpet. The gray.

"I'm sorry," Two said, still in character. "Please, forgive me."

I felt tears on my cheeks. I shook my head.

"I beg you, Tom."

I wanted him to shut the fuck up.

"Fine," I glowered at him. "I forgive you."

He commended my "good work." In our next session, when I brought up Lauz, he changed the subject to priesthood. When I brought up my desires for men, he did the same. Apparently, his role-playing exercise should have fixed me.

I wasn't the only one who was broken. Mom told me my brother was staying home from school a lot, though Jeff rarely got sick. He shot baskets in the snow, wearing only a sweatshirt and shorts. He was indestructible. Like Mom, he rarely showed feelings. When she asked why he'd been crying so much, he'd said nothing, but I knew what it was.

He was in eighth grade.

He was fourteen.

He was Lauz's patient.

Dealing with my own crap, I'd ignored the safety of my brother and sister. Maria went to Lauz too, and my cousins and many other kids. How many had he violated?

Each day I didn't tell my parents about Lauz, I conspired in his abuse. God became distant, hiding just around dusty corners. Number Two was worthless. Father Scott increased my spiritual direction sessions to two or three a week. "There's power in community," he assured me. "Even Jesus let Simon carry the cross. Trust your church family to carry this burden with you." I told my prayer group. Father helped me write a letter to my nuclear family. He walked me to the mailbox. This was the essence of priesthood: being present to people in pain. Someday I'd do the same.

While waiting for the letter's delivery, my friends prayed. Father gave me cleaning projects to occupy my "overactive noggin." On the third day, Mom left a message to call home. I prayed. I dialed. I listened. They were devastated.

Jeff and Maria said they hadn't been abused. My cousins were also safe. That weekend, Mom, Maria, and Jenny came to visit. Dad apologized for having to work. Jeff had sports. We checked into the Heartland Inn, collapsed onto a bed, curled into a mass, and wailed.

I further immersed myself at St. Stephen's. Going to Mass two or three times a weekend, I analyzed how Father Scott tailored his homilies. I applied what I gleaned to my witness talk for the coming Antioch retreat—my first homily.

After Masses, Father and I went to Big Boy. We decorated the chapel for the various liturgical seasons and holidays. I arrived at events before the first guest and left after sweeping the final crumb. He drove Josie and me to Clinton to eat at the restaurant. With her, we celebrated my twenty-first birthday and his fortieth. He took me to Father Hunter's rectory for an Italian feast with my parents. Whenever I got down about the abuse—he called it "obsessing"—he'd burst into a pop song parody. His baritone foghorn resounded throughout the chapel: "All I wanna do is date some nun. I got a feelin' I'm not the only one." If I didn't laugh, he'd widen his eyes and flare his nostrils until I did. The students nicknamed him Taco Bell; they rechristened me Taquito.

On the Antioch retreat, I sat on the floor in a circle of my peers and delivered my talk, "Growth." Using "Move On," a song from Sondheim's *Sunday in the Park with George* as a foil, I shared my healing from the anger, hurt, and abuse of the past. To grow in God's love, we had to forgive and "move on." Preaching God's word felt as natural to my mouth as sucking off Tobey had. Proclaiming the Gospel was my salvation.

But the nightmares persisted. Lauz was everywhere: in the Communion line, in my parents' clothes, in Grandma's old spot behind the restaurant's cash register passing out bubble gum, and in my bed. I woke screaming. While awake, scents similar to his musk or antiseptic office transported me back into his grasp. His tongue. When I masturbated, his face projected itself over my fantasies.

I decided to stop the doctor. Dad found me a lawyer, who suggested filing a complaint with the Iowa Medical Board of Examiners. They would investigate Lauz and take action. If they failed, we'd sue. My lawyer told me to focus on school and my support network at church.

Jane, the staff supervisor for Antioch, called me into her office. She brushed a dirty-blonde curl from her forehead. "You've got a lot going on. How're you doing?" Her peppy voice sounded tinny.

"OK. My family's hanging in. We appreciate the retreat team's prayers. Father Scott's been great."

She picked some black lint from her jeans. "How are things between you two?"

The dark fluff drifted onto the carpet beneath her desk. "Fine. Great." I noted the lint's location for my next pass with the vacuum.

"He's not the best at friendships," she said. "There was another student, a seminarian. They were close. When the guy decided not to be a priest, Scott cut him off."

Through the second story window and a line of conifers, I could see my apartment.

"I don't want you to get hurt," she said.

Her office was above Father's residence. Had she seen me watching him? Did she think he was attracted to me? No, he roughhoused with all the guys.

"I won't get hurt."

Later, as I dropped a fluorescent pink, hockey-puck-shaped air freshener into the urinal—Father referred to them as "cough drops"—I concluded that Jane had issues with him. So did the amorphous ex-seminarian. I didn't. I was fine. But I had to control myself, my window peeping. I needed a new apartment.

Father Scott chose light gray for the walls, dark gray for the trim. My new place was two lots closer to St. Stephen's. A frat house blocked Father's apartment from my view.

At his request, Josie and I remained in Cedar Falls over the summer to deep clean St. Stephen's. I was also his exercise partner. One humid morning after a run, I invited him to my apartment for breakfast. He said this was a "boundary violation."

Late one night, I pulled into St. Stephen's parking lot—Father Scott allowed me to park there because I was "staff." Through his office's cracked vertical blinds, his round face shone in the computer's light. What did he do in there for twelve to sixteen hours a day?

I bounded into his office. "Take a break already. It's vacation."

Without looking away from the computer, he said, "Go home, Tom."

"Wow." I lowered my voice and leaned against the doorframe. "Sorry."

"I don't need you butting into my business." He spun from the computer to his desk and rummaged through some papers in a binder. "Running a parish is more than preaching and socials. If I don't do it, it won't get done. I'm sick of people bugging me to take a break." He smacked the binder closed and whirled back to the computer. "You don't get it. Why do you think I use a tanning booth? So parishioners think I'm getting outside and quit hounding me. You don't know what it's like." He ripped a sheet of paper from the printer and filed it. "But you'll learn. In the meanwhile," he slammed the drawer, pinched the back of my triceps, and hustled me through the vacant lobby, "deal with your own junk."

"Jesus," I yanked away and cut for the exit, "I was just giving you a hard time."

"Get your own life, Tom." His voice trailed. "Ask Josie out."

I parked the car in front of Josie's house. Dinner had been awkward. The movie was dumb. All the while, I'd worried about kissing her at the end of the night. Tobey and I had never kissed. Too gay. Barring an onstage smooch, my only kiss had been with the doctor. The tongue. This was my first collegiate date. She'd expect a kiss.

"Does this feel weird?" I said. Incestuous felt more accurate.

"Definitely," she nodded. "What was Father thinking?"

We shared our mutual desire to be friends and hugged. No kissing. No doctor.

What had Father been thinking? He knew I liked men. He knew God wanted me to be a priest. And Josie had just been through a breakup with Jason, the former seminarian who had worked at St. Stephen's during the school year. "Things got too weird," she'd said.

A few months earlier, before they dated, I almost told Jason that I had attractions to men. He'd picked me up after the St. Stephen's blood drive to run an errand out of town. Because of "irreconcilable issues" with

Father Hunter and Father Scott, he said he was leaving seminary. My emotions were a mess because, at the blood drive, I'd answered affirmatively when asked: "Are you a male who has had sexual contact with a male, even once, since 1977?" The phlebotomist rejected me, right there in St. Stephen's hall. She might as well have proclaimed: "The American Red Cross doesn't take queer blood. Get out of this church."

As the barbed wire and cornfields blurred by, I wondered how Jason had answered the phlebotomist's question. His eyes often lingered on guys. But if I asked about his truth or confessed mine, he'd take the next exit and park on a dirt road. We'd touch. And suck. And fuck. That's how gay men lived.

"I almost told Jason the truth about my attractions," I told Father Scott, after telling him the date with Josie failed. He spun to his computer, clicked the mouse, and called me over. He entered a gay chat room that he'd investigated "to understand how homosexuals operate." I'd just begun using email and didn't even know there were chat rooms. He signed in as SCB. Within seconds, he received a sexual proposition. "Is this how you want to live?" he said. "A few minutes of carnal pleasure aren't worth getting AIDS and an eternity in hell. Do you want to have sex with Jason?"

"No."

I believed it. I had to. But as I went about my summer cleaning, I couldn't forget a chat message Father had received: "What are you hiding SCB?"

Sometimes he hugged me after spiritual direction. Other times he refused, calling me "too clingy." He told me about a high school boy he'd taught in Dubuque. Once, when they'd hugged, the kid got hard. "Irrelevant." He released the boy and went on his way. What priests felt didn't matter, only that they offered up their attractions to God. That was celibacy.

One night after the church emptied, Father Scott flipped off the lobby's lights and pulled me into a shadow. His chest, belly and hips pressed against me. One of his hands cradled the back of my head; the other pulled the small of my back. I felt his growth against my mine. He released me. We said nothing. It meant nothing.

When I arrived at sunrise to mow the lawn, he castigated me for my "dependency." He seemed confused. Lonely. When I asked about this, he turned things back to me. I was the "problem child." "Histrionic." I needed to be honest in my seminary application and tell Father Hunter the truth about Lauz.

Sitting on an angular couch like something out of a 1950s magazine, I waited in the lobby of the Archdiocesan Pastoral Center—in priestly shorthand, "the chancery." I imagined Father Hunter's possible responses to my news of the abuse and probable litigation. He was a lawyer. He understood the system and could help me understand the process. As the archbishop's judicial vicar, chancellor, director of seminarians, and head of the metropolitan tribunal, he was on the fast track to bishop. Perhaps he'd take me under his wing. But what if he freaked out?

I followed his secretary down a long hallway lined with pairs of doors labeled things like lay formation, liturgy and worship, finance, religious education, and family life. She pointed out the door at the end of the hall: Archbishop Jacob Haggis's office. Two doors shy, we turned into Father Hunter's.

He greeted me with a handshake. No hug. The secretary closed the door on her way out. "I know why you're here. Please, sit." I shuffled in the stiff armchair. He set aside a file. "I must apologize," His face turned sullen. "I didn't have time to purchase wine coolers."

My tension released in a deep laugh. "I've developed a taste for red wine."

"Your father must be proud." He said he'd enjoyed entertaining my parents at his rectory a while back. "They're delightful. And Jill's a knockout."

"Thank God for giving me her genes."

He guffawed, but then the joviality left his eyes. "How's Scott? I haven't heard from him."

"He's busy. So much to do."

"Tell him dust bunnies can wait." He waved off his melancholy. "Enough about Scott." His eyes were soft again, like a velvet teddy bear's. "So what brings you to the bowels of Dubuque?"

I told him about Lauz, my case with the medical board, and how it might become public knowledge.

"I commend your courage, Tom. You have my full support. But I have to be honest with you. I'm not sure how Jacob will respond. It's my duty to inform him."

He explained what I'd feared. The priest-perpetrated sexual abuse cases had colored the public's understanding. Bishops were paranoid. Some believed that victims became abusers. He wasn't sure whether the archbishop would risk taking a seminarian with a history of abuse, but my being in therapy helped. "Jacob is traveling. I'll speak to him when he returns. In the meanwhile, take care of yourself and tell Scott to call me."

When I pulled into St. Stephen's lot, the sky and building were dark. The stained glass hanging in Father Scott's windows shimmered amber, cobalt, and crimson. My rusting Oldsmobile popped after I stopped the engine. The church's back door was unlocked. Periodic nightlights illuminated the hallways. I turned the corner to approach Father's apartment. His door opened in a blinding light.

"How'd it go, Pastrone?"

I told him that I didn't know whether the archbishop would accept me and cried.

He put his arm around me and led me through the shadowed hallway into a windowless lounge. He closed the door and left off the lights. He pulled me to the edge of a couch and sat. He pushed on my shoulders, guiding me to the floor. His arms and legs cradled me. His lips moved against the crown of my head, "Let it out, Pastrone."

I wailed as he held me in the darkness. Lauz had robbed me of my past and now my future.

Over the next week, Father didn't pick on me. It felt like the months after I'd first told him I was going to be a priest. Then Father Hunter called. The archbishop would still consider me for seminary. "Tell Scott to call me," Father Hunter demanded.

"Tell Jim that communication is a two-way street," Father Scott said.

"Why don't you just call him?" I said.

"That's none of your business." He ran his fingers down the vertical blinds. "These need cleaning."

"I'm not your go-between."

"It's all about Tom."

The next day, he gave me a bear hug. The day after that, he kept his office door closed.

By summer's end, I'd had enough of his vacillations. In my family, we didn't treat each other like crap. We told each other we loved them. I did the same with my friends. I dropped my cleaning rag in a pew and marched into his office. "I have something to tell you."

He stared at his computer. "Well, spit it out already, Pastrone." He clicked his mouse. Always busy.

Fuck it. I didn't care that he wasn't looking at me or that I was dressed in holey tennis shoes and cutoffs. I looked at the side of his face.

"Scott, I want you to know that I love you."

His tanned fingers plucked at the keyboard. He focused on the monitor. "Thank you for being honest, Tom." His voice had less emotion than a corpse.

I returned to the chapel and scrubbed the pews with lemon soap. I felt like a cancer that had metastasized to him. He was right. I was out of control. Infatuated. We needed space. It was time to talk to a different priest.

CONFESSIONS

After receiving my "I'm going to be a priest and in large part thanks to your positive influence on my youth" letter, Father Pete Foley invited me to his southern Iowa parish for Labor Day weekend. I hadn't seen him since I was fifteen. Early in his priesthood, while stationed in my hometown, he'd attended my Dad's bachelor party. Years later, when my family's parish blacklisted us for transferring to the public schools, he'd welcomed us to his parish. He was the most human priest of my childhood. When I arrived at his ranch-style rectory, he waved me into the garage to park by his white Ford Explorer.

As I stepped out of my car, I was surprised to be slightly taller than he was.

"My God, Thomas, you're a man." Nobody called me by my baptismal name, but it sounded right coming from him. We hugged. He smelled like Irish Spring. "Just let me look at you," he said, with his hands gripping my shoulders. "My God, you look like your mother. But that's your nonna's nose."

"Thanks for having me, Father."

"Thomas, what's all this Father crap? Call me Pete."

Despite soft wrinkles, his blue eyes, broad cheeks and smile were the same, but his gut, to which he referred as "the spare tire," had grown. The horseshoe of hair around his scalp was now white.

"I hope you brought your laundry," he said. "There's nothing like free laundry for a college boy."

We toured the church-rectory complex. His small white terrier, named Tree, trailed us. After unpacking, I joined him in the den. As we reminisced, he became giddy. "You're not gonna believe this," he said. He scrambled to his office and returned with the letter of intent that I'd been required to write before confirmation. I marveled at the foreign words written in my handwriting.

I recalled Bishop O'Keefe's eyes when he anointed my head with oil during the confirmation rite—the moment the Holy Spirit entered me, as it had the apostles on Pentecost. "When the bishop anointed my head and looked at me, I almost passed out."

"You got zapped," Pete said from his cardinal La-Z-Boy. He rested his hands on his belly and frayed shirt. He was beaming. He'd never stopped caring for my family. I admitted what had really been going on at fourteen, Dr. Lauz, and my confusing attractions to males. He didn't judge. He offered apologies and scotch.

I spit it out. "That tastes like it was wrung from dirty old church pews."

He smiled and said, "It grows on you."

He didn't bully me into the hard stuff. I had wine. Buzzed, we fell asleep in our recliners watching *The Last Temptation of Christ.*

The next night, after Mass and supper, I confessed my frustration with Father Scott and his avoidance of discussing the mechanics of celibacy.

"I'm here," Pete said from his chair with Tree in his lap. "Ask me anything."

He admitted celibacy was difficult and that he was attracted to men. He always had been, even during his military days in Korea. As a teen, he'd escape the farmhouse, hike into the fields, strip, lie on the grass, and masturbate as the sun set.

"I love sunsets," I said.

He refilled my glass. I confessed that since seeing *The Fisher King*, the scene in which Robin Williams and Jeff Daniels lie under the stars nude in Central Park, I'd always wanted to do the same, but fear of being seen by the neighbors had deterred me. My face was warm with wine. He was answering my questions. So I asked. "Were you able to stop masturbating after ordination?"

He chuckled. Then he told me the truth.

Priests still had sexual feelings. They were human; they jacked off. They were attracted to parishioners, even to priests. He claimed to be celibate since ordination, but I knew otherwise. A few years earlier, a friend told me Tom hit on her brother, a University of Iowa student. I asked about this.

"We acted out." He gently stroked Tree. "I'm not proud of it. We masturbated. Once. It wasn't sex."

I felt relieved but confused. I was technically a virgin because I'd never had vaginal sex. Was he still celibate because they'd only jacked off? I was too afraid to ask. I took another swig.

He explained how he exchanged back rubs on vacations with a priest friend. Priests needed close friends with whom to release their feelings.

As I listened, I tried to understand. Maybe priests could have one relationship with another priest or seminarian with whom they could share massages and jack off. Were blow jobs okay? Maybe Father Hunter and Father Scott had this, and I was messing it up.

After another drink, Pete and I decided to lie under the stars. Clothed.

His parish bordered the cornfields edging a farm community. The rectory's backyard was perfectly dark, shielded from the dimly illuminated parking lot by the shadow of the church. We stumbled around and found a spot. We laid side by side, gazing at constellations. We'd missed the Perseid meteor shower by a few weeks. "No problem," he said, "Come next August. Come often."

Then, as if it were the natural thing to do, he removed his shirt saying, "It's not Central Park, but it'll do."

No big deal. I pulled off mine.

He lost his shoes and unbuckled his belt. He stripped his pants and underwear and sprawled out on the ground. "That's more like it."

The priest, who had hugged my grandmother and heard my childhood confessions, was lying naked beside me.

We weren't touching. What was the harm? I shed my shorts and briefs.

The chilly grass prickled my backside. My skin tingled. My penis rose over my stomach like Polaris, beckoning me toward the fixed nature of my being. The silhouette of an erection stood over his gut. I wanted to feel him but didn't move. What if that wasn't celibacy?

The cold breeze intensified. My jaw chattered.

"Let's go inside, where it's warm," he said.

As we dressed, he watched me and I him, imagining what the darkness veiled.

The only other erection I'd seen was Tobey's. I wondered what an older man's was like. But clothed, Pete was Father Foley again. I hurried inside past Tree to the guest bathroom and waited until my erection relaxed and the near occasion of sin had passed. I retrieved my clothes from the dryer and returned to the den.

With a tumbler of scotch in hand and Tree at his feet, Pete sat in the cardinal La-Z-Boy. Naked. Erect.

I stared from the doorway. In my childhood memoires, he wore layers of holiness: green chasuble over white alb over black clerics. How could the exposed flesh before me be the same priest?

"Well you've already seen it." He smiled with open legs.

But I hadn't really seen it. It had been dark. Still, I wanted to see it. I wanted to know how priesthood worked for him. I poured my laundry in the center of the room, trying not to act overly interested.

"It's nothing to be ashamed of." He stood and turned around. "Just the way God made us." He plopped into his seat. "Natural."

I couldn't tell whether he was circumcised; I'd never seen foreskin before. Black and gray hair covered his body. Like a gorilla under surveillance, he watched me watching him. If I wanted to learn, I had to follow his lead. I stripped.

As I folded clothes, we discussed Scorsese's interpretation of the crucifixion. We drank more wine and scotch. We rubbed Tree's belly. The conversation seemed normal, in spite of our erections. Then he invited me to his bedroom for a backrub. Nothing more. No pressure.

I froze next to his bed, on which Tree nestled. Was it a sin, sitting on priest's bed naked? Pete gathered towels and Johnson & Johnson's baby oil from the bathroom. He spread a towel on the floor and directed me to lie on my stomach. He anointed me, kneading my muscles from neck to buttocks. Occasionally, his legs or belly brushed my skin. I wanted him against me, but worried we'd gone too far.

He told me to turn over. His aquamarine eyes demanded trust. I let him continue. He massaged my chest and abdomen. My erection popped up and down as he stroked my perineum within an inch of my scrotum. But he didn't touch my genitals. I assumed that was a boundary violation.

We swapped. As I straddled his legs and massaged the oil through his back hair, my erection nicked his buns. "I'm sorry."

"That's OK," he said. I wondered if he wanted my dick in his ass. If he'd massaged many guys. If he had AIDS. I moved on to his arms, knuckles, legs, and feet.

He rolled over, still vein-hard and dripping precum. Why was I attracted to a sixty-something, overweight priest? Because of Lauz? Was I infected, reprogrammed to be sexually attracted to old men until I was their age and returned the favor by preying on the young?

He thanked me, stood, and hugged me. His oiled hair stuck to my skin as he stepped away and led me onto the bed. He pushed Tree to the far side.

I hesitated. "Is this celibacy?"

He directed me to lie next to him with my feet by his head. I did. He masturbated. I watched, trying to ignore the crucifix over his head. I wanted what we were doing to feel, to be, okay, so I stroked myself. We didn't touch. Apparently, this was celibacy. I could handle a lifetime of this.

After orgasm, self-loathing squeezed into the spaces flushed out by testosterone, as it always did. And I knew in my baby-oiled gut: this was definitely not celibacy.

I retreated to my room, locked the door, and dressed. When I bent over to pack my suitcase, the room spun. Such a lightweight. I couldn't drive. He had me for the night.

He knocked. "Thomas, let's just talk. Please."

He stood in the doorway, assuring me that "it" wouldn't happen again. I tried not to look at him, focusing instead on the carpeting at his feet. He was still naked. His skinny legs, shrunken dick, and hairy belly should have repulsed me, as I repulsed God. Why did I want him to throw me onto the bed?

His eyes softened. He sensed my attraction. "Let's move into the den, where it's more comfortable."

"I can't." I packed my freshly folded clothes. He begged from the door and periodically shooed Tree to the den. Eventually, he returned to his room.

I rose early and rushed to the garage. Pete entered, already dressed for Mass, and extended his arms. "Just a hug before you go."

His embrace was soft; his soapy scent, benign. I was frightened to hug back. If I did, my body would respond. I pulled away, but he pressed against me. I gave him a few fraternal pats. His hands migrated down my back. One slid into the front pocket of my shorts. "A little something to cover your gas."

I pulled a fifty from my pocket. "I can't—."

"I won't take 'No' for an answer."

I felt like a whore.

On Labor Day, I mowed and edged St. Stephen's lawn. I vacuumed the chapel and scrubbed the toilets. When there was nothing more to clean, I knocked on Father Scott's door.

"What?" He didn't look up from his desk.

"I need to go to confession."

"Fine."

I sat in the black rocking chair, which smelled Murphy's Oil Soap clean. I stared at my grass-stained Reeboks. The gray carpeting was immaculate, not a dirt clod or shred of paper to be found. I made the sign of the cross. "It's been a month since my last confession."

Father Scott scribbled at his desk. The plastic floor protector crunched as he spun in his chair to face his computer on the opposing wall. I still hadn't figured out what he did all day.

I scanned the office. Every item had its place. Except me.

Volumes of theology lined the floor-to-ceiling bookshelves, yet I'd never seen him reading. Between the shelves, a window revealed the decaying ΣAE house. At night, drunken frat boys pissed from their porch toward the church, which ticked off Father. The sun split the vertical blinds, throwing columns of light onto an end table, where a wooden stand bore a Bible opened to his favorite passage, Sirach, chapter 2:

> My son, when you come to serve the Lord,
> prepare yourself for trials.
> Be sincere of heart and steadfast,
> undisturbed in times of adversity
> Cling to him, forsake him not;
> thus will your future be great . . .

I knew the chapter by heart. Praying it was one of Father's spiritual exercises. God, the devil, the Church, everyone was conspiring to test my vocation, to see if it was genuine. I should have prayed harder. My dry tongue tasted of soil and rust. My eyes grew moist. Sirach shamed me:

> Woe to craven hearts and drooping hands,
>   to the sinner who treads a double path . . .
> Let us fall into the hands of the Lord,
>   and not into the hands of men . . .

I plucked a hair from my forearm. When had I become so bestial? I picked the frayed edge of my loose-fitting jean shorts. Nothing fit my boney body.

Father stared at the computer. His gnawed fingers punched the keyboard. "Well, spill it already, Pastrone."

I hated the nonsensical nickname he'd given me, but it did its magic. I told him my sin.

". . . then we massaged each other and masturbated."

His fingers halted.

"But we didn't touch each other's genitals."

From across the office, he turned. His eyes flared behind his lenses. The vinyl mat crackled as his chair rumbled toward me. He stuck his face into mine. His warm coffee breath brushed my lips. His mustache nicked my nose. My body froze. His fingers dug into my knees.

"This is appropriate touch," he said.

His hands slid from my knees, up my inner thighs, under my shorts, and grasped my briefs, my soft penis and balls. He squeezed hard. It hurt.

"This is inappropriate touch!"

My body remained stupefied as my mind transported to another time, another rectangular room, smaller, brighter, and purer. Antiseptic. The paper of the examination bed crinkled under my exposed buttocks. My mind remained in the doctor's office as Father Scott held my genitals.

"I'm sorry, Father. Please, let go."

He released me and rolled onto the mat. I stared at the boundary of the gray carpeting and the translucent vinyl. His ashy voice prescribed my penance. "Can you do this?"

I nodded.

Again, the casters squealed toward me. I wanted to run, but my body refused, betraying me as it had in the doctor's office. His boxy loafers halted toe-to-toe with my tennis shoes. I felt his hands bear down on my head as he prayed: "God the Father of mercies, through the death and resurrection of his Son, has reconciled the world to Himself and sent the Holy Spirit among us for the forgiveness of sins; through the ministry of the Church may God give you pardon and peace, and I absolve you from your sins in the name of the Father, and of the Son, and of the Holy Spirit."

I kept my head bowed and begged God to forgive, hoping Father Scott would as well.

As penance, he required me to put my vocation in God's hands. I couldn't become a priest on a lie. He ordered me to tell Father Hunter.

Discarded peanut shells crunched under my feet as I entered the Ground Round's bar. Wearing an azure oxford, Father Hunter waved from a darkened booth, scotch in one hand and a cigarette in the other.

We engaged in the usual banter. After I finished a strawberry margarita, his eyebrows raised. "So, Pastrami—whatever Scott calls you—why are we in a dump, drinking bad booze?"

"I fucked up, Jim."

He extinguished his cigarette, "OK?"

"I acted out. Sexually."

His face was wooden. "OK."

"With a priest."

I thought he winced. But it was dark. "Who?"

"My old pastor from Clinton. Pete Foley. We exchanged back rubs and masturbated. We didn't touch each other's dicks."

His eyes tightened. He lifted his lighter to a cigarette. His pupils filled with flame. "This behavior doesn't befit someone hoping to attend seminary." His whisper whipped across the table, "I thought you were more mature than this. I just defended you to the archbishop, in spite of your sexual abuse. What should I say to him now? I should call this Foley's bishop and out him."

"Please don't. It's my fault. It won't happen again." My voice sounded loud. People chatted nearby. I hoped they hadn't heard. I lowered my voice, "Please, Jim. I'm sorry."

He scrutinized me as he took a drag. "You've betrayed my trust. You've so many gifts for priesthood. It would be a shame to squander them on a man old enough to be your grandfather."

"I know. It's sick. I'll do whatever you ask."

He waved off my apologies. "I'm quite fond of you and your parents, as is Scott. You have so much promise." He squeezed his hands together. His knuckles turned white. "For your parents' sake, I'll forgive this failing. But if you act out with this Foley again, your career in Dubuque is over."

His thick fingers pinched the cigarette butt and mashed it into the ashtray. Just as easily, he could have extinguished my vocation. He hadn't. For that, I was grateful.

When I returned to Cedar Falls, Father Scott wasn't waiting downstairs to hold me. He was at the computer. I told him I'd survived.

"Go home, Tom." His keyboard popped like green wood on a fire.

A few weeks later, I met with the Iowa Medical Board of Examiners. I needed a conference call–capable telephone so my lawyer could participate remotely. Father Scott offered his office. As the investigator questioned me about Lauz, I sat in Father's caster-mounted chair. The plastic mat rustled. I recalled his lesson about inappropriate touch. What had motivated him to react violently? Jealousy? Maybe he was in love with me.

When the investigator's questioning grew painful, I looked at the Bible by the window and silently recited Sirach's words:

> Trust God and he will help you;
> make straight your ways and hope in him.

THE CLOUD OF UNKNOWING

I slid through a small square door into the pipe organ. A twenty-five-foot-tall and six-foot-deep wooden box, the newly installed instrument mimicked the minimalist architecture of St. Stephen's; its wheat stain matched the pews and rafters. Pewter pipes lined the organ's façade, camouflaging large speakers and a dozen or so different-sized ranks. They blasted the chapel with a faux symphony: part pipe organ, part synthetic, indistinguishable to the lay ear. At the side of the sanctuary, Father Scott rocked back and forth at the organ console, his fingers and gold-toed socks pounding the pedals and manuals. I squatted in the organ's crawlspace, hoping to exorcise the outside world.

The police had called. Having retrieved my name from the Iowa Medical Board of Examiners, they begged me to go on record against Lauz. My lawyer advised against it. If I spoke, the case would be out of our control. The police would scare other victims, potential witnesses, away. Lauz would get off. The news would land in the papers, and the archbishop would deny my seminary application. I needed to be patient and let the medical board do its work. But each minute I did nothing, I allowed the pediatrician to abuse other kids. And Father Scott wasn't helping with his rapid shifts between consonance and dissonance. He never said anything about grabbing me during my confession. Father Foley wouldn't shut up. His letters filled my mailbox with legato apologies and fifty-dollar checks. Father Hunter's phone messages were staccato commands about application deadlines, punishing in their monotony.

I sang to the music, unable to hear my voice. Leaning against the reverberating wall, I surrendered to the maelstrom of sound shaking my bones. One with the music. I wanted to be one with God, to have my every cell quiver with devotion, power, presence, and life—to be obliterated by love.

After fifteen minutes of bliss, I crawled out of the instrument and returned to my cleaning duties. Father Scott conjured canons and concertos late into the night. As I passed behind him with the vacuum, I looked over his shoulder. His arms and fingers bounced between keyboards. His face shone with a vibrancy that I hadn't seen in months. He thanked me for sticking around to clean up after the installers and played the rumbling, bass opening from *The Phantom of the Opera*. I sang as he played late into the night.

"Do you miss music?" I asked, as he slid to the end of the bench and retrieved a shoe.

"Not at all." He pulled the black shoelace into a bow. "God made me a priest."

I missed acting. Auditions for the final productions of my undergraduate career were approaching. The shows had perfect roles for me. My vocal range matched *Fiddler on the Roof*'s lead and supporting roles. Since reading *Equus* in high school, I'd been salivating over its lead: a young man in therapy after jabbing out the eyes of six horses. Before mutilating the steeds, he worshipped them as gods. It was the ultimate play, rife with spiritual, religious, philosophical, psychological, and sexual themes. I wanted the part. But the last twenty pages called for the lead to be naked. My grandparents, the folks from St. Stephen's, and Father's nun friends would attend. They'd be six feet from my dick. Pope John Paul II had been an actor before becoming a priest. But as far as I knew, he'd never done nudity.

"I want to audition. But is this a temptation to lure me away from priesthood?"

"Take it to prayer," Father said.

Lying in bed, I scribbled in my journal, performing an examen. Father taught me the Jesuit exercise in which I examined the events of the day, wrote, prayed, and reflected on them with the goal of discerning God's presence or absence in each moment. I exposed the areas where I failed to notice God and concocted a plan to do better the next day. But my problem wasn't the lure of curtain call. It was Father Scott.

When he jumped me from behind, put me in a headlock, or tickled the soft spots above my hips, I wanted him to grasp my genitals, only tenderly this time. But when he pushed me away, I wanted to chisel out his eyes. When he roughhoused with other male students, I filled with jealousy. My journal revealed that he was more central in my life than God. He was my *Equus*.

Still, I fanaticized about him, Father Foley, the archbishop, and other priests. I wanted to know what it was like to be them. I coveted their priesthood. But was that a sin? Was God working through my attractions to men to bring me into the priesthood? I couldn't ask Father Scott. I knew his answer: *God doesn't work that way*. Besides, I sensed God's beauty and presence in so many other things: the browning leaves twirling down the street, the wind whipping a chill through my hair, and Josie's hands folding rags. God was in the atheist professor who supported my priestly discernment and even in my memories of the sexual abuse. God was in the trauma.

"God's in everything," I said in spiritual direction.

"That's pantheism," Father Scott said, "a heresy. If God's everything, then He's sin. And everything's gray." He insisted that there were things of which God wasn't a part. When it came to right and wrong, there were no "shades of gray."

God wasn't part of my lust. I had to stop fantasizing, doing anything that made me desire anything but God. My feelings for Father Scott had become an obstacle. I took my spiritual cleansing elsewhere.

Counselor Number Three worked on campus but wasn't a graduate student. A licensed psychologist, Three was African American, had a molded beard and round glasses. I assumed he was a Christian because he confirmed my spiritual conversion and resulting peace. The more he affirmed my feelings, the more I shared about what had happened with the doctor. But I stopped shy of revealing what happed with Father Foley or how Father Scott had grabbed my genitals. I deserved that punishment.

Three diagnosed me with post-traumatic stress disorder (PTSD). Because I'd survived my teenage years by disassociating myself from the emotional and physical impact of the doctor's abuse, I'd become accustomed to nightmares and intrusive thoughts. I didn't qualify them as traumatic or abnormal. He coached me to counter these symptoms of PTSD with breathing exercises, tactile actions, such as touching a tree or feeling the grass beneath my feet, or reciting a mantra—anything to pull myself out of the doctor's office and ground myself in the present.

Just like acting. Just like music. Just like prayer. Focusing on the present moment was the key to success. But I couldn't imagine the day when the sight of a Filipino man, a call from my lawyer, or the thought of kissing wouldn't conjure debilitating anxiety. I didn't tell Three that Father Scott had triggered a flashback when he'd grabbed me during confession. Despite the panic of that moment, I liked having him focused on me. Even when he hurt me, he made me feel loved.

Father told me that I had to do more than Three prescribed. Jesus had instructed his followers to love their enemies and pray for their persecutors, so each night, after writing in my journal, I was to pray for Lauz's repentance and salvation. "That's the only way, you'll find true healing," he said. "If you're gonna be a priest, start acting like one. You have to model even Jesus's most difficult commands."

At night, I prayed for Doctor Lauz. I said the words but hoped for his death or dismemberment. *Fake it till you make it*, my dad and his BMW-obsessed sales associates said. I hated their philosophy, but maybe the Church was the same. We were all sinners, but we still went to Communion as if we were pure. Therefore, I coordinated student movie nights to focus on peers rather than Father. At the Antioch retreat that I led, I composed what I believed was the greatest commission since the Gospel according to Matthew. Musing over biblical images of fire, I challenged the retreatants to enter the fire of God's presence, to let it burn us and mold us into tools of God's grace. Afterward, I sent Father Foley a letter and ordered him to cease communication. I was celibate.

Father Hunter applauded my "mature handling of the situation" and summoned me. He needed to prepare me for the seminary application process.

Under the sunset, the hills of ripe corn and soybeans surrounding Father Hunter's rectory looked like loaves of bread in an oven. I hadn't seen him since he'd rebuked me for "acting out" with Father Foley. I needed his support. Father Hunter headed the seminary board. If they had doubts, he could sway them. After they approved me, the archbishop had the final decision. Father Hunter could influence him too. I put on a penitent face and rang the doorbell.

"I'm sorry," he said. "Dinner will be late." He hugged me and patted my back. "I was tied up at the chancery and just got home." His ashy breath indicated that he'd failed to quit smoking again.

"Oh well," I said, "more time for cocktails."

He grinned, "Come in where it's warm." He led me down a hallway lined with framed Caravaggio prints—scriptural scenes of David, Jesus, and religious men draped in sheets; half-naked, sepia-toned skin against backgrounds of pure darkness; passion and pain. We entered the guest room across the hall from the master suite. I set my duffle bag on the bed.

"I'm concerned something's wrong with Scott," he said. But it was a question.

I could feel his scrutinizing gaze as I unzipped my bag. "Like he tells me anything."

He left me to unpack. Why couldn't they leave me out of their conflict? But everyone had problems. And I was in good care. At Mass in Clinton, Mom had met a visitor from Dubuque, who said Father Scott and Father Hunter were the best priests in Dubuque.

I joined Father Hunter in the kitchen and reached for the cutting board.

"Don't do that," he handed me a fuzzy navel—not the wine cooler version—and snatched up the Cutco knife my dad had sold him. "You really *are* a people pleaser." I had never thought of that as a bad thing, but watching him mutilate a cucumber with the cleaver-like blade, I wasn't going to argue. I did as he ordered: "Sit down. Relax."

After affirming my dad's promises about the superior quality of the cutlery and inquiring about my "gorgeous" mother, he mentioned Father Scott still hadn't returned his calls. "Some people are incapable of intimacy," he said. The knife scraped the surface of the cutting board as he slid the vegetables into the salad. I didn't want to talk about Father Scott. I swallowed my drink. Father Hunter apologized for smoking, lit up, and exhaled into the stove's fan intake.

"You're quiet tonight," he opened the fridge. "Refill?"

During my third drink and over antipasti, he divulged that Father Scott's roommate on a trip to Rome had said, "Scott's a real dangler."

I froze midswig, hoping my eyes hadn't bulged. He scrutinized my next move, as if he sensed my attraction to Father Scott. I set down my glass and ate something from the platter of cheeses, peppers, and olives. Was he telling me it was okay to talk about it? Or would he block my application if I told the truth?

In the dim dining room, over angel hair puttanesca and halfway through a bottle of Chianti, Father Hunter delved into the seminary application process. This exhaustive procedure consisted of psychological questionnaires, an assessment by the archdiocese's psychologist, another by a local psychiatrist who would give me an IQ test, and an interview with the seminary board, which was composed of four or five priests and a token nun and layperson.

"Don't worry about the psych tests," he said. "Just a formality to be sure you're not a serial killer or a molester." We drank to my sanity. He cursed other dioceses, more conservative than ours, where older priests like Father Foley preyed on seminarians. He told me a story about a nun friend. While they were studying canon law in Rome, she had botched the pronunciation of *penne* and ordered not a bowl of hot pasta but hot penis.

After dinner, we settled in the living room. The fire popped under our conversation. Father Hunter sipped his *digestivo* from a cordial glass, which his huge hands could easily have crushed. I was thankful we were back on good terms following the Father Foley debacle, and that I'd discovered a taste for sambuca. Before he poured my second, he complimented how relaxed and funny I'd become after drinking.

"How's your new therapist?" The smoke swirled from his cigarette.

I praised Three and preached the details of PTSD recovery, how I struggled when smells and sounds transported me back to Lauz's office, and how his face even intruded into my sexual fantasies.

"So what were you fantasizing about?"

"You know . . . men," I laughed. "I'm a homosexual."

Then he told me to lie.

In my coming interview with the archdiocese's psychologist, who was a deacon and bigshot canon lawyer with Father Hunter, I was not to share that I was homosexual. I could tell the progressive psychiatrist who would administer the IQ test, but not the deacon. If I wanted to pass the deacon's evaluation, I was to answer affirmatively when he inquired about my attractions to women. When he asked about men, I was simply to say no.

My buzz dulled. I didn't want to become a priest on a lie. The light and shadows from the fire danced on the carpeting.

"It's for the greater good," Hunter said. "There are too many repressed conservatives in the seminary. The Church needs men like you. Men who embrace progress. And therapy. You're doing your work. Why should you be punished for being more integrated than a bunch of closeted, self-hating nellies?"

His eyes reflected the fire, but his voice was cool. He explained how Dubuque passed over the staunchest conservatives, who were afraid even to masturbate, because repression of sexual development resulted in abusing children and such. Those rejects absconded to dioceses like Davenport or Lincoln.

"Peoria's director of vocations takes his seminarians to bed." Without betraying his opinion, he stated, "What do you think of that?"

I fumbled through my thoughts. He'd asked about my fantasies. He'd revealed the size of Father Scott's dick. Half-naked men hung on his walls. Maybe the alcohol was just screwing with my judgment, but I sensed his attraction. He'd told me that he was "very fond" of me, the same words he'd used to describe Father Scott's feelings for me. Was that priestly code for "I want to grab your dick"?

"Well, it's wrong," I said. "A boundary violation."

He lifted his cordial. He had the largest mouth of anyone I'd ever known. A lot could fit in that opening. "Of course it is." He drained the remaining contents.

Later, after I'd brushed and flossed, I stumbled into the hallway. Father Hunter's room was dark, but his door was cracked open, not an accidental slit caused by a resistant latch, not the wide-open assuredness of someone who sleeps with their door open, but four inches of calculated temptation. Peoria.

I entered my room and closed the door.

Sitting at a table in St. Stephen's lobby, I spent hours filling circles on written psychological assessments. When Father Scott passed, he gave me a quick shoulder massage, but he did that to other students, even some of the girls. After the written tests, Father Hunter kidded me about whether I'd answered true or false on the MMPI's absurd questions, such as "Evil spirits possess me at times" and "My stools are black and tarry." He told me not to worry about the interviews.

My meeting with the progressive psychiatrist, Counselor Number Four, was first. When he asked about my sexual orientation, I answered "homosexual," as Father Hunter had instructed.

Counselor Number Five, the deacon psychologist, interviewed me exactly as Father Hunter had outlined.

"Do you have attractions to women?"

"Yes."

"Men?"

"Nope."

I lamented. Could God be present in a lie?

When I brought my feelings to prayer, a new truth flooded my mind: that deacon had no right to stop God's calling. I was more than my urges, more than my dick. The Church taught that all homosexual desires were "intrinsically disordered"; therefore, I had to be chaste—meaning no sexual activity outside marital relations culminating in vaginal sex open to procreation. Because of my lack of desire for vaginas, being a priest made sense. If I had to give up dick, I might as well get praised for my sacrifice by giving it up for Jesus.

URGENT LONGINGS

I felt like a priest. After St. Stephen's staff had gone home to be with their families, I remained on a couch in the lobby consoling the organist, a student from a former Eastern Bloc nation. Being single and celibate, I had nowhere to be.

Her best friend, the liturgist, had been missing since the night before, when they'd had a row. The organist feared she'd killed herself. Father Scott was on his day off. No one in the office knew what to do, so I'd taken charge. I'd gone to the liturgist's apartment, gaining entry with her handyman, and found nothing.

The organist cried. Imagining our roles reversed, I gave her what I would have needed: calm reassurance and words that indicated I'd understood. Unlike Father Scott, who stared at his computer during meetings, I listened.

Later, when he bustled through the lobby with shopping bags, I relayed what had happened.

"You did what?" His mustache hurled quills. It wasn't my place to manage his staff. His students. "Go home, Tom." I wandered back to my apartment dazed. The anxiety of the day pummeled me in waves. Acting like a priest had been exhilarating, but how did they handle being alone after a difficult day?

The next morning, the liturgist reappeared. I asked Father what had happened. "That's not your business." The other staff members avoided asking the liturgist for fear she might implode. They worked extra to cover for her. Unspoken tensions between Father and everyone ballooned. He barked at Josie and me about each streaked window and random pubic hair on the bathroom floors.

One afternoon, I walked into his office, sat, and said, "Stop working for a second and look at me."

He stared at the computer. "Go home, Tom."

"No."

He sighed, rolled away from the screen, and faced me, "What is it now?"

"Are you OK?" I asked. Calmly. Sincerely.

The creases across his forehead softened.

Then he yipped that I was just like Marv, a pimple-faced sophomore, who had the heart of a puppy and nagged for constant coddling. I felt like the grime I scraped from the toilets.

After the student Mass that night, while doing dishes in the church's kitchen, Father tussled playfully with Marv, whipping him with dishrags, giving him noogies, and tweaking his love handles. Maybe I was wrong. Maybe he didn't love me.

"Pastrone! There's Kool-Aid on the tile. Get the mop," he yelled, tightening Marv in a headlock.

"Get it yourself." I slammed my dishrag into the dirty sink. Gray water streaked the immaculate backsplash. Students gasped. I didn't care. The asshole needed to be put in his place.

I was wrong. Or so Josie and I deduced the next day while clearing cobwebs from the rafters. Father Scott wasn't an asshole; he was overstressed. We concocted a plan to save the staff: we needed to get away from St. Stephen's over Christmas break and have some fun.

I followed the bluffs along the frozen Mississippi from Clinton to Bellevue, a small town set between forested hills at Lock and Dam No. 12. At the shore, stocking-capped townsfolk viewed bald eagles that swooped and snatched fish from a break in the river's ice below the cascading spillway. The remnants of Christmas—garland candy canes and angels—embellished the main street's electrical posts. Looming over the rooftops, a Pepto-Bismol-pink Victorian home protruded from forested bluffs like a pop-up book. Mont Rest. There, the St. Stephen's staff would heal.

To save money, the three single women, Josie, Jane, and the liturgist, split the only room with multiple beds. The deacon and his wife had a suite to themselves. Father and I remained to split accommodations. I hoped to bond like my early days at St. Stephen's, but which Father Scott would I get? A part of me didn't want to be in the same room, let alone bed, with him.

The deacon and his wife rose from a loveseat near the great room's fireplace to greet me with hugs. Father remained in an armchair sounding off a nasal "Pastrone." A petite hostess showed me to our upstairs bedroom. Father's black suitcase lay zipped by the drawn curtains of the window. A lacy quilt adorned our queen bed.

After all the guests were present, including some non–St. Stephen's interlopers, the hostess assigned roles and handed out costumes for our Hollywood murder-mystery dinner. I was the bellboy with an unpublished screenplay, desperate to make it with the big boys. Father was the rich producer with a scandalous past that the murder victim had exploited. The list of unimaginative Hollywood stereotypes went on. In the end, it was the deacon's wife, playing the aged, jealous diva, who did the deed. The non–St. Stephen's guests mused that we were "too fun" to be a church staff and were "so lucky" to have one another.

What the other guests didn't notice was Father's going out of his way to avoid me. When I returned from cleaning up in the bathroom, he lay in bed reading a book with the blankets pulled up to the neckline of his shockingly white undershirt. I stripped down to my underwear and crawled under the sheets. Waiting for the blankets to warm, I examined the ceiling's cracks. Father asked, "You OK?"

"No." A blizzard of unspoken doubts about seminary and priesthood plowed over me. Why had I lied about my homosexuality? Would God punish me? What if studying theology, scripture, and church history caused me to lose my faith? I was a logical person. Faith was illogical. I'd doubted God's existence since I was seven years old and figured out that there was no Tooth Fairy, Easter Bunny, or Santa Claus. My dad's response to my question, "Is the Tooth Fairy for real?," had been, "She is if you want her to be." He answered the same way when I questioned the door-opening bunny and reindeer-exploiting elf. I'd wanted to ask about God but had been too afraid Dad might answer, "God's real if you want him to be." I'd wanted God to be real. I still did. I wanted to know that God loved me. The terror of losing my faith and God's love landed on me like a dead Christmas tree.

Father placed his book on the bedside bureau, folded his glasses, laid them on the book, and told me to place my head against his heart. I rolled onto my side and lowered my cheek to his chest. He stroked my hair. His ribs vibrated with a voice no longer nasal, barking, or biting, but velvet assurance that God wouldn't abandon me or allow me to lose my faith. Listening to his heart, feeling the weight of his arm on my back and his fingertips against my scalp, I knew beyond doubt that I was loved. We rolled to the opposite sides of the bed and turned out the lights.

I lay still, trying to sleep, but couldn't. The mattress wobbled. He was restless. A few minutes later, it shook again. The mattress dropped slightly in his direction. I shifted my weight so that I didn't roll back into him. Was he moving closer to me? I chastised myself: *No, you pervert. He's a priest. He's just not used to sharing a bed.* But again, the bed coils rustled. The air between us warmed. He was less than an inch from me. I shortened my breaths, frightened that the full expansion of my ribs might cause us to touch and wake him. The heated cotton of his T-shirt pressed against my skin. His spine rubbed mine.

For what seemed an eternity but was probably only minutes, our backs remained in contact. Blood sloshed through my ears. His breathing remained the same: slow, rhythmic, normal. I felt anything but normal. What did his pressing against me mean? I decided to let him think that I was asleep, to move slowly as he had, afraid that any sudden move might cause him to pull away. Over the course of a minute, without my skin losing contact with his T-shirt, I turned through the darkness, until my chest was against his back. He didn't pull away. I wove my hand through the sheets and around his stomach, expecting he'd toss me aside with a scolding. But he pulled my arm and pressed his lower half into our spoon. Within a few silent moments, we were chest to chest in a tight embrace, his T-shirt lost to the floor. Then he pried his hands between our skin, lifted me into the cold darkness and tossed me to my side of the bed.

"That's enough," he said, before retreating to his side.

Facing away from him, I stared into the night. What had happened? I'd felt his hairy sternum against me, his erection against mine. His sweaty, soapy scent lingered on my face. I contemplated going to the bathroom to masturbate—a lesser sin and a sleep aid.

Again, the mattress moved. He pushed his back against mine. I rolled over. He pulled me into another spoon. I moved my hand around his belly, searching the depths. "So that's what you wanted," he whispered, moaning as my fingers slid beneath his elastic waistline. Then he was on top of me, his mustache against my upper lip, his tongue invading my mouth. I was hurled into the doctor's office. I wanted the tongue to stop, but it didn't. It wouldn't. My body kept moving, hugging, kissing, as if separated from my mind. But this was different from the doctor's office. I told myself to give in, to trust. This had to be love. Still, I wanted the tongue to stop.

Without a break in his kissing, he rolled and pulled me onto himself. No longer trapped under his weight, I moved my mouth to where it had felt most natural with Tobey. After a few seconds, I gagged and pulled away, but he grabbed my hair and held me in place, thrusting until he was finished. He shoved me to my side of the bed, telling me what we'd done was wrong.

I asked him to reciprocate and blow me. He refused.

"Just like Tobey," I said.

He spit in his palm and begrudgingly jacked me off: no kissing or words of love, just the procedural fist of a distant, unknown man stroking me to orgasm.

The guilt followed. I wanted to talk about what had happened, but Father refused. "Go to sleep, Tom." After hours of tossing about in desolation, silently begging God for comfort but feeling nothing but hell's gravity, I fell asleep. I awoke to an alarm clock and an empty bed. Father's suitcase had vanished.

When I entered the dining room, the deacon's wife gave me a slanted smirk. When the breakfast conversation required Father to acknowledge me, he did so without eye contact. I worried everyone knew. What if in the middle of the night someone had gone downstairs for a glass of water and heard us? I added sugar to my coffee and buttered my conversation.

After checkout, Father, the deacon, and his wife visited the local parish, where Father had worked early in his priesthood. I tagged along, hoping to catch him alone. I feared that I'd destroyed his vocation. He was a popular priest. He helped so many. That had to continue. But I also wanted him to love me so much that he'd throw it all away.

He plunked out a few tunes on the organ. I felt as hollow as a broken pipe.

After the miniconcert, the deacon and his wife left. Father rushed down the sidewalk toward his black sedan. The sun's glare on the snow blinded me.

“Wait,” I said. He yanked open the car door. “Scott, we need to talk.”

He met my eyes, the first time since the night. He looked terrified. His mustache scowled: “Go home, Tom.”

He dropped into the car, slammed the door, and sped off heading north.

I couldn’t move or catch my breath. The wind burrowed through the hillside of denuded trees and scraped across my skin before screeching over the icy river. A bald eagle shrilled, splashed, and flapped away from a break in the ice. A skewered meal squirmed in its talons. In the darkness of the night, I had been unable to see Father Scott’s face, the face of someone who loved me but now loathed me. I drove south, following the river.

IN PRAISE OF FOLLY

At home, I opened the curtains of the picture window and stared down the steep driveway. When I was a tween, Mom had scolded me for hosing down the incline to build a bobsled course midwinter. Beyond the memory, across Scenic Drive and down Meadowview Lane, I imagined Father Scott's car climbing the pavement. I waited until the glass grew cloudy and then icy from my breath. Father wasn't coming to Clinton. I was home. Alone.

I slunk into the lower-level family room, tossed my duffle bag and shoes into my bedroom, and checked the answering machine on the faded black Formica counter. Mom and Dad spoke of their safe arrival at our cousin's wedding in Michigan and hoped that I'd had fun at Mont Rest. Why hadn't I gone with them? If I'd put family first, I wouldn't have had sex with Father. I swaddled myself in earth-toned afghans, wedged myself into the loveseat, and burrowed into the darkness.

For two days, I left my cocoon only to eat and relieve myself. Television voices rambled: disjointed guttural sounds, background noise to my inner monologue. I was too ashamed to pray. I didn't understand what it meant to have had sex with Father. I needed to know: Had he used me to get off, or did he love me? On the third day, I rose and drove to Cedar Falls.

When I reached St. Stephen's, Father met me halfway across the lobby by the trickling holy water font. "Go home, Tom." He grabbed my coat, dragged me into his office, and closed the door. I sat in the rocking chair, arms crossed. My fingers strangled my biceps. His voice lowered into a razor-sharp whisper. After leaving Mont Rest, he drove to his confessor and unloaded our sin. He ordered me to do the same, saying I'd seduced him and needed to repent if I were to be forgiven by him or God, if I still hoped to be a priest. When I tried to respond, he interrupted: "Haven't you already done enough?"

He punched numbers on his desktop phone and told his confessor I was on my way—canon law forbade me from confessing to Father Scott himself because he was the one with whom I'd sinned. I didn't protest. I'd planned the trip to Mont Rest. I'd been the one who'd rolled over. I'd blown him, just as I had Tobey and almost Father Foley. I was the depraved gay who had ensnared a holy priest.

Thirty minutes later, the frozen black cornfields grew darker as the sun set behind the overcast sky. I drove on unfamiliar county roads, leading me to Father Scott's confessor, Father Schulhaus. They'd known each other for years. Father Schulhaus was the one who'd told Father Hunter about seeing Father Scott's "dangler" in Rome. I wondered whether he and Father Scott had shared a bed on that trip. Was Father Scott sending me to have sex with him? Was this the reality of celibacy? But I didn't want to have sex with another priest. I wanted forgiveness.

Father Schulhaus greeted me with a paint-speckled handshake and a grave smile before inviting me into his rectory. Dented tubes of paint, rainbow-lathered palettes, and half-finished canvases cluttered the rooms. The mess shocked me. The other priests I knew were so tidy—or "anal retentive" as Father Scott called them (and me). Father Schulhaus had thinning blonde curls. He spoke with a voice like a down comforter. I chose the chair across the coffee table from him and told him what I'd done to Father Scott. He nodded and didn't say much, only that he couldn't hear my confession because it was a conflict of interest with his relationship with Father Scott. He walked me to the door and shook my hand. I drove the curvy roads back to Clinton feeling worse.

The next day, I crossed the Mississippi to Fulton, Illinois, a Dutch Reformed town with one Catholic parish. The priest there didn't know me. He wouldn't recognize me as a Rastrelli. The inner voices of my childhood conditioning remained intact: *Family comes first. Don't do anything that will damage the family name and Grandpa's legacy. If you screw up, you hurt the business.*

In Catholic grade school I'd learned that going to confession was like leveling a wall of sin that I'd built between God and me. Venial sins—lesser infractions such as swearing, disobeying, gossiping, or cheating—were pebbles that over time piled up into a small but surmountable barrier, over which I could still see and hear God. Mortal sins—grave infractions involving adultery, murder, or blasphemy against the Holy

Spirit—were wall-sized sins that formed an impenetrable monolith between God's grace and my soul. Sex with a priest was a Great Wall of China–sized sin. Confession, contrition, absolution, and penance—telling a priest, feeling "heartily sorry," receiving God's forgiveness through the proxy of the confessor, and completing good deeds that proved my conversion—were the ritualistic wrecking ball. I worried whether the fragile, bald priest with fishbowl glasses who sat in his office staring at me, shocked that a college boy had come knocking on New Year's Eve, was up to the task.

He made the sign of the cross, invoked God's loving mercy, and prompted me to confess. Staring at his scuffed wingtips, I admitted having sex with my confessor, who was also my spiritual director and campus minister, who was helping me prepare for seminary, but that we didn't have anal sex, just oral, well me giving him oral after which he jacked me off. I'd put our vocations to the priesthood at risk and wanted to do better. I'd failed God, the Church, and myself. As I spoke, the priest's eyes blinked behind the lenses, normal periodic blinks. No staring. No looking away. I expected him to grow angry, to yell at me, maybe grab me, or to gasp and cover his ears, or at least blush, shocked by the fact that a priest and his future seminarian had done the unthinkable. But his monotonous voice prescribed a rosary using the sorrowful mysteries and encouraged me to start the new year sin free. His lack of affect left me feeling more confused. Was it commonplace for college students who were planning to be priests to confess they'd blown their pastors?

When I got home, I dug through the keepsakes in my top dresser drawer until I found a rosary and the prayer book Grandma and Grandpa Figgins gave me for first Communion. The book's pages crackled as I pried them apart for the first time in a dozen years. I looked up the five sorrowful mysteries—Jesus's agony in the garden, scourging at the pillar, crowning with thorns, carrying the cross, and crucifixion. I prayed to Mary, asking her to beseech God on my behalf. As the fifty beads representing Hail Marys slid through my fingertips, I imagined Jesus sweating blood, his skin torn by barbed whips, and thorns puncturing his skull. I imagined the cross driving splinters into his gouged flesh, the spikes splitting the bones in his forearms and ankles, and the fluid filling his lungs until he suffocated. Each of my sins corresponded to a drop of Jesus's blood, a snap of the whip, a nail piercing his flesh, or twinge of pain. My sins, I, had crucified him. I swore never to compound his suffering again. I would be the celibate priest he'd called me to be.

Two weeks later, I reported to St. Stephen's for my cleaning duties. Two steps into the lobby, a boisterous "Pastrone!" sideswiped me. "What took you so long to get back?" Father Scott shook my hand, yanked me into a headlock, and ground his knuckles against my scalp. A few students, including Marv, leapt from couches, egging him on.

Father increased his grip and twisted one of my nipples. "Say, 'uncle.' Beg for mercy, Pastrone."

I wriggled like a severed earthworm. Marv pried him off me. Apparently, we were to pretend that nothing had happened.

A few minutes later, I stood in the janitor's closet reading Father's to-do list. The heating system hummed. "Pastrone!" he shouted from behind.

I recoiled against the wall. "Holy shit."

His head curled around the doorframe like an old *Laugh-In* comedian. "Got ya," he said. "I'm fixing you dinner. We've got a lot to talk about." He opened his eyes wide and flared his nostrils over his mustache. "See you at six." And disappeared.

In the back corner of St. Stephen's walkout lower level, Father's apartment bordered the parking lot, a walled patio, a grassy yard, a classroom, and a hallway. The staff's offices were above. Even at home, he was surrounded by work. The apartment had two bedrooms, two bathrooms, and a compact kitchen that blended into a tiny dining and living room. The simple space had shredded-wheat Berber carpeting. Father had spiced it up with a mulberry couch and cobalt recliner. Multicolored stained-glass lamps opened like fragile umbrellas on the end tables. In the hallway leading back to the bedrooms, his collection of crucifixes hung: a cornucopia of corpora—silver, gold, wooden, painted—dying for the salvation of the world. Waist-high shelving lined the walls. They held small stained-glass versions of his previous churches. In one of the small frames speckling the spaces between the churches, I noticed my picture.

Over dinner, he spoke of coming events at St. Stephen's before asking how my interview with the seminary board had gone. Father Hunter had assured me that the board had no issues and that my acceptance by the archbishop was "merely a formality." As we spoke and ate—there was no drinking in Father Scott's apartment—he bounced with an enthusiasm I'd never seen. I wanted to enjoy myself. But had he lured me to castigate me for seducing him? After dinner, we settled into the living room. He sat in the recliner and I on the couch.

He flattened the creases on the sides of his baggy jeans. "Since I shooed you away a few weeks ago, I've been thinking. A lot. And praying about what happened." His brow furrowed. His breathing grew shallow. As his plum lips opened, I expected him to lash out.

"When I was in sixth grade, my scoutmaster abused me. He performed oral sex on me and the other boys."

"I'm so sorry."

His eyes closed. "There's more."

He admitted a sexual relationship with his best friend during college in Clinton. He and his friend would drive to the south end of town to his friend's parents' motel and do it "like rabbits."

"Are you still in touch with him?" I asked.

"No." His lips shrunk as if preparing to spit.

He'd had his Tobey. He'd had his Doctor Lauz. We were the same. "I don't think any less of you," I said, watching him bite his thumbnail. "You're human. You sin."

He nodded his head and lowered his elbow onto the arm of the recliner. His mustache and chin pressed against his fist: "There's more."

In college, he stayed at the parish rectory during breaks to avoid his drunken father. A middle-aged priest enticed him into an ongoing sexual relationship. After graduation, he lived with the priest for a year before going to seminary. His eyes were moist. He looked away and spoke into his fist: "He had me use this ringlike thing around my stuff while we—" He shook his head. "Disgusting."

I tried not to look shocked, but I was. Even though I felt awful for him, my body was betraying me, just as it had with the doctor. I shifted my black jeans and baggy sweatshirt to hide my erection. The last thing I wanted him to think was that I wanted sex. He was confessing. To me. I had to be the priest. But I also wanted more details about the genital device.

"I'm sorry," I said.

He lowered his hands into his lap. His shoulders rounded forward. "I don't want to be that lecherous old priest."

"You're not."

He looked me in the eyes. "I don't want to hurt you."

"I don't want to hurt you either."

His face blushed. He squinted and rubbed his eyes. I leaned forward, trying to indicate that I wouldn't reject him.

He said, "You're the first person who's really cared about me in years. You asked me how I was doing and wanted a real answer. You looked past the priest."

Just as he had during my first confession with him, I reached and took his hand. It was trembling. I said, "What you've told me doesn't change anything. I still care." He pulled away. His sad eyes looked to the floor. Over his head, picture frames crowded the wall. Enshrined black-and-white portraits of ancestors intermixed with color photos of his numerous siblings, friends, and parishioners. They surrounded him, but none of them knew him. None of them loved him for who he really was.

"I care about you, Scott." He shook his head. "Even more so because of what you just told me. I love you."

Fear or joy filled his eyes. "I care about you too, Pastrone." He sat up. "God has blessed us with this connection," he said. "This is a gift. He wouldn't have graced us with it if He didn't want us to realize it."

He stood and extended his thick hand. I placed my palm against his. He led me past the generations of portraits, the stained-glass churches, and the wall of crucifixes into the guest room, where he embraced me. I opened my lips and received his tongue. Images of the pediatrician ripped through my mind, but I persevered, focusing on Father's touch. We shed our clothes and ripped the comforter from the bed. As one body, we rolled onto the mattress. Within minutes, he lowered his head and took me into his mouth. I was lost in communion.

After orgasm, the standard guilt consumed me. I gathered my clothes, hurried to the guest bathroom, shut the door, and hopped into the shower. My skin still tingled with excitement, but my thoughts oscillated between elation—he really loved me—and panic—we'd sinned. I abraded my body with a soapy cloth. Suds swirled down the drain.

When finished and clothed, I stepped into the hallway. With his back to the wall of crucifixes, he stuffed the bedding into the washing machine. "You OK, Pastrone?"

I retrieved my boots from the guest room floor, my eyes avoiding the bed. "Yeah." I leaned against the wall at the foot of the bed and pulled on my boots. "I'm fine."

Lit from behind, he stood in the doorway watching me tie the laces. His torso and head cast conjoined elliptical shadows that stretched over me.

"Thank you," he said.

I froze, shoelace in my fingers. "For what . . . ?" I silently chastised myself, *seducing you?*

"For being here."

"Oh." I finished the bow and stood up. "You too."

We hugged. He showed me to the back door. I snuck out through the wooden door of his patio's seven-foot-tall fence. As I passed through the small halos of light lining the driveway, the four windows of his apartment were already dark.

I walked his driveway most nights as my final semester progressed. One afternoon while I worked, he snuck into the janitor's closet and jumped me from behind, kissing my neck and reaching around to stroke me. I pushed him away, whispering, "Settle down, Father. Someone might see." He laughed and came at me again. One night, when a female friend was staying in his guest room, he threw himself on me in the lobby and pulled me into the coat closet, only seconds after he'd locked the front doors. I worried someone was praying in the chapel or his friend might hear. "Stop," I tried to pry free. After another student and I finished shoveling the sidewalks, Father invited us in for chili. When the other fellow left, Father pulled me into his bedroom. I was embarrassed that my body reeked of sweat and my feet of drenched leather, but he didn't care. The bed jostled. Less than twenty feet above, the secretary answered the phone. Through the wall, an elderly granny prepped for the sacraments of initiation class. I didn't understand how he could be so unconcerned or even excited by the possibility that someone might discover us.

"We have to stop," I said, as I washed at his sink.

"I know," he said from the bed. He rolled over, facing away.

I knew the drill and showed myself out.

In spite of my guilt, I returned the next night: patio gate unlatched, back door unlocked. He waited in bed. Later, as I walked home, students passed, heading to the bars. The animosity I held toward their "Why Don't We Get Drunk and Screw" attitudes vanished. We were all sinners. At least they had alcohol. What was my excuse?

"It's taken the edge off of our relationship," Father said in my next spiritual direction meeting. "It's been good for us."

I nodded. We weren't bickering any more. I stopped seeing Number Three.

On my birthday, a letter from the archbishop arrived. I ran to St. Stephen's with it. Father rushed me down to his apartment. We ripped it open: I was accepted to begin pretheology courses at Loras College in Dubuque. I was going to seminary. We embraced. Then he knelt and blew me.

In April, the Iowa Medical Board of Examiners dropped my case against Lauz due to lack of evidence. Father held me in my grief and then pulled me into the bedroom. When we were finished, I said, "I love you."

As usual, he quoted the Budweiser commercial saying, "I love you, man!" in a pretend drunken voice. I walked up the driveway doubting his words.

I sat before a mirror in the theatre's dressing room applying makeup. Graduation was a week away. For months, I'd been preparing my senior recital—a thirty-minute theatrical piece: monologues, short scenes, and musical numbers. Father and I had brainstormed the showcase over post-Mass omelets. To frame the entire piece, I'd used Deuteronomy 30:15–19, "The Choice before Israel," whether to choose God and life or to serve other gods and perish. The performance traced my spiritual journey from birth to rejecting the Church to my return and ultimately the priesthood. My sisters, who both performed, sat next to me, readying their hair and faces. Old friends from Clinton, family members, theatre folks, and St. Stephenites filled up the black box theatre. I said some precurtain prayers and the show began. We sang songs from *Big River*, *The Fantasticks*, *Sweeney Todd*, *Into the Woods*, and *Sunday in the Park with George*. I poured my soul into monologues from *Mass Appeal* and St. Paul's witness of conversion in Acts 22. I raised my arms to the heavens singing “Move on! Move on!” before my sisters adorned me in an alb and we closed with the show’s title number, *The Tie That Binds*, an old hymn Father Scott had passed on to me.

After curtain call, I scanned the lobby but couldn’t find Father. The directors of *Assassins* and *Wild Honey* congratulated and hugged me. Over their shoulders, I saw Father’s nun friends and moved to intercept them. An old theatre friend with whom I’d bashed religion before my calling, yanked me aside. Tears filled his eyes. He said, “I understand now.” Josie and students from the Antioch retreats swarmed. My grandmother asked what the show meant. My parents and grandfather nodded. They knew: the priesthood bound me to the world, God’s people, and to life itself. It was me. And Father was nowhere to be found.

The next day, I cornered him in his apartment. “Why’d you avoid me after the recital? Did I do something wrong?”

“Come here, Paddlefoot.” His private nickname for me, after my wide feet, eased my fear that he was mad. He caressed my shoulder. “If I’d have spoken to you last night, I would’ve lost it.” He explained: throughout the performance, in the back-row darkness, he’d sobbed. His eyes filled with tears, “God’s working through you. I’m just damaging your vocation.”

I felt like the wind had been knocked out of me. He was right. We were living a double life. We needed to stop. I had to move on from our sin. But instead, I pulled him into a hug and whispered, “I’m fine.”

We retreated into the bedroom.

THE SEVEN STOREY MOUNTAIN

Early on a July morning, before the sun stirred the muggy midwestern air into a convection oven, I hunched over a small spherical barbecue. A few months earlier, at the Easter Vigil, it housed the fire that represented the redemptive light of Christ coming into the darkness of the world. My solo vigil was of a different nature, more personal, but just as integral to my salvation, my future in the priesthood. At the side of the empty parking lot and in the shadow of St. Stephen's, I placed my spiritual journals into the metal bowl, doused them with lighter fluid, lit a match, and tossed it in. They erupted in a whooshing flame.

Weeks earlier, I had filed a civil lawsuit against Lauz in Clinton County Court. The medical board's failure left me no other option. I sued under the pseudonym *John Doe.* The doctor and his practice also remained anonymous. My lawyer hoped this would show the judge and jury that I wasn't out to destroy reputations but to protect potential victims. I hoped it would keep my name out of the papers, which Father Hunter warned might spook the archbishop into dismissing me from seminary. During the discovery phase, where each side gathered witnesses and written evidence, the defense could summon anything I'd written: poetry, songs, monologues, diaries. My spiritual journals, six spiral-bound notebooks, held my deepest desires, fantasies, and sins: everything about Father Scott and our failure. Father had assured me the journals were privileged information because I'd used them in spiritual direction. "It's under the seal of the Confessional. They can't touch it in court." But he wasn't a lawyer.

In Dubuque for a meeting, Father couldn't stop me. The staff was off for the month. Students slept in their beds. No one would be party to my destruction of evidence. I prodded the pages with a poker.

As the sun emerged over the university bookstore next to the church, the dewy grass glistened like the candles of the Easter Vigil, Christ's light passed from one believer to the next until the unified congregation became a beacon in the darkness. I wanted Christ to burn away my sin, my attractions to men and to Father. The past needed to die. What remained ahead was resurrection: seminary.

A beige pickup rattled down the driveway and parked a few feet from my bonfire. The deacon, a retired professor with a runner's build, stepped out and approached. "That's the Tom I know. Hard at work."

"Just getting rid of old class stuff. Who needs acting notes in seminary?" I stirred the flames, hoping to disintegrate any legible scribbles.

He stood at my side. If he and his wife suspected anything about Father and me, they'd said nothing. Instead, they'd invited us for dinners. They'd promised to send me fifty dollars per month throughout seminary. Nonnegotiable. They prayed for my vocation and loved me like a son. I hated myself for deceiving them.

"Enjoy the catharsis," the deacon said, before heading inside.

I flipped the notebooks exposing more pages. Flames lapped at the unblemished sheets. I stabbed, swatted, and stirred the charcoaled text into ash. The notebooks' metal spirals became molten orange, the color of hell. The little barbeque collapsed onto the ground. A leg had pierced the base. I'd failed to notice how the heat of the liquefied spirals had weakened the hull. The grill had seen its last Easter fire.

After all had turned to dust, I doused the remains with a garden hose and left the grill to cool. I set about my yardwork: mowing, edging, pruning, weeding, raking. No blade of grass or decomposing leaf escaped my scouring. My palms blistered as I swept the sidewalk and driveway. I blasted the parking lot with a hose. As a whirlpool of coffee-colored runoff and plant matter swirled through the grate in the center of the lot, I tossed the damaged grill and ashen remains of my sin into the dumpster. I left St. Stephen's immaculate.

PART II

ST. PIUS X, POPE

Patron Saint of
First Communicants
and Pilgrims
1996–98

I firmly hold, then, and shall hold to my dying breath the belief of the Fathers in the charism of truth, which certainly is, was, and always will be in the succession of the episcopacy from the apostles.
—Pius X, *The Oath against Modernism* (1910)

THE CONSOLATION OF PHILOSOPHY

I straightened my tie in the rearview mirror of my Ford Escort. The vehicle was a postaccident rebuild, white with aquamarine stripes on the sides. The junker only had to get me through six years of seminary, after which my priestly paycheck would buy something new. I grabbed my sports coat and got out. Vehicles crowded the curb of the residential Dubuque cul-de-sac. I checked my watch: five minutes until the meeting started. Apparently celibates arrived early to official functions.

The archbishop's beige ranch home occupied a corner lot in a neighborhood with streets named after women: Adeline, Ramona, Pamela. The verdant lawn defied the late summer sun. The pruned bushes resembled coffins.

I rang the bell. The door whipped open.

"Tom, welcome." Archbishop Haggis's hand enveloped mine. Grandma Figgins had heard him preach about milking cows in his Nebraska youth and how that strengthened his broad hands. I'd inherited Grandpa's large hands, but they looked girlish compared to the archbishop's. I shook firmly, as Grandma had taught me, to impress.

"Thank you, Archbishop."

He bucked the stereotype of candy-cane-postured bishops with cloudy pupils. His athletic frame filled the doorway. Despite his graying hair, he was rumored to be a monster on the racquetball court.

"Any trouble finding the place?"

"Not at all."

A smile broadened over his dimpled chin. "Did you notice the street names?" He set his hand on my shoulder and leaned in. "I tell folks that you have to get past three women to get into the archbishop's home."

I laughed and entered.

A modest chandelier hung over a long table with china set for more than twenty. Throughout the room, seminarians and priests in navy sports coats or black clerical attire clustered, toddies in hand. My trendy tweed sports coat and paisley tie suddenly felt tight.

"How about a julep?" The archbishop asked. "I used fresh mint from the garden."

I followed him past the kitchen and his multitasking chef into a den, where more men mingled. The room looked like any family room: two recliners facing a television flanked by end tables, lamps, and bookshelves. He passed me off to the seminarian who'd had the bicycle-bell mug at Father Hunter's Christmas party. From behind a small bar, he poured me a julep.

Father Hunter approached offering a handshake. "It's great to have you here, Mister Rastrelli." Apparently hugging in the archbishop's presence was out of the question.

"Thank you," we clinked our glasses, "*Father*."

I looked around at the seminarians and priests exchanging the latest jokes and pastoral war stories. I had arrived. This was seminary.

"How's Scott?" Father Hunter asked with furrowed brow.

I wanted to say, *Call him yourself and ask*. The last thing I wanted to discuss in the archbishop's presence was Father Scott. I said, "I don't know."

Father Hunter introduced me to Father Rich Dixon, a skinny priest in his thirties whose teeth sparkled with orthodontics. Father Dixon was also a canon lawyer and worked at the chancery. "He'll become director of seminarians next year when I return to Rome for my JCD," Father Hunter said. "Not to be confused with a pontifical STD. I don't need another one of those."

I wasn't sure whether to laugh. Father Dixon chuckled and moved on. Father Hunter recognized my confusion. "Really, Mister Rastrelli. Did Scott teach you nothing? STD. *Sacrae Theologiae Doctor*."

I congratulated him. A JCD was a huge step toward bishop. He shrugged off my enthusiasm.

"What's wrong?"

"Rome," he said, as if repeating a courtroom sentence. He threw back the last of his scotch and returned to the bar.

The archbishop sat not at the head of the table but in the middle, surrounded by those of us who were new. Conversation remained light: questions about our hometowns, relatives, and previous lives. Someone explained that "previous lives" meant everything that happened before seminary. All the nonpriests were in white or light blue shirts. Every couple of bites, I readjusted the sleeves of my jacket to cover my mustard-colored cuffs.

The other new guys were cordial. I imagined sharing meals, becoming close, working in neighboring parishes, supporting one another through the coming decades, vacationing together, and eventually burying one another.

After the meal, we descended into a large room with cinderblock walls in the basement. Sitting in a circle of folding chairs, we prayed Evening Prayer. I had never done Evening Prayer before. During my last year at UNI, I'd met with Father Scott and a couple of students for Morning Prayer, but we'd always been too busy at night. As the other seminarians used their color-coded ribbons to open their breviaries, I felt exposed. The bald guy next to me whispered for me to look off his book. "We'll get you a set from the dead priests' library after the meeting," he snickered.

After prayer, Archbishop Haggis invited each seminarian to ask him one question—a tradition at the annual gathering. The guys rustled in their seats. A few loosened their shoulders and jaws, as if they were cracking their mind's knuckles and prepping for battle. Most inquiries fell into the following categories: seminary procedures, liturgical arguments, and shortage of priests. As the role of questioner approached me, I conjured an obvious question to which I thought everyone could relate.

"Tom, fire away," the archbishop said, with open hands.

I leaned forward. "Archbishop, how did you receive your calling to the priesthood?"

He looked at his hands. The grinding squeaks of the chairs marred the silence. I glanced around the room. A few seminarians averted their eyes. Others focused on the archbishop, anticipating his response. I relaxed, until I noticed a couple veterans shielding smirks. The archbishop looked perturbed or amused. Nobody moved. I wasn't the only curious one. They'd never heard the archbishop's story either.

"Thank you for your question, Tom." He flashed a quick smile. "I promise to answer it at a future date."

Without thinking, I kindly said, "I look forward to it, Archbishop." Or had I said it with a passive-aggressive tint, or even worse, laced with stalker-like eagerness? I slunk into my chair. The archbishop nodded graciously, or with forced tolerance, and moved on to the next seminarian.

Whatever his intention, I got this message: respect means silence. Keep your mouth shut and mind your own business.

Afterward, the archbishop wished us a splendid school year, offered us his blessing, and dismissed us. A priest in his late fifties with saggy eyelids and the wounded scowl of a basset hound showed us new guys to the dead priest's library: shelves of dusty books in the corner of the basement. The rector of St. Pius X Seminary at Loras College in Dubuque, he was my on-campus superior for the coming two years of "pretheology"—shorthand for graduate-level seminary prerequisites in philosophy and religious studies. He instructed us to take whatever books we needed. I snatched a four-volume set of the Liturgy of the Hours, boxed in white cardboard aged with coffee-like splatters. Inside, the red, blue, tan, and green breviaries looked as if they'd never been opened.

"Nice find," the rector said. "Hopefully you'll put them to more use than their previous owner." He handed me a thick book with a weathered black cover and silver lettering titled *Liber Usualis.* "A singer like you should have one of these."

I flipped through the pages of music. I'd never seen four-lined staves, stemless square and diamond notes, and Latin lyrics. "What is it?"

The other seminarians looked at me as if I were a moron.

"It's the official book of Gregorian chant used before Vatican II," the rector said. "Didn't Bell teach you anything at UNI? No matter. We'll take care of you at Loras."

My forehead dripped under the August sun in the heart of campus as I lugged my possessions into Smyth Hall—Loras College's buildings were named for Dubuque's deceased bishops. The eastward view from my modest room overlooked the lower campus and, farther down, neighborhoods in the flats of the Mississippi. I covered my walls with pictures of my family and church friends, just like Father Scott's apartment. The lamp he'd given me I placed on my desk. I scraped the dust from the heating pipe that crossed above my bed and sanitized my dresser drawers. I excused the bass thumping from the floor below and the cackling upstairs. The undergraduate dorm wasn't ideal, but I could do anything for two years.

My three classmates weren't as forgiving. Because of our undergraduate degrees in secular fields, we were classified "nontraditional" seminarians, unlike the undergraduate seminarians majoring in philosophy or religious studies. Rob, a high school teacher from Chicago, had returned to Dubuque, where his uncle was a priest. Like my father, Rob was a Hodgkin's survivor, so I felt connected, even though he smelled like the inside of a vitamin bottle. He was the eldest of our group, thirty-three or thirty-four, and the shortest by seven inches. A year younger than Rob, Matthew was the tallest and skinniest, with an angular, aristocratic face. He was a grant writer, held a master's degree from the University of Iowa, and seemed to come from money. We connected through our love of musicals, although he preferred the older shows, such as *Mame* and *Thoroughly Modern Millie*, to my Sondheim. Gerald was a big-boned, Germanic farm boy from the hills of western Dubuque County. He had a Union Jack bedspread and an affinity for World War II documentaries.

At our first meal in the dining center, I couldn't wait to share our stories of being called to the priesthood. Instead, they bitched about the dorm and being the oldest students on a campus of 1,200 puerile undergrads. Anything positive I voiced was doused like cotton candy in a downpour.

"You're so naïve," Rob said. "When you're our age, you'll understand."

My routine developed much like life at UNI, with a few changes. After breakfast in the dining center with my classmates, I went to campus ministry for Morning Prayer. My classmates passed. They disapproved of the "crazy hippy" campus pastor, Father Vince, who used a translation with gender-neutral pronouns referring to the Father, Son, and Holy Spirit as Creator, Redeemer, and Sanctifier. Father Vince opened my eyes to the social repercussions of the Gospel, what liberation theologians called God's preferential option for the poor and oppressed. I chose him as my spiritual director. His refusal to pay taxes to "a corrupt government" seemed extreme, but he practiced what he preached. On Monday nights, I assisted him at the Catholic Worker House, preparing meals for and eating alongside Dubuque's poor.

Classes were always with my classmates and a sprinkling of undergrads. I loved scripture, history, and philosophy but loathed Latin. Our comic-book-like text used tales from an ancient Roman boy's life and instructed us in useful Latin phrases: *Quintus throws the stick to Flacus. Flacus retrieves the stick. Quintus says, "Good dog, Flacus."* It was simpler than eighth-grade Spanish. To fill my boredom, I rewrote Quintus's caption bubbles to include alien abduction and a stint as a serial killer.

Mass felt like a regression too. For the first time since sixth grade, I served as an acolyte. At St. Stephen's, congregants in street clothes simply stepped forward from pews to assist at the altar or distribute Communion. At Loras, two seminarians dressed in albs tailed the priest like overgrown altar boys. Before my debut, a young seminarian had to teach me how to tie a knot in my cincture—the rope that goes around one's waist. As the priest prayed from the *Sacramentary* that rested on my palms and against my chest, I resisted the itch of the alb around my neck. I preferred the noncostumed role of cantor, with Matthew accompanying me at the piano. Leading the congregation in song reminded me of St. Stephen's.

Determined to build friendships with my classmates, I shared every meal with them. Shortly after Cardinal Bernadine of Chicago died of cancer, I plopped into the booth. Rob looked up from his tater tots and said, "It's devastating. First Bernadine. Now the pope."

"No," I set down my fork. "When did he die?"

They laughed. "Jesus, Tom," Rob said, "you're so gullible."

I wanted to fling my peas at him. *Turn the other cheek.* I changed the subject. Before long, Gerald defaulted to Churchill references and the hippie liberals ruining the Church. He was close to Father Scott's predecessor at UNI, who Josie said assaulted one of our female friends. I hesitated to trust him. I focused on Matthew, but when Gerald and Rob were present, I was the outsider. The kid.

After a few months, I ate breakfast alone in my room. At lunch, I sat with the religious studies majors, who were female and reminded me of my college friends. Some felt called to the priesthood. "Well, if I'm ever bishop, I'll ordain you," I said.

I brought my frustrations with my classmates to Counselor Number Six. A puffy man with thick glasses and a comb-over, Six spoke after long silences during which his brain seemed to flip through dusty textbooks, searching for appropriate things to say. He was gentle, but I felt uncomfortable with him. I withheld my homosexual experiences. I saw him to assure the seminary faculty and archbishop that I wasn't a sexual threat to children.

Each week, the rector gathered the undergraduate seminarians and pretheologians for a private Mass. During the intercessions—the prayers of the faithful to which all responded, "Lord, hear our prayer"—we voiced spontaneous prayers. The conservative seminarians, who longed for the pre–Vatican II Church, prayed for the pope, the "happy repose of the poor souls in purgatory," the conversion of non-Catholics, and the overturn of *Roe v. Wade*. The progressive, left-leaning seminarians prayed for an end to the unjust distribution of wealth between First and Third World nations, successful ecumenical and interreligious dialogue, and the abolition of the death penalty. Those in the center prayed for benign things, such as a loved one's recovery from illness. Those who were frustrated with the prayerful posturing prayed for unity in the Church. I sided with the poor and oppressed.

On Thursdays, we pretheologians were invited—seminary code for required—to dine in the priests' private dining room to "build community" with those on the faculty. In the days leading up to our first meal, I filled with excitement, hoping to befriend priests outside Father Scott's circle. Most of them were shy, cordial, and intelligent. The exception, a silver-bearded curmudgeon with a smoker's growl, pontificated about Hillary Clinton's running the White House and highlighted some medieval pope's scandalous proclivities. A month into the semester, he compared African Americans to monkeys. The moral theologian walked out in protest, never again to eat in the priests' dining room. As the weeks passed, others followed suit. By December, only the racist drunk and those beyond retirement age, men who'd spent their entire careers living in the male dormitories, remained. We concluded they were at Loras because they couldn't survive in a parish. We learned to stuff our opinions and ignore the ranting insanity. I questioned whether I could survive priesthood to age seventy, or—more likely with the vocations' shortage and ever-rising retirement age—eighty or eighty-five. Would the isolation and loneliness mold me into an idiosyncratic outcast?

After the Thursday night meals, when my brothers had settled into their rooms, I snuck out and drove to a retreat center on the edge of town. In the private apartment of a satellite building, a "hermitage" as

Father Scott called it, he waited for me, in town for his Friday off. Under cover of darkness, I parked my white Escort in the shadows. As always, his door remained unlocked. After checking that no one watched from a lit window in the neighboring retreat house, I entered. Father waited in bed or the tub. For a few moments, I didn't feel so alone.

A THEOLOGY OF LIBERATION

I pulled the blankets, careful not to make Father Scott's twin bed squeak. Moonlight penetrated the blinds. Outside, across the snowy lot, even the ΣAE house was silent. But not my mind. Things were supposed to have been different once I started seminary. I traced my finger along the headboard that matched the custom-built, single-occupancy church pew in the corner. The first time I'd seen it I'd wondered, *What kind of person has a pew in his bedroom?* Now I knew.

Father's exhales rose from the sleeping bag on the floor. It was our first night sharing a bedroom. I normally slept in the guestroom. I would have preferred to snuggle, but after orgasm, he was done. On occasion, he stood behind me, watching in his bathroom mirror as he fondled me. I wondered whether he imagined having my tall, skinny body. I fantasized about anal sex but didn't ask. Following his lead, I concluded oral wasn't as sinful. Our limited behaviors weren't really violating his celibate commitment.

Tonight was different. When I arrived at St. Stephen's, he'd greeted me with disappointment. Unexpected guests were coming. I'd offered to leave, but he begged me to stay. Now, I hoped the adjoining room's occupants, his brother and sister-in-law, were sound sleepers. We'd done it on the floor so they wouldn't hear the bed rattling.

In the morning we all made small talk over breakfast. I fretted my face was pink from rubbing against Father's stubble. God would out me somehow, punishing my duplicity. But if Father's family suspected anything, they didn't mention it.

Later, when he and I were alone on his couch, I said, "We have to stop." My second semester at Loras had started. I needed to be celibate. Our behavior was too risky.

"You're right," he said. I couldn't recall the last time he'd agreed with me. I wanted to blow him on the spot. He must have sensed my energy, because he told me to close my eyes. "I won't do anything bad."

His fingertips pressed against my eyelids. Gently, he massaged my eyes. "This is intimacy," he said. "We can do other things together besides acting out."

I believed him.

I believed I could redeem us. When volunteering at the Catholic Worker House, I saw the people with *real* problems: poverty, addiction, and unemployment—things outside their control and often imposed by powerful institutions. Compared to the corrupt systems that caused the evils of the world, my sexual failings were miniscule and self-imposed. I had to fix my life.

Focusing on my lawsuit against the doctor, I completed stacks of interrogatories. My lawyer and I investigated leads for other victims. Third parties informed us these men had mentioned that Lauz had molested them. When we contacted them, they refused to speak.

On weekends when I wasn't handling the litigation, I escaped my jaded classmates and retreated to Cedar Falls. My trips were easy to sex proof. When Father Scott and I ate at his apartment, we included two old nuns who liked to play hearts. I stayed with married friends. When he came to Dubuque on Thursdays, we tried going to movies, but he talked through them, comparing me to every male character with an ounce of flamboyance. After seeing *The Birdcage*, he called me Agador Spartacus, the Guatemalan pool boy, who strutted around barefoot in Daisy Dukes. My pleas to stop only egged him on. For him, flirtation and annoyance were indistinguishable. We needed other options.

The oncoming headlights glared across my glasses. Bored with driving by the homes of Father Scott's old students from Dubuque's Catholic high school, I half joked: "We should drop by the archbishop's. He's probably the loneliest guy in the archdiocese."

Father laughed. His eyes widened. "Great idea, Pastrone." He cranked the wheel. His new black minivan squealed through a U-turn.

I clenched the overhead handle. "I was just kidding."

Ten minutes later, we stood outside the archbishop's door.

"You ring it, Pastrone. This was your harebrained idea."

There wasn't a protocol for dropping in on the archbishop at night. Would he be annoyed? Would he realize that we were a couple? Would he answer the door in a bathrobe and invite us to join him for a nightcap? I pressed the doorbell.

Father pinched my chest though my coat. I pushed him away. The light above the door clicked on. His frozen breath wafted across my field of vision as he whispered, "Agador Spartacus reporting for duty." The door opened. The archbishop, whose thinning hair was mussed, wore a white undershirt tucked into black dress pants. And no socks. "Father Bell. Tom. Please, come in!"

He led us to the den where he sat in his recliner and introduced us to his guest, an older man with a five-o'clock shadow with whom he was watching the news. Father and I sat in opposing armchairs that flanked the recliners. The guest wore only dress pants and a white T-shirt tucked around his small gut. As the archbishop asked about our families, I couldn't stop wondering why he and his guest were barefoot. The archbihop's feet were wide, his ankles lacked varicose veins, and his toes were well groomed, except his second toe was growing a new nail, recovering from a racquetball injury perhaps. I wondered whether he showered in the gym at Loras after working out. After twenty minutes, he showed us to the door, shook our hands, and thanked us for visiting.

Back in the minivan, Father Scott cackled. "You should have seen the look on your face when I called you Agador. Priceless."

I gave him the look of death. "We're never doing that again."

An hour later, I exited the hermitage and tiptoed to my car through the shadows.

We weren't the only ones struggling with celibacy. Father Vince announced he was leaving the priesthood to marry the manager of the Catholic Worker House. In our final spiritual direction session, he described the Church as an ancient building erected in the desert over a life-giving spring that had provided nourishment for millennia. But now the fountain was dry. It bubbled elsewhere. Those with power refused to follow the spring by moving the Church. Father Vince assured me, "I love the Church. Because of that, I'm moving on."

Although sad, I understood. I would help lead the Church back to life-giving waters. The post–Vatican II Church would survive. Father Vince would return to the priesthood once John Paul II died and a more progressive pope ended mandatory celibacy. After all, priests could marry for centuries in the early Church. There were still married Catholic priests: Episcopal and Anglican priests who'd converted to Catholicism kept their wives. It seemed unjust that Father Vince had to leave but converts could stay. They could have sex. Why couldn't we?

I sang at Father Vince's wedding. Father Scott disapproved. According to the Gospel of Father Scott, God couldn't call a man to priesthood and then to marriage. "The Holy Spirit doesn't work that way," he said from his computer.

"The Holy Spirit is more powerful than your imagination," I said from the rocking chair.

He spun on his chair and rolled toward me. His hands gripped his knees. My ribs constricted. Over his shoulder through the window, a parking officer with long blonde hair and an athletic build slid a ticket under a windshield wiper. I wondered what it would be like to be her: outside the Church's control, walking the streets in the warmth of the spring sun. Father Scott laid into me. I was "so predictable," "projecting unresolved anger" with my father onto him. I didn't know anything about the real world of priesthood. I'd become the clichéd rebellious seminarian who thinks he's outgrown his mentor.

I wanted to outgrow him, to be a better priest than he was and better than my jaded classmates would be. I'd heard that less than half of seminarians survived to ordination. I'd outlasted Rob, who announced he was quitting at the end of the school year, thank God. I'd outlast the others too.

I wrote Father Foley, venting my frustration with the negative seminarians and disjointed priests at Loras. He replied, "Dear Thomas," and concluded his note with, "Love and prayers, Pete." I cashed his fifty-dollar check. He advised me on dealing with miserable clergy and offered advice on staying positive. The key was having one or two close priest friends like the buddy with whom he exchanged backrubs. I'd thought mine would be Father Scott, but whenever I tried to talk to him about our sexual failures, he changed the subject. I needed to know what I meant to him: did he love me or was I just a celibacy relief valve?

A rare May snow had been melting all day. After sunset, the clouds faded into anemic lavender. My Ford Escort had survived the first year of seminary despite the road salt rust creeping its way around the doors. I needed to halt my vocation's corrosion. Instead of sex, Father Scott and I needed a "Come to Jesus" talk. I pulled up the retreat house's driveway and slid into the spot next to his minivan.

When I entered the single-room hermitage, Father Scott sat in an armchair, dressed in black jeans and a red sweatshirt, illuminated by a crown of light from a floor lamp. "Pastrone!" Before I could pass the bed and get to the couch, he stuck his tongue in my mouth and clamped onto my ass. I tried to wriggle free. He continued to peck at my chin and neck.

"Wait," I said. One of his hands latched onto my front. "We need to talk."

He stroked me through my denims. "Come on, Paddlefoot."

"Scott, wait."

He jostled against me, clutching tightly. Almost biting my neck.

"No." I pushed at his chest. "Stop!"

He ceased and looked at me. I could see my tired reflection in his pupils as I said, "Please, let's talk instead."

He batted his eyelashes and flared his nostrils. "No talking," he said, as he tripped me backward onto the bed and threw himself on me. "I've been waiting for this all week."

After he came, he returned to the armchair. "Well? You wanted to talk." His head cast a shadow over his raccoon eyes, belly, and dick.

I rolled to the side of the bed, laughed, and pulled up my underwear. "Now that I've paid the price of admission, you'll talk."

"That's not fair."

I slid on my jeans. "It's accurate."

As I dressed, he backpedaled, throwing the blame on me for coming to meet him when I knew that we'd act out. Again, I was both tempter and occasion for sin, the unholy creator and satanic sanctifier. I let him spew his apologetics, his justification. A sudden clarity overwhelmed me. I couldn't fix Father, but I could fix myself.

Before leaving for Rome, Father Hunter referred me to Counselor Number Seven, saying, "He's helped other priests and seminarians with issues like yours. Plus, he's Italian."

Seven said I'd been straight before Lauz abused me. The doctor's kiss had "conditioned" me to avoid kissing the girls I'd taken to high school dances. Since I didn't kiss them—"There's a reason they call it first base," he said—I didn't advance to the heavy petting bases. Had I hit a home run, my pitcher/catcher fantasies would have been history.

Following Seven's prescriptions, I pictured actress Kate Winslet as I jacked off. I tried to convince myself that she could arouse me. But after ten seconds she morphed into Leonardo DiCaprio, who quickly became my über-masculine philosophy professor with thick, shoulder-length hair. I failed to climax with Kate or any woman I pictured. Having sex with them felt unnatural. Incestuous.

"You're trying. That's a start," Seven said.

He led me on guided meditations to recover my unsullied childhood sexual urges, before the doctor's kiss. He focused on my memory of kissing a girl on the cheek in front of her locker during preschool. Her mother was dying of cancer. I'd wanted her to know everything was going to be okay. Buried somewhere in that innocent kiss was a lost boy—a lost straight boy.

I recalled a football game I attended in eighth grade. The bleachers were frigid. I gave the girl I was going with my jean jacket, even though it was too small; she'd beaten me to the pubescent growth spurt. I told myself to kiss her lips. But as with the girl in preschool, I pecked her cheek. The next day, I called her and broke up.

"What were you feeling before you kissed her?" Seven said from his armchair.

"I felt like I needed to kiss her. To be like my sister and her boyfriend. Like my friends."

"No. What were your feelings for your girlfriend?"

"Affection. Like for my sisters. I wanted to be with a popular girl, to be seen as cool."

"But you wanted to kiss her, right?"

"I guess." What Seven wasn't concerned with was how I'd messed around with boys in elementary school, playing naughty doctor or all-star wrestling. "If not for the abuse, you would have grown out of that," he said. But in my middle school reality, I prayed not to get hard in the gym showers. While football manager, I tried not to stare at the star linebacker's Clydesdale dick. I knew I was programmed to stroke, lick, and suck men long before the doctor.

"Pastrone, aren't you a sight for sore eyes?" Father Scott got up from the small candlelit dinner table. I'd spent July in a Spanish-language immersion program in Miami. Within days of my return, he called: things had changed since our fight and he needed to talk. He invited me to join him at a 1960s supper club and motel on the bluffs overlooking the Mississippi. Overnight. Apparently, none of the couple thousand people living in East Dubuque, Illinois, would recognize him and see through the camouflage of two queen beds. I gave him a half hug and sat.

From across the table, his bleached smile seemed brighter under his tanned upper lip. He'd shaved the mustache and replaced his black glasses with rimless oval frames that matched mine. His gut was nearly gone. When I noted the changes, he said, "It was time for a fresh start."

We overate, drank, and acted out sexually.

As he slept in the next bed, I stared at the ceiling, feeling alone. Before going to Miami, I'd spent a celibate month living with a married couple from St. Stephen's while training a skinny, handsome student to do Father's summer cleaning and yardwork. I observed the disproportionate number of titty twisters and love-handle jabs Father directed his way. My friends called him "the new Tom." Was he the real reason for Father's physical improvements?

A few weeks later, I let Father fuck me. It was the final boundary. If I showed him that I trusted him enough to let him cum in me, maybe he'd love me again. He thrust in and out of me like a crazed animal. I bled.

Guilt consumed me.

Father was right. I was the seductive one. Maybe I finally earned the punishment my duplicity deserved: HIV.

Seven was right. Lauz had baptized me into gayness. I'd been able to suck Tobey without kissing him. Father had confirmed my initiation. When men were with men, there was no lovemaking or tender kissing, just hardcore fucking. Blood. Cum. Disease.

In the days before classes resumed, I read St. Paul. He and I were the same: unable to stop choosing that which we knew was sin over that which was righteous. If I didn't rip the sexual thorn from my side, if I didn't eradicate my sexuality, I was going to destroy my life and my vocation.

THE LONG LONELINESS

Awestruck, I gazed upward at the statues and golden woodwork of the high altar of St. Boniface Church in my hometown. It looked exactly as it had when I'd learned to serve Mass in third grade. My favorite duty had been at Communion, when I flipped a hidden switch to illuminate dozens of lights dotting the high altar and the treelike scepters held by two angels that flanked the Communion rail.

I relaxed into my pew surrounded by Rastrelli relatives who were back in town for my cousin's wedding. I needed to be back where it all started, where God had sown the early seeds of my vocation before everything became so messy. I reminisced and chuckled. The lights were easier to turn on and off than the numerous candles I had to light and extinguish when I'd served Mass at the limestone church four blocks up the hill: St. Irenaeus. The pastor there, Father Hoenig, liked nobody, and nobody liked him—except for Christian, an eighth grader with a bowl cut, whom even Protestants thought should be a priest. He trained me to serve just the way Father liked it. Perfectly.

After my first Mass with Father Hoenig, I retrieved my bronze snuffer from the sacristy. Christian, who remained to empty Father's iniquity from the bowl into which I'd washed it, ordered me to put out all the candles. The pews were empty save for a granny mumbling rosaries in the back. I ascended the three steps at the back of the sanctuary to the high altar whose climbing wooden arches held paint-chipped statues of Peter holding the key to the Church, Paul holding a sword, and three Marys crying at the crucified Christ's bleeding feet. I had to stand on tiptoe to lower the extinguisher over the four candles lining the gradine. When I passed the center of the sanctuary, I genuflected and made the sign of the cross just like Christian.

Next were the two flames on the central altar, where Father stood for the consecration. A circular stained-glass window cast a kaleidoscope of color over the altar, making it look like an electrified fruitcake. As threads of smoke curled upward from its extinguished candles, I scanned the sanctuary for other flames. To the right, a side altar enshrined a statue of Mary draped in blue. Her bare feet stood on a snake, which kind of grossed me out. To her side hung an elevated candle encircled by a red glass cylinder. I extended the snuffer but couldn't reach high enough. I set it on the marble counter in front of a little golden closet with lace curtains, pushed up the sleeves of my alb, and climbed into a kneeling position on the altar. I figured that kneeling was better than standing. From there, it was simple to lift the extinguisher over the red glass cylinder and smother the last candle. Mission accomplished. I hopped down. My first Mass for Father Hoenig was perfect.

"Not the tabernacle light!" Christian stood aghast. "You killed Jesus!" He rushed to the sacristy. "Father, Jesus is gone."

A ring of black soot lined the red cylinder. I froze, expecting the stained-glass windows to implode and chunks of limestone to crumble. In the back pew, the old lady babbled, "Hailmaryfullofgracethelordis withtheeblessedarethouamongwomenandblessedisthefruit . . ."

Father shot across the sanctuary with a stepladder, "You smothered the light of Christ." He ripped the snuffer from my hands and handed it to Christian, who frantically struck matches, until one flared. He lit the taper on the backside of the snuffer and handed it to Father, who ignited the candle.

They exhaled in unison.

"Never extinguish *that* candle," Father Hoenig ordered. "Your salvation depends on it."

Stifling tears, I ditched my robe in the sacristy. I walked to school believing I'd recrucified Jesus and questioning God's decision to entrust such power to a candle.

I chuckled as the wedding guests filled St. Boniface. When I'd gone to daily Mass there from first to third grades, the girls sat in the pews that were now the bride's side. I looked to the groom's side where I used to sit with the boys and saw Dr. Lauz.

I wanted to leave, but this was my family. Not his. In childhood, my cousin had been like a sister. As teens, we'd watched our dads' relationship crumble under the weight of the struggling family restaurant. We'd vowed to remain close but had hardly spoken since high school. She needed to see that I still loved her. I wasn't going to miss her wedding.

"What the hell is he doing here?" I asked my parents after the wedding.

They pulled me around the side of the church and apologized. They'd forgotten that the groom's mother was Lauz's nurse. They understood if I needed to skip the reception but couldn't do the same. That could break the fragile peace between Dad and my uncle.

"Damn Lauz," I said. "If he thinks he can push me out of my own family, he's wrong."

Later, at the Clinton Country Club, I sat at a table, ignoring my relatives whooping it up on the dance floor. A waitress I'd worked with three summers earlier, when I'd seen Lauz and lost it, reached over my shoulder to fill my water. "Welcome home, Tom," she said over the 80s dance mix.

"You too." My voice sounded metallic. Flat. Like a cracked cymbal. Under the white tablecloth, my fingertips dug into my palms. Lauz sat a few tables behind me.

Across the table, my brother, Jeff, seventeen but still shy, stamped his fingerprints into the softened rim of the centerpiece's candle. Maria, now a woman of twenty, danced with Dad, keeping tabs from over his shoulder. At weddings, I usually danced with everyone. I overheard some cousins asking Mom what was wrong with me. As she ushered them off, I heard: "Maybe an old girlfriend's here."

I inhaled deeply. That was in the past. I exhaled. But it wasn't. It was now. Lauz had infiltrated my family.

The music pounded. Panic, like boiling acid, rolled between my heart and gut, spreading into my thighs and biceps. My neck. And jaw. When it reached my eyes, I'd cry. Everyone would see how damaged I was, and I'd know that I couldn't face Lauz.

I pushed away from the table. The tears streamed down my cheeks like the molten wax of a damaged altar candle. With my eyes fixed to the green carpeting, I passed the doctor's table. I rushed down the stairway, around the landing into the basement. Everything was dark; the golfers had finished their day, leaving the locker and weight rooms empty. I crumbed into a ball by a rack of dumbbells.

After a few minutes, I felt my father's arms cradling me. His fingers stroked my hair. His tears cooled the back of my neck. No words. Only his warmth. His grief. His oversplashed cologne. He'd been led to me by Maria and Jeff, who waited tables at the club and knew where I might be. After what seemed like minutes of sensory confusion, my ears began working again. I heard Dad's voice beseeching God to calm me. "Take his pain and give it me," he prayed.

As his sobs increased, mine decreased. My gasps became breaths. My skin cooled. I opened my eyes. Backlit from the hallway, Maria and Jeff watched in shock. Dad waved them over. As we hugged, I realized what I had to do.

I needed to leave, but not until I'd spoken to Lauz. I said, "If I can't confront him now, how will I face him in court?"

Maria latched onto my hand, "I'm going with you."

We ascended the stairs and pressed through the crowded banquet hall to Lauz's table. Her grip tightened as he looked up. His pasty lip dropped from his mustache. This time, he was the one caught off guard. I inhaled his stench. It filled me with power.

"I want you to know: I pray for you every day."

It was the truth. Twice a day. During Morning Prayer, I prayed for him to repent and for his patients' protection. At night, I prayed for his peace and healing and to be able to forgive him. But now, seeing his frightened, pathetic face, I felt pity.

I tried to walk away, but Maria's hand tethered me. She remained frozen in his gaze. Without looking back, I nudged her. We escaped through a side door that opened onto a tee box and fairway. The sun had set, leaving the sky a bruised violet.

In the safety of my Escort, I finally looked at Maria. Black tears streaked her ivory cheeks. I pulled her into an embrace. She trembled. "It's OK," I lied.

"He licked his lips," she said. "After you turned to leave. That sick fucker ran his tongue across his lips."

I pounded my fists into the steering wheel and screamed. For Lauz hadn't abused only me, he'd abused my family.

Once home, I called my lawyer and relayed what had happened. I worried I'd made a mistake. She felt awful. Had either of us known Lauz would have been there, she would have advised me not to attend. The damage was done. Lauz's lawyers convinced the court to slap me with an injunction, for the protection of his "good reputation." The judge's ruling was so obtuse that legally it sounded as if I could only speak about the "alleged sexual abuse" with my lawyer. I was forbidden from talking to friends, spiritual directors, priests, seminarians, and family. The lawyer's assistant had to inform my parents of developments, even when I was in the same room.

I felt I'd ruined my cousin's wedding. Our dads took sides and warred. I could speak to no one to facilitate reconciliation. Father Scott stopped returning my calls. When I caught him on the phone, he was distant, as if he were afraid of what I might do. The injunction sounded like I couldn't even discuss the abuse with Seven. My recklessness was being punished, but part of me didn't care. If need be, I'd throw everything away, even the priesthood. To keep even one child safe, I'd take the martyr's arrow.

Still, I feared hurting more people. I continued to live, eat, and attend classes with my brother seminarians. Having replaced Father Hunter as director of seminarians, Father Dixon moved in with us. He observed my frenetic rush to finish homework so I could drive to Clinton on Friday afternoons to handle the litigation. He offered his thoughts and prayers. My brothers were supportive but equally helpless. Besides, my mind wasn't with my seminary community. I was focused on my coming deposition.

My lawyer, Dolores O'Connell, had taken the case pro bono. I'd known her since transferring to the public schools in seventh grade. She'd married the widowed father of my preschool "girlfriend." Growing up, I'd been intimidated by Dolores's height, savvy, cropped auburn hair, and retention of her maiden name. Now, her feminist strength was my asset; her passion for justice, my ally. For Dolores, stopping Lauz, who'd attended parties for foreign exchange students and their hosts at her house, was personal. Like the rest of Clinton, he'd hoodwinked her with his benefactor persona. To prepare me for the depositions, she brought in her legal aid, Shawn. Having suffered her own lawsuit against Clinton's medical establishment and the surgeon who'd assaulted her, Shawn knew what to do. If a question could be answered yes or no, that was all I should provide. If I couldn't remember, I'd admit it. If the defense tried to back me into a specific answer, I was to add "to the best of my recollection." I felt like an actor learning my lines, only the script was my life. The stakes were real and the motivation less self-serving than a standing ovation.

But it was impossible to compose the entire script. At some point, the defense would go for blood. Lauz's spicy scent could trigger my PTSD. Shawn instructed me to improvise, devising ways to temper my anxiety. She encouraged me to bring a small object to ground myself in the world apart from the abuse. I chose a crucifix that fit inside my closed palm. Father Scott had given it to me on a retreat, before we'd ruined things. Holding it, I listened to David Haas's contemporary chant adaptation of St. Patrick's Breastplate, "Prayer for Peace." I grounded my breathing in the lyric's repetition and the crucifix's warm metal. Recalling the serenity experienced when I'd first heard my calling to the priesthood, I armed myself with God's presence.

The autumn morning of the deposition, Mom, Dad, and I went to 7 a.m. Mass in Clinton. Sitting in the cold pew, I concentrated on the crucifix behind the altar; I prayed God's will be done. On the forty-five-minute drive to Davenport, my parents were strangely quiet. When we spoke, it was about other topics: my sister Jenny and her husband's move to California, Maria's change of major from dramaturgy to Catholic studies, Jeff's choir repertoire, Dad's hope for a sales record, and Mom's upcoming school concerts. I sensed they weren't saying what was really on their minds, as if voicing their worry would shatter my eggshell illusion of peace. Once at Dolores's office, they hugged me tightly and left to wait at Uncle Jim and Aunt Karen's nearby house.

As Dolores drove Shawn and me to the defense lawyer's office, they rattled off final reminders and encouragements. During the elevator's ascent to the firm, I rubbed my thumb over my crucifix totem. *Peace before me.* I recalled Maria sobbing in my car, the outrage that consumed me. *Peace behind me.* What if Lauz licks his tongue during the deposition? *Peace under my feet.* I inhaled. *Peace within me.* I exhaled. *Peace over me.* I'd survived it. *Let all around me be peace.* I could face him again.

We entered the deposition room.

The chickenshit hadn't come.

Whether he'd been ordered or had chosen to stay away didn't matter. I strode into the small, bland room and took my place between Dolores and Shawn. The court reporter swore me in. Across the table, the lawyers representing the doctor, insurance company, and medical practice began questioning me: name, date of birth, place of birth, address, parents, siblings, and schools attended. They were testing my memory. When they asked what teachers I had in middle and high school, I did as Shawn had instructed. I provided them with first and last names, subjects, and class periods. In order. When it served our purposes, I answered succinctly. They scrutinized my timeline concerning the abuse. I maintained my consistency and won the day.

Afterward, Dolores congratulated me. Shawn informed my parents, aunt, and uncle of the day's events. All day, Mom and Dad had been horrified, for during the morning Mass in Clinton, Lauz had appeared from behind us to receive Communion. They didn't know how I'd missed seeing him. The awkwardness of the morning car ride suddenly made sense. They'd known that bringing him up would rattle me. That bastard actually believed God would answer his prayers, that God would offer his Son for the forgiveness of kid fuckers.

He'd picked the wrong God. The God of Jesus had been looking out for me, protecting me. Together, we'd defeat Lauz.

Throughout the remaining weeks of the semester, Dolores filed to lift the injunction and then to have it defined more clearly. Each time, the judge refused. The defense's request to delay the court date to summer succeeded. If they delayed it again, it would affect my ability to go to major seminary—graduate-level studies—in the fall. Studying in Rome was now completely out of the question. Our possible witnesses, including Lauz's former maid, who'd discovered his secret basement room equipped with only a mattress and a table holding a TV and VCR, backed out. Without another victim, our case was doomed.

I asked Dolores to petition the court to refile the case, not as *John Doe v. John Doe, MD*, but as *Thomas P. Rastrelli v. Gregorio Lauz, MD*. The newspapers would cover the story. Other victims would join the charge. The Dubuque Archdiocese would likely release me. I didn't care. Father Scott didn't seem to either; he refused to talk to me about anything.

There were other dioceses. God would get me to the priesthood, but not if I didn't risk it all to stop Lauz.

The judge denied our request, citing precedent from cases of alleged sexual abuse against Catholic priests in which the court allowed accused clerics to remain anonymous to protect their reputations from money-hungry opportunists. Suddenly, I felt like the one on trial. The judge thought I was a liar. My nightmares returned. My focus dwindled. I dared my metaphysics professor to fail me after all but one person in our class received an F on our midterm. My right eyelid twitched. My appetite diminished. I couldn't continue at such a scattered pace.

I petitioned to take spring semester off. Father Dixon agreed. Because I had some philosophy credits from UNI, I'd only be three credits behind if I entered major seminary in the fall. "Take care of yourself," he said. "Seminary will be there when you're finished."

I woke up to "Für Elise" being mutilated on the piano. Every morning at seven, Mom gave kids piano lessons. I pulled my pillow over my head. When I woke again, the house was mine. My sisters were grown and gone. Jeff, now an eleventh grader, had a full social calendar. Dad had risen from knife salesman to regional manager and now commuted to Davenport and Dubuque. Mom taught full time. I earned my keep cleaning, doing laundry, shoveling snow, running errands, and assisting with supper. For the first time in months, I relaxed.

Shawn and I spoke daily. She encouraged me to see Lauz's upcoming deposition as his moment of judgment. "He'll lie. But no matter what front he puts up, he's not the one in control. You are," she said. "Your presence alone will intimidate him." During the deposition, I should occupy myself by jotting his inconsistencies and my questions. I was to record anything of possible assistance to Dolores's line of questioning on a Post-it and hand it to Shawn, who would determine whether to pass it on. She had become my mediator, my high priest.

Lauz wore a suit and a dry black toupee that clashed with his sweaty gray crown. When I caught a whiff of his musk and met his eyes, the deposition room disappeared. Shawn nudged my thigh and wrote on a fluorescent pink Post-it, *He's the one squirming.* I focused my rage and revulsion into an unwavering stare that shamed him until he looked away. The panic that had previously fueled my PTSD, I welded into power and calm. Dolores channeled the February wind and whipped him with questions.

He claimed not to be sexually attracted to adolescent boys. He'd had sex with a woman and even proposed to one who rejected him. Speaking of his great love for children, he aggrandized his overseas medical mission work. His story changed with each answer: I'd come to him with a venereal disease. I'd been dangerously sexually active. I was jealous of his friendships with other boys. My dad had abused me, and I was projecting that onto him out of some misguided vendetta. I was mentally ill. At fourteen, I'd had priapism—chronic and long-lasting painful erections; he'd merely treated me. Dolores let him babble. I went through a pack of Post-its before noon.

Throughout the afternoon, Dolores combed through my medical records, reading Lauz's notes and pointing out inconsistencies. She asked why he'd never reported to my parents that their fourteen-year-old son allegedly had a sexually transmitted disease. Why hadn't he informed the proper state authority of the infection as law required? He stuttered. He didn't understand the question. She repeated it. He'd been afraid that my dad was going to beat me. I nearly laughed at the absurdity of his answer. This man, who had stalked my nightmares and haunted my body with panic, was a pathetic, puny liar.

Dolores pounded back. He was a mandatory reporter. Why hadn't he reported my dad to the police? Where was this in his medical notes? His lawyers repeatedly objected. They claimed that because English was Lauz's second language, he couldn't understand the questions. But as Dolores pointed out, the majority of his working life, he'd lived in the United States among English speakers. My medical records, written in English, proved that he was either lying, guilty of malpractice, or both. Deposition number two was ours. It was only a matter of time before he begged settlement.

A week later, we returned to the defense's stuffy deposition room. Having assured my parents I was fine and they could go to work, I caught a ride through snowy cornfields with Shawn. With all luck, this would be my final deposition.

I assumed my lead role and answered the gruff head attorney's questions. He had an oval face with drawn cheeks and unkempt eyebrows that rested on the rims of his glasses like soot on a barbeque grate. Again, Lauz was a no-show. After his debacle of a deposition, his lawyers weren't going to let him anywhere near Dolores. The morning progressed as expected: more memory games and recounting office visits during the year of the abuse. They wanted to see whether my story had changed. I relaxed into the tide of questions, crucifix totem in hand.

"Name the priests that have been instrumental in your, whatever you called it, 'priestly formation,'" eyebrow lawyer said.

Dolores objected, but he countered that it was important to understand how widespread the damage to Lauz's reputation had been from my talking about the abuse. He demanded the names of everyone with whom I'd spoken about my allegations before the injunction, everyone in Clinton, Cedar Falls, and Dubuque. Unable to remember everyone, I tagged "to the best of my recollection" to each answer. He wanted the names of the seminary board and any other professionals who'd interviewed me during my seminary application. I listed them. He asked whether I knew Father Tim DeVenney, who'd been convicted of sexually abusing boys in Dubuque. I'd met the priest on a few occasions. Where? At Father Hunter's. How did the priest know him? They were in a group of priests that met monthly to support one another's ministry and celibacy. Who else was in the group? Father Scott.

My mind raced, trying to decipher his line of questioning. What if he summoned my seminary application interviews? He'd see I lied to Counselor Number Five about my homosexuality. He was going after my vocation.

My thumbprint ground against the crucifix totem. He was going after more than my vocation. He wanted dirt on my brother priests. He was going to put the archdiocese on trial. I looked at Dolores, but she was fixed on objecting to his questions. I tried to see past her to Shawn, who, recognizing my distress, would call for a break, but Dolores's marble profile and spiky hair blocked me. I squirmed, silently praying: *Peace within me. Let all around me be peace.*

God took heed. The defense lawyer took note of Dolores's mounting objections and announced a different line of questioning. I breathed, hoping the worst was over.

He slapped a document on the table, our expert witness's psychological assessment of me. I'd flown to Seattle earlier in the year, where Counselor Number Eight evaluated me. Eyebrows pointed at the transcription of my interview, "Who's Tobey?"

"One of my close friends from high school. My roommate sophomore year at UNI."

I silently cursed. Why had I told Eight? Now Tobey was outed. Thank God I hadn't told her about Father Scott.

"But you were more than roommates," his eyebrows sharpened over a grin. He asked about our sexual relations: timeline, activities, everything we'd ever done. Earlier, he'd spoken of homosexuality and sexual abuse being connected. The bastard was shaming me, calling me a perpetrator. My lungs halted. My brain twirled. The cross-totem: *Let all around me be peace.* Inhale. Exhale. Dolores objected. My sexual life after the abuse had no bearing on my accusations. He countered that he needed to better understand the level of "alleged damage" that I'd endured and quoted Eight, who'd concluded that my sexual development was halted by the abuse, which had marred me with an aversion to kissing.

"OK then," his eyebrows curled over his lenses. "Let me be more direct. After the defendant allegedly kissed you, have you ever kissed another . . . person?"

Dolores objected on the grounds of something I didn't understand. She demanded this be noted in the records but then conceded to my answering.

"Could you repeat the question?" I stalled. He did. Under the table, I clenched my crucifix. "I'm not sure how you define kissing."

His eyes rolled behind his lenses like the last shot swirling in the bottom of a bottle. "Not a peck on your grandma's cheek. A romantic kiss." His eyebrows scrunched together and fired, "With *tongue*."

Lauz's tongue filled my mouth. The recorder stopped punching her dictation keys. The silence pounded my skull like a mallet. I looked to Dolores. She nodded for me to answer. My thumb slid over the sweaty cross. *Please, God, let this be the end of it.* I met the defense attorney's smug brows and tried to sound calm.

"Yes."

The wind pelted the window with grains of snow from a neighboring rooftop.

"With whom?"

There was only one answer. One person. And no time to think. If I answered, my future as a priest was dead. Father Scott's career could end. If I lied and named Tobey, would they depose him? After our falling out, would he lie for me? Would God forgive me for sacrificing the truth to stop a sexual molester?

Again, I looked to Dolores. She nodded, indicating that I answer.

"I need to take a break," I said.

"Just answer the question. And then we'll break," she waved me on. I didn't know whether she was mad at me or just frustrated with the questioning.

My fingers tightened around the crucifix, pressing it into my skin. "I can't." I looked to the court reporter, as if she'd be merciful and stop typing. "I need to speak to Ms. O'Connell privately."

Dolores raised her hand for me to be silent, "Could we break for lunch?"

"I can wait for this," the attorney said. His eyebrows relaxed over a smile.

Dolores led me by the arm from the deposition room. Shawn followed. Within seconds, we entered what must have been a legal library. Ceiling-high shelves stacked with books dwarfed us. Dolores and Shawn crowded me into a corner, their faces contorted with concern or anger.

Dolores whispered, "Who was it?"

My shoulders quivered. "Father Scott Bell." I sobbed.

Shawn held me up with a hug, "Oh, Tom. I'm so sorry,"

Dolores's head shook. "This is bad." Betrayal tinged her voice. "I could have protected you."

"I'm sorry. I'm sorry," I said. It felt like my first real contrition in years.

Dolores explained what was to come. Shawn would take me to lunch while she revised her strategy for the afternoon. She promised not to let the defense make me answer that question. I thanked her. But she scolded, "For us to be successful, you can't keep secrets. Especially not ones of this magnitude."

"I know. I'm so sorry."

The afternoon passed, a blur of objections and eyebrows. I squeezed my crucifix totem, beseeching God, but there was no answer. No presence. My affair with Father Scott would exonerate the doctor. I'd extinguished God's candle, the sanctuary lamp of my soul. What remained was the soot-stained husk of a sinner.

In the month that followed, the defense declared total war, asking the judge to force me to answer the objected questions. They submitted lists of potential witnesses to depose: my parents, my siblings, my friends, the archbishop, the seminary board, Father Scott. I couldn't bear to put my family through it. Or to have Father's career destroyed. Around every street corner and down each supermarket aisle, I feared seeing Lauz. There was no peace at Mass, where he'd approach the altar with folded hands and bowed head, receive the Body of Christ on his tongue, cross himself, and circle around the front of the pews, grateful that God had saved him. Not me.

My spiritual life was dead. I was too weak to keep fighting my sexuality and the doctor. Dolores and I agreed: it was time to settle the case, not to spare the others but myself.

It could take months. In that time, Dolores encouraged me to get out of Iowa. I took Maria to New Orleans for her spring break. In April, an old high school friend and I embarked on a road trip, camping our way toward Los Angeles.

In the pure silence of the bleached-white gypsum dunes of south-central New Mexico, I heard the blood squishing through the capillaries in my ears. The beating of my heart was louder than my footsteps on the soft sand. I stood in that awesome tranquility and realized why Jesus went to the desert to pray: nothingness—not the barren loneliness following my botched deposition, but the calming, purifying focus of solitude. My life was full of so many voices: the abused boy seeking to prove perfection, the angry young man demanding that the world yield to his will, and the selfish beast seeking communion in men rather than God. In the nothingness of the desert, there was only God. The God that had called me to the priesthood. Before the lawsuit. Before Father Scott.

I returned to Clinton and settled the case. At least, I was on record against Lauz. When other victims eventually came forward, the court records would lead them to Dolores and, if I wanted, she could refer them to me. She assured me Lauz would suffer. No insurance company would cover him without a huge premium increase. His medical partners couldn't afford to leave him alone in an examination room with a child. Shawn concurred. I wanted to believe them, but the doctor had escaped only a few dollars poorer and free to be with children outside the office.

Father Scott greeted me with a boisterous "Pastrone!" and a lingering embrace. After receiving news of the settlement, he'd invited me to visit him at his new apartment, separate from St. Stephen's. Having made changes to his lifestyle so work and home didn't bleed together, he assured me his boundaries were intact. He also wanted to help me car shop.

He hadn't had time to clean up before I arrived, so he invited me to chat with him as he showered. I sat on the toilet and spoke through the curtain. When he exited, he was hard and pressed his dick toward my lips. I took him into my mouth, longing for something tender, anything to forget the pain of my failure. But he grasped my hair and thrust against my face. My spine winched against the toilet handle. After orgasm, he left to dress. Not even a hug. I remained on the toilet feeling familiar. Like myself. Abused.

Under an early morning August haze, my new black Nissan Frontier sat perched atop the driveway at home. My parents, siblings, and I packed my belongings into the back of the compact pickup, paid for by the settlement. I didn't think of the vehicle as a sign of my failure. It was my escape eastward over the Mississippi River to Baltimore, into a future beyond Dr. Lauz and Father Scott.

I slammed the lid covering the truck bed. Everything was secure, ready for the journey to St. Mary's Seminary and University.

"I love you," my sisters and brother said. I hugged them, saying the same. Jenny had taken a break from her acting auditions in LA to see

Maria and me off. Maria was flying to Italy to study Catholic art. Jeff was entering his final year of high school with grades that could take him to any college. We didn't know when we'd be together again, maybe not until my ordination.

Mom and Dad waited by the truck's door. Mom embraced me. "I love you and am so proud of you, Thomas. For doing this, being yourself. You're courageous." She rarely called me by my full name.

"Thanks, Mom. I love you."

Dad grasped my shoulders, gazed at me with his light brown eyes and said, "Your Grandpa Rastrelli used to say, 'Never forget: A priest is a man first.' "

"I know, Dad."

We hugged, pecked on the lips, and said, "I love you."

"It's a new chapter, Tommy," he said.

I nodded, hoping to convince myself he was right.

I climbed into the cab and turned the ignition.

PART III

ST. MARY, MOTHER OF GOD

Patron Saint of
Crusaders, Needle and
Pin Makers, and Virgins
1998–2002

The Mighty One has done great things for me, and holy is his name. His mercy is from age to age to those who fear him.—The Canticle of Mary, Luke 1:49–50

INTERIOR CASTLE

Titanic oaks and tulip trees with leaves large enough to swaddle newborns shaded the blacktop driveway. The hardwoods looked older than any growing back in Iowa. I slowed the pickup, silenced the cassette player, and offered a prayer for guidance, fortitude, and growth to do what God had planned for me, if there still was a plan.

Through the breaks in the foliage, St. Mary's Seminary emerged. Four stories of pale gray stone towered before me, as if guarding the sky. One of the three-dozen windows lining each story would be my room. I worried I'd made a mistake. It looked more like Versailles than home.

A young man dressed in jean shorts and a pine-green shirt with embroidered lettering, "St. Mary's Seminary and University, Roland Park," directed me to the base of the wide staircase at the main entrance. I parked and stepped into the oppressive August humidity.

"Welcome to St. Mary's." The guy shook my hand and told me his name, diocese, and year in the program, all of which I immediately forgot as I gawked up the stairway. Six ionic columns framed three arched wooden doors that looked solid enough to withstand the assault of a neighboring fiefdom. Atop the columns, a triangular pediment housed a sculpted relief of the Twelve Apostles flanking a haloed Jesus, who pointed assuredly toward the world. Over his head, an engraved, ovular crest proclaimed, GO TEACH ALL NATIONS.

"You'll get used to it," he said.

A mosquito buzzed my ear. I swatted at it. "I doubt it."

We passed through the large central door into an expansive vestibule with checkered marble floor, vaulted ceiling, and stone columns. Along the walls, golden statues of Matthew, Mark, Luke, and John vogued. A scent of damp dust and waxy funeral flowers lingered in the heavy air. From behind a ruffled table, three or four women who looked like they could have been my mother's friends smiled. Before I could introduce myself, a stout seminarian dressed in clerical blacks introduced himself as a fourth theologian and deacon—meaning he was entering his final year. We exchanged names and dioceses as he directed me past the women. He led me across an arched hallway into a shadowed atrium. In the center of the space under a cloudy glass ceiling, peace lilies and anthuriums encircled a pearly statue of Mary cradling the infant Christ. The deacon explained she was the *Sedes Sapientiae*, which meant Mary, Seat of Wisdom, the patron of the seminary around which the community prayed something called the *Angelus*. I looked more closely at the anthuriums, never before having seen the veiny heart-shaped, waxy red flowers sprouting middle-finger-sized white phalluses.

"I don't know why they use those to decorate." The deacon shook his head before escorting me into the neo-Gothic chapel.

Stone walls lined with arched stained-glass windows drew my eyes forward to the sanctuary. Four marble columns circumscribed the high altar over which a large wooden crucifix hung from a golden roof.

"It's a beautiful baldachino. Isn't it?" he said.

I'd never been in a church with anything quite like it. "Yeah." I genuflected and made the sign of the cross.

"The Blessed Sacrament is in a side chapel," the deacon corrected me. "We bow to the cross to show reverence when we enter." He did so, solemnly bending from the waist. I hopped up and did likewise.

The pews were different too, not arranged in front-facing rows but in two choirs of five rows that ran the length of the chapel. They faced each other like opposed rakes of a stadium-seating theatre. He instructed me to sit in the pew closest to the door. A metal plaque marking my spot proclaimed that three years earlier Pope John Paul II had prayed in this pew. The deacon spoke of how the pope's visit had affirmed his vocation and moved him to tears. When the pope's security swept the chapel with bomb-sniffing canines, the mutts had stopped and bowed before the Blessed Sacrament. He spoke of the seminary's founding more than two hundred years before by the Society of San Sulpice, which originated in seventeenth-century France in response to the Reformation. Father Jean-Jacques Olier founded the Sulpicians and charged them to form future priests. Tradition. Dedication. Calling. He mused on, but all I could think about was how the pope's butt had touched the same wood as mine.

The deacon instructed me to kneel and prayed over me. When we returned to the entrance hall, the ladies showered me with folders of information. "We love the Dubuque guys," one said. She told me that my DB (seminary shorthand for diocesan brother), who'd just graduated, had prepped them for me. He'd been in charge of the chapel's décor and flowers—the deacon rolled his eyes—always taking the time to bring the ladies working in administration a few blooms. She continued: "You midwestern folk are so down-to-earth. We'll take good care of you."

The seminarian in the green shirt hurried things. Per his instructions, I drove to the loading dock on the east side of the building, where other seminarians in green knit shirts greeted me. More smiles. More names. More dioceses. They unloaded my truck while one led me down a barren, basement hallway into the Donnelly Lounge, the seminary's private pub, which continued the bomb-shelter look of the hallway. From behind the chipped counter, a seminarian asked what I wanted.

"A pop."

"It's soda out here."

"Of course. Soda. Coke, Pepsi, please."

He slid me one, "We're saving the hard stuff for later."

I sat on one of three worn green sofas. Two other new guys waited on the other couches. They must have been nervous because they answered my enthusiastic questions with one-word answers befitting a deposition. I tried reading my folder's orientation materials, but there wasn't enough light. The barkeep said, "Don't worry. It'll all make sense later."

The sweat-soaked movers came for one fellow, the other, and then me. They had moved my stuff to my room and parked my truck.

"Don't expect the same when you move out," the mustached and middle-aged mover quipped.

"He'll be here long after your liberal-grandpa-ass gets booted," the impish fellow slammed.

"Don't mind them," said the bald one. He extended a well-groomed hand, "I'm Pat Cameron. From Baltimore. We're classmates. And neighbors." We shook.

During the previous year, Pat had completed pretheology at St. Mary's. He volunteered to be on the orientation team so that he could "get to know the newbies." In his previous life, he'd been a banker in New York City. I asked him about life in the metropolis, apologizing that I'd wanted to be a Broadway star when I was a teen.

"Do you have a trained voice?" the mustached one interrupted.

"I had voice lessons in high school and college."

"Stay hydrated." The bartender tossed me a bottle of water, which I fumbled. "Those liturgy nuts are gonna eat you up."

Pat led me into the elevator just outside the Donnelly. "Not having AC stinks." He pressed 3. "But not having to cook is good." He patted his belly. "Too good." The doors closed. "Let me know if you ever want to go for a walk."

"Sure."

He explained the seminary was shaped like a giant letter E and had five wings, three for the arms and two for the spine of the E. The seminarians and Sulpician faculty members lived on the third and fourth floors. Offices were on the second floor. The first floor housed the chapel, library, classrooms, dining room, and lecture hall. The basement, where we'd been, had the bar, mailboxes, rec room, and bookstore. Pat said, "I know it's a lot, but—"

"It'll all make sense," I interrupted.

He giggled. "And all you really need to know is where the bathrooms are."

I laughed. He was all right.

The third floor had crimson-and-indigo brocade carpeting and a drop ceiling. Evenly spaced doors dotted the beige walls. It reminded me of something out of a clichéd nightmare, where one is being chased down a never-ending hallway. Then we rounded the corner into the B wing. I froze. The corridor ran uninterrupted the entire length of the seminary. The floor seemed to rise as the ceiling fell until, nearly a quarter-mile distant, the hallway ended with a speck of light. Pat said that my flower-wielding DB had roller-bladed the stretch, and according to legend, seminarians used the hallway as a bowling alley after Vatican II to crush the pin-sized *Sedes Sapientiae* statues stripped from their rooms. "So much for tradition," he said.

When we reached the hallway's halfway point, Pat explained we were above the main vestibule, where I'd first entered the building. Two stories above, a miniscule fifth floor supported the main façade. On that floor, our moral theology professor engineered his toy train collection, equipped with tunnels connecting the adjacent rooms. Far below, in the hauntingly dark stretch of basement along the building's spine, was the

Sulpician K-Mart, where graduates and dropouts left furniture for the next generation.

"Get down there before the others arrive," Pat said. "The best shelves have glass windows on the front. If you're lucky enough to find any."

My DB had told me a house legend about that stretch of basement. In the 70s, deviant seminarians operated an underground gay bar there. Maybe that's when conservatives had started calling St. Mary's "The Pink Palace." Pat didn't mention that on our walk.

Three quarters of the way down the corridor, we arrived.

"Welcome home," Pat opened the door.

My room was small, maybe nine by twelve feet, with one window that opened to a courtyard on the backside of the building. My boxes and suitcases sat piled between a twin bed, desk, chair, bookshelf, and an immaculate cherry-wood dresser. The closet, built for the two cassocks that seminarians required in the 1930s, would overflow with my dress-code-required collection of clothing. Next to the closet, a basketball-sized sink and medicine cabinet offered me privacy, at least for shaving.

"I hope you like the dresser," Pat said. "I had it locked up all summer." He explained that it had been "willed" to me by my DB. Pat had guarded it loyally, even though poachers promised him a better couch in exchange.

"You fit a couch in your room?" I said.

His room looked like a graveyard for mismatched IKEA floor models. An albino ferret watched us from a cage.

"Will he bite?"

"Not unless you scare him."

I knelt down and gently extended a finger. The weasel's pink nose sniffed it, feeling cool compared to the air. "Does he make a lot of noise?"

"Not at all. But I snore." Pat shrugged. "Sorry."

He wasn't lying. That night, after I'd unpacked and blanketed my walls with photos, the frames rumbled with his snores.

The next morning, I packed a bag and moved for the orientation retreat into the newly constructed Center for Continuing Formation of Priests attached to backside of seminary. It was the Hilton of retreat houses. For the next few nights, I slept in a queen bed, enjoying an air-conditioned room and private bathroom. The dress code was not yet in effect, so we shivered in our shorts in the refrigerated conference room as the rector, Father Brock Lowell, S.S.—Society of St. Sulpice—and his staff welcomed three dozen of us to the fold. We were the biggest incoming class in years, a sign that things were turning around, the vocations shortage was ending, and God was at work in the internet age.

The orientation team indoctrinated us with *The Rule of Life*, the thick seminary handbook that explained everything about our new lives: academic requirements; formation of our spiritual, social, pastoral, intellectual, and celibate-sexual beings; the theology and logic behind every statute that would govern our lives for the next four or five years; and so on. We were caravanned to the original seminary building in downtown Baltimore, where St. Elizabeth Ann Seton, the first American-born saint, had briefly lived. When our baptism into the Sulpician story was complete, Father Lowell promised, "You will leave here someone different. Someone new." I hoped he was right.

That night, we seminarians gathered in the center's lobby. Some of us encircled the grand piano, singing. Others congregated on the lobby's plush furniture. We emptied bottles and estimated the cost of the exotic carpet that looked as if it had been pillaged during the Crusades. We exchanged the latest priest jokes, quoted our favorite movies, and gleaned acquaintances from our dioceses and "past lives."

A gregarious Irish-American Baltimorean named Mick Casey had been a film major. As I struggled to convince him that *Titanic* deserved its Oscar, his gesturing arm sent a beer tumbling onto the priceless carpet. The guys laughed and hedged bets that Mick would be the first sent packing. With handfuls of embossed napkins, I helped him soak up the mess while joking about the Sulpician's insurance policy. He thanked me. I had my first friend.

An Italian New Yorker who was studying for the Paterson Diocese confessed nerves about returning to school in his forties. I assured him he wouldn't have been accepted if they didn't think he could handle the academics. The half-dozen guys from South America (studying for Worchester and Raleigh) struggled to speak English. In return, I offered my inebriated Spanish. I waxed philosophical with the smokers, even though I didn't smoke. One of them, a fellow extrovert from Puerto Rico named Abdel (Worchester), and I bonded over our love of musicals. With a wide smile and dimpled cheeks, he spoke with vowels of pure Spanish but dropped his Rs like a Bostonian. Felix (Erie), the retreat team's mustached melancholy seminarian, outed Abdel and me as singers. Everyone volunteered us to provide music at the morning's grotto Mass.

The grotto looked like a sliced-open, twenty-five-foot-tall, hollowed-out cement football—or womb—with a statue of Mary enshrined in its gut. A verdant canopy domed the area, muffling the nearby expressway. At Mary's feet, white splatters of melted wax streaked a stone altar. A slow-moving stream snaked through the space and provided sanctuary to mosquito larvae. Abdel and I arrived before the others with a guitar, hymnals, and music stand. The short hike through waist-high ferns and ivy-webbed trunks had been beautiful, perfect for a romantic stroll. We praised God for nature and stifled our opinions of the concrete Easter egg shrine. When the others arrived, we hadn't had time to rehearse the closing song, which I didn't know.

"Just follow my lead," Abdel assured me.

When it came time for the piece, I picked it up quickly. For the second refrain, I decided to improvise a harmony. I met Abdel's brown eyes. He understood. His bass and my baritone reverberated throughout the woods: "We are companions on the journey, breaking bread and sharing life; for in the love we bear is the hope we share, for we believe in the love of our God." Even in the heat, I had goose bumps. We bellowed all four verses. Afterward, the Guamanian priest who'd celebrated the Mass informed us he was the director of liturgy. In the future, we were to sing only two verses of each song. After he left, Abdel and I laughed, congratulating each other on our role as liturgical upstarts.

Orientation bled into a full seminary retreat, for which we had to move back into our broiling dorm rooms and begin strict adherence to the dress code. Third- and fourth-year guys wore black slacks, clerical shirts, and Roman collars. The rest of us sported dress pants and shirts with neckties. The hallways filled with men of all ages and colors, from a blonde deacon studying for La Crosse, who barely met the twenty-five-year-old requirement for ordination, to one of my classmates, a silver-haired, sixty-one-year-old Bostonian studying for Grand Rapids, who emanated the honeyed scent of pipe tobacco.

The recently elevated auxiliary bishop of Baltimore, one of the few African American bishops, led the retreat. He was a Jesuit from California. "That's code for liberal," Felix said. The bishop challenged us to consider the priests in our dioceses and find men whose spiritual lives we hoped to model. After the session, I introduced myself to him and admitted I didn't have any priest friends at home that I wanted to emulate. Discovering I was from Iowa, he broke into song from *The Music Man*, "Oh there's nothing halfway about the Iowa way."

In the privacy of my room, I did as he suggested. I focused on my priestly models' strengths rather than their flaws. With no lawyers to subpoena my words and no priests to take me to bed, I wrote freely in my journal. Father Scott could find a connection with people that allowed him to preach to the core of their struggles. Father Foley had a sense of humor about life and an earthiness that made him approachable, easy to trust. Father Vince's prophetic honesty and compassion for the poor may have led him to leave the priesthood, but these qualities made his ministry and preaching relevant. With his intelligence and cunning, Father Hunter got things done. They all had flaws, but so did I. I needed see my own flaws as clearly as I'd come to see theirs, so that God could mold my flaws into strengths. I also needed new role models.

The seminary had a plan to assist with this: mentors, professors who would guide us through the formation process and write our yearly evaluations. This person was different from our required spiritual director in that anything said to a mentor was considered "external forum," meaning fodder for discussion among the faculty and our diocesan superiors, whereas information shared with spiritual directors was "internal forum," privileged and private information equivalent to the confessional. We could share anything in spiritual direction with no fear of expulsion, whereas mentors were mandatory reporters.

My mentor was the vice-rector, Father Tim Quinn, O.SS.T., Order of the Most Holy Trinity, founded during the Crusades by holy men who exchanged themselves as ransom for Christian prisoners-of-war. The alphabet soup following the faculty member's names confused me. I'd grown up knowing them as nuns and monks with no idea there were so many breeds.

Father Quinn stood at about five-four, even with the thick industrial soles that were in fashion. I'd observed him cracking jokes with the smokers on breaks during the opening retreats, but word in the pew was you didn't want to cross him. As vice-rector, he was the disciplinarian, the vocational executioner. I called home to my flower-loving DB and asked about Father Quinn.

"You'll love him. Just don't piss him off," he laughed.

As I approached Father Quinn's office, I messed with my sweaty hair, hoping I looked presentable. With his back to the door, Father Quinn sat at his desk smoking a cigarette, with his silver head of hair hunched over a file. I knocked.

"Jesus!" He leapt in his seat.

"I'm sorry." *Shit!* I scolded myself. "I didn't mean to scare you."

He swiveled around with a hand on his chest. "No worries. I get startled when I look in the mirror." He eyed the file, closed it, and hopped up. "You must be Rastrelli."

"Reporting for duty." *The military? Really, Tom. Stupid.* I offered a handshake.

"Tim Quinn," he said, with a firm grip. "Let's go next door."

In the next room, he had a couple armchairs, end tables, and a few lamps. He directed me to a chair and closed the door. "Looks like you're melting," he said in a sandy bass. He cranked up the window unit. "Will the noise bother you?"

"Not at all." I straightened my tie. "Was I supposed to bring anything?"

He plopped in the seat across from me. "Registration and proof of insurance."

I hesitated.

His blue eyes met mine. "Relax, Thomas. This is just a getting-to-know-you meeting."

He asked about my DBs who'd graduated recently, Father Hunter, my background, the pretheology program at Loras, and my family. He asked what I thought of Father Dixon as compared to Hunter. When I responded to his questions, I avoided calling him by name. I wasn't sure whether I should call him Father, Father Quinn, Father Tim, Vice-Rector, Brother Tim, Brother Quinn, or Tim. He was dressed like a regular priest. But how did one address a Trinitarian? He shared the basic information about his order, how long he'd been at the seminary, and that he'd be teaching me theological anthropology. His shoe bopped to the beat of the conversation. His black clerical collar was unbuttoned, its white plastic tab jutting forward from its cotton-polyester neck holster. Before long, we just talked.

When he stood for me to leave, I finally asked, "What do I call you?"

He squinted with his head tilted to the side. "Excuse me?"

"I don't want to offend you by addressing you incorrectly."

"Call me anything but Father." He grinned slyly. "And Butthead."

"All right then, Father Butthead."

His eyes popped. His jaw went slack. I froze, shocked by my bold jocularity. I expected him to lay into me, as Father Scott had.

He laughed. I joined in. He shook my hand and promised to kick my butt in class the following week.

Hoping to escape the heat for Labor Day weekend, I tried to organize a group to go to the beach. Only one, a former cop and fellow landlocked prairie-dweller from Little Rock named Luke, was eager for the Atlantic. He'd become acquainted with one of the newbies, another ex-cop, Naylor, from the Wilmington Diocese, which covered the Delmarva Peninsula and included Ocean City, MD. Luke's southern accent charmed us into a friend of Naylor's rectory near Rehoboth, supposedly a "really nice" beach.

When we arrived, Father Stout greeted us with hugs. Shaved head, with a healthy tan, hint of a gut, and glasses, Father Stout wore tropical attire, including flip-flops. He showed us our rooms, which were not in the rectory but in a neighboring six-unit building where the parish housed priests who assisted with overflow masses during summer. Two bedrooms were available for us, but we'd be staying in different apartments, splitting our quarters with the visiting weekender priests. Father Stout invited us to dinner in his rectory. Two visitors named Ben were staying there: the vocations director of Wilmington and a third theologian from St. Mary's. They were preparing some sort of expensive fish. A few others would attend, including Naylor, who was staying with a friend. I hoped that the meal would yield new friends and role models.

Throughout dinner, Father Stout orchestrated the conversation from the head of the table. When he inquired about my theatrical past, he and the others raised their eyebrows at one another and roared at my mention of dance rehearsals and make-up-room etiquette. Even Luke laughed along, seeming to get it. After the meal, Father Stout and Vocations Director Ben bustled off to get dessert. I scooped up a pile of plates. When I entered the kitchen, Father Stout had VD Ben pressed against the sink and was thrusting his pelvis against his butt. They looked at me and howled. Father Stout jumped away and relieved me of the plates. "We're just joking."

After dessert, I locked the door to my room.

The next morning, we hauled our chairs, towels, and cooler across the coastal highway to the beach. A reflective wall of high-rise hotels stretched the length of the strand, choking it against the sea. As we navigated a patchwork of towels, Father Stout apologized for not having time before the Saturday evening Masses to drive up to the more scenic beach in Rehoboth. I concurred. I recalled the natural beauty of Key Biscayne in Miami.

"Did you get to South Beach?" Father Stout asked, as he dropped his load onto the first empty tract of sand and pulled off his T-shirt.

I spread my towel. "Yeah. I loved the art deco."

The Bens laughed and ran for the water with Luke. I took off my shirt, revealing my blinding white torso, and applied my sunblock as we spoke about Miami. Father Stout was particularly interested that I'd been there when Versace was assassinated. I didn't know much about Versace and couldn't reach the middle of my back. "I'm sorry to ask, but could you help me with the sunblock?"

"If I must." Father Stout rubbed his palms in circles from my shoulders to my waistline, just like my brother, sisters, and friends had done for years.

"Thanks."

"My pleasure."

I joined the others in the water.

After the Masses, eleven of us squeezed around a long table at a posh seafood restaurant. Father Stout, who sat at the head, insisted I sit at his right. He ordered a round of cocktails. Mine was Miami Beach blue. "It matches your eyes," he said. He instructed us to eat anything we desired: "The parish must reward its hardworking priests and feed its future spawn." As the staff refilled our drinks and we downed mussel, skate, shark, and blue crab, the conversation returned to my acting days in Podunk, Iowa. The alcohol enhanced the jokes. I laughed even when they were at my expense. After all, someone at the orientation retreat had said, "If you can't laugh at yourself, you won't survive seminary."

When Father Stout cracked one about farm boys and animal husbandry, I realized he'd been licking his lips a lot. *Probably butter dripping from his lobster,* I concluded. I forced a giggle. Under the table, his knee rested against mine. *Because of the close quarters.* His steel blue eyes fixed on me. His eyebrows bounced twice over his glasses before his tongue slid over his upper lip. I recognized that gaze. That leer. I looked away. They all laughed.

After a few bites, I glanced up. Again, the eyebrows. The tongue. He batted his eyelashes and puckered his lips. Laughs. His knee nestled my thigh. I snapped my legs together and slid to the far side of my chair. His jokes became more biting. The Bens, Naylor, and the priests continued to roar. I caught a glimpse of Luke at the other end of the table. His face was the color of a steamed crab; his lips pursed into a pincher.

On the ride back, Father Stout invited me to the rectory for drinks, "I won't take no for an answer." He ignored Luke. When we arrived, Luke stomped off to his room. The Bens, Naylor, and Father Stout begged my presence. "No, thank you," I repeated. I locked my door and tried to sleep.

I couldn't. Part of me wanted to go to the rectory. I imagined them all having sex. Then I chastised myself. They were just messing with me. My sick, homo brain always reverted to sex. Not everyone was like Father Scott. Like me. And I didn't want Father Stout. Why had I let him lather me with sunblock? He'd probably thought I'd led him on. I didn't know whether I had.

In the morning, while the priests were at their Masses, I grabbed my stuff and beelined for Luke's room. "We need to leave." He was relieved that I hadn't joined their "homo circus." His cop instincts kicked in. He wanted to club their orifices. "Let's just leave," I begged.

The doorbell rang. Luke answered. Father Stout insisted we come to breakfast. Luke informed him we were leaving to beat the holiday traffic. Stout protested and pushed his way in. He plopped onto the ottoman before the couch and placed his hands on my knees. I yanked away: "Don't touch me."

He recoiled a bit. "I'm sorry. I didn't mean anything. We were just messing with you last night. Having fun." He begged me to stay for one more night, he'd take me out for a greater meal.

"We need to get back. Settle in before classes."

He persisted. After a few minutes, his eyes lost their salesman sparkle. He left.

In the time it took him to get to the rectory and for someone else to return, another knock rattled the door. Luke tightened his fists. I rushed past him and yanked the door open.

Seminarian Ben stood, his young face lined with penitence.

"Are you fucking kidding me?" I said.

He begged *me* to stay: don't waste such a beautiful day; Stout's a great guy; traffic won't be that bad; if Luke needs to go, I could catch a ride with someone; I needed some fun before the stress of the semester.

"I can't believe he got you to beg for him," I said, shutting the door.

Luke and I sped past the brown poultry farms of southern Delaware. I spilled my guts about having been sexually abused, the lawsuit, and the shame of the settlement. Luke grew angrier, wishing he could beat all pedophiles to death. We cursed the kid fuckers. We cursed the gays. The weekend followed us like the stink of the state's overcrowded broiler coops.

Back in the safety of my room, I contemplated my next move. If word got back to the seminary that we'd stayed with Stout, if he were a known homosexual, I might get kicked out of seminary. I called my DB in Iowa and Father Dixon. They concurred that I should talk to Quinn.

I fidgeted in a leather chair. Across a polished desk, the seminary rector, Father Lowell, stared at me through lenses as thick as the glass in the popemobile. I'd told Quinn everything, but as seminarian Ben's spiritual director, he had to recuse himself from his disciplinarian duties. Therefore, the case went directly to Father Lowell. I'd hoped to leave sex, abuse, and my attractions to men in Iowa, but even before classes had started, I'd landed myself in a scandal.

Like Quinn, Lowell was short with a ruddy complexion. They could have been brothers, but Lowell had less gray hair and his was curly. He wore hearing aids and spoke out of one side of his mouth with a New

England accent. He thanked me for coming forward and invited me to recount the weekend's events. Calming my nerves as I'd learned during my depositions, I focused on the essentials, stripped my emotions, and testified. He wrote on a pad.

When I finished, he explained that he'd speak to the other seminarians involved and the bishop of Wilmington. "We don't mess around with these types of situations," he said. "Thank you, Tom. You did the right thing." He wished me a great semester and looked forward to having me in spirituality and practice class.

Back in my room, I tried to clear my mind by playing *StarCraft* on my computer. I might have done the right thing but didn't want to be labeled a rat.

Pat slid into the doorway, ferret on his shoulder: "Hello, neighbor!" I looked up, depleted. His smile and goatee dropped. "Let's get out of here."

As we walked Roland Park's rolling blocks of Cape Cod and Victorian homes, I confessed what had happened. He listened, shaking his head and affirming my anger. When I finished, he turned to me and said, "Welcome to Saint Mary's."

THE RULE OF LIFE

I stood in the back row of the chapel's right choir. My stomach growled. The sharp sweetness of the Communion wine teased my appetite. Nearly a hundred seminarians and lay faculty members peppered the pews. Ordained professors robed in chasubles and stoles lined the front rows. With hands folded into a point, the celebrant, our director of liturgy, loomed before his chair in the sanctuary with an expression as bland as a Communion host. A tanned deacon known for wearing kimonos around the dormitory and a silver-bearded acolyte who collected vintage nun habits flanked him. After the presider offered the final blessing, the deacon proclaimed with a lisp, "Our closing hymn is number seventy-six, 'Hail Holy Queen.' "

Across the chapel, Abdel's eyes popped. I averted my gaze but met Mick's. He was biting his lips. I looked at the pew rail, retrieved my red hymnal, and fought the burning well of laughter within. Beside me, Felix swallowed a giggle. On my other side, oblivious or perhaps just more mature, Pat sang the opening line, hailing the holy queens.

Monday through Friday, 11:30 a.m. Mass was the pinnacle of our day, the cornerstone of community life, but my day began with the alarm clock at 7:15. I threw on my bathrobe, slid into my shower flip-flops, and stumbled toward the bathroom. The scent of coffee emanated from Pat's door. I silently cursed morning people. The bathroom—four of which relieved nearly ninety men—contained its original white fixtures, a dozen marble stalls with impenetrable wooden doors, and a few washers and driers. Some fellows even conversed while on adjacent johns. Rumor had it that one of my DBs, who'd graduated a few years earlier, had taken it upon himself to rescrub the toilets after the cleaning ladies had. Word around the seminary was that my DB had been a closeted queer obsessively purifying the stools because he couldn't deal with his own shit.

In the adjacent room stood eight individual showers, the marble of which matched the bathroom. Each stall contained two white plastic curtains. The first provided privacy from the others; the second splash proofed one's tiny dressing area. The building had water pressure problems that often left us with no more than a trickle of water. Felix said it was like having someone pee on him. I'd never thought of that possibility. Some guys conversed while lathering, rinsing, and repeating, but most remained silent.

I sloshed back to my room to dress and groom. After grabbing my breviary and stuffing my backpack, I hopped down one of the worn marble stairwells, rushed to the cafeteria, and squeezed into a table with the other late risers. I scarfed down cereal, a banana, and orange juice, making occasional contributions to the conversation, which centered on the coming day's assignments, readings, or tests. At 7:54, we sped down the hallway to the chapel. We deposited our bags on one of the arched windows' sills and slid into our pews seconds before Morning Prayer was intoned at 8:00.

"God, come to my assistance," the leader began.

"Lord, make haste to help me," we responded, while crossing ourselves. Some of us said "our" and "us" because we were praying as a group. Liturgical purists argued that the rubrics—the official instructions for Catholic liturgy written in red words—called for the singular and should not be changed for the sake of proper grammar.

On holy days and special occasions, we chanted the Psalter—the Psalms—around which the four-week cycle of the Breviary, or Liturgy of the Hours, was based. I was drafted into a rotation of a dozen or so singers who split the cantors' load. The chapel's opposing choirs alternated stanzas. When somebody rushed the tempo or lagged behind, the group voice nudged him into submission. When somebody wandered in late, hungover from the previous night's consumption in the basement bar, we silently shamed him. When somebody offered a specific request at the intercessions that differed from our preferred theological perspective, we silently judged him.

The faculty who lived with us in the dorms joined us for prayer. And to take roll. We didn't have assigned seats, but most of us settled into a two-pew radius. Periodically, I'd swap choirs. But that stirred dirty looks from guys whose space I'd invaded. It became easier—and less noticeable—to settle.

Father Quinn lived off campus, so I could have skipped periodically and gotten away with it, but absences were frowned on. Too many, and one was diagnosed with a "formation issue"—an apparently minor problem indicating something dastardly that could undermine his entire celibate commitment, priestly calling, and humanity (like my DB who oversanitized the bathrooms). A healthy prayer life reflected a healthy vocation, so the first question asked of those suspected of floundering was "how's your prayer life?" We were to nurture, guard, and defend our prayer at all costs, for without it, one had no relationship with God. One's vocation had no security. I may have sleepily mumbled through Morning Prayer, but I never missed it.

Classes began at 8:30, followed by Mass at 11:30 and lunch. The dining room was large enough to seat two hundred and fifty at its round wooden tables. Large arched windows brightened the space in spite of its dark paneling. In pre–Vatican II times, a seminarian or faculty member would have read excerpts from a saint's spiritual confessions during meals, and all would have paused to pray before stuffing their faces. We were trusted to pray on our own and encouraged to "break bread together" and "build community" during meals. At first, we newbies filled the tables one after another. Eventually, we became more discerning. Cliques developed along theological and liturgical lines: those who preferred *Worship*, the red hymnal with the "traditional" sounding hymns, versus those who preferred *Gather*, the blue book. Even though I didn't care where the music originated as long as it was good, I sided with *Gather* and its piano- and guitar-friendly songs that reminded me of Mom's old praise group. I couldn't understand why the conservative guys preferred *Worship* and its collection of Reformation dirges composed by Luther and Calvin. Before long, I knew which tables a left-leaning thinker should avoid.

We shared the dining room with the faculty and the lay staff, mostly women who ran the administrative offices. The priests had a private dining room; only the more laid-back ones ate with us. Periodically, when the monotony of male conversation became tedious, I'd sit with the ladies. Doing this too often was frowned on: "formation issue."

Afternoons varied with classes, meetings, and offsite pastoral internships. I spent free afternoons attending counseling, mentoring, and spiritual direction sessions or studying in the air-conditioned library. Wednesday afternoons were reserved for communitywide formation events—various activities meant to mold our personalities, spiritualities, intellects, pastoral skills, and sexualities into those of celibate priests. Each week, Father Lowell held a rector's conference, during which he stood at a podium before the great hall and lectured about the various challenges facing priests. When he spoke of celibacy, he mentioned his niece's coming of age and how on a family sailing event in Connecticut he'd noticed how attractive she'd become in her teens. This spawned a wave of incest and statutory rape jokes throughout the house. When he'd missed a number of consecutive daily Masses—he rarely came to prayer—Lowell waxed apologetic and spun his rationale: work was prayer. Disgruntled students, who moaned that he wasn't "part of the community," needed to realize that he was absent because he was working for the preservation of the community, courting donors, bishops, and alumni. Most often, he mused about his latest building project, an expansion of the library, including state-of-the-art archives. A systematic theologian whose expertise was in the postmodern philosophy of Paul Ricoeur, Father Lowell seemed incapable of transcending the academic plane. He claimed that the seminary was his parish and we were his parishioners. But he was a philosopher, CEO, and philanthropist first.

In addition to the rector's conferences, we met in "theological reflection" groups of four students, facilitated by a professor. During these meetings, we presented "verbatims"—written reconstructions of challenging situations, such as an encounter with a beggar in Baltimore's Inner Harbor, talking with our grandparents or parents about their living wills, or confronting a friend who had an addiction. In the discussions that followed, we parsed our experiences to glean insight into our limitations and strengths. We discerned the presence of God in each situation, making connections to scripture in hopes of applying this knowledge in our homilies.

When we weren't in classes or meetings, we were encouraged to make time for fitness, private prayer, and recreation. At 5:15 p.m., we returned to the chapel for Evening Prayer, which was like Morning Prayer only with different psalms and readings. The dress code was relaxed, meaning no ties and clerical collars; slacks were still required. On Wednesdays, an hour of adoration before the Blessed Sacrament preceded Evening Prayer. A consecrated host was placed between slides of glass that fit into a monstrance, which looked like an ornate, gold-plated tennis racquet standing on end. A deacon placed the monstrance on the altar, knelt before it, and wafted thick clouds of incense toward it. We knelt in pews to worship and pray before the consecrated bread, the Real Presence of Jesus Christ. Felix referred to adoration as "cookie worship." I agreed. The rite seemed a relic of the pre–Vatican II Church and a conservative litmus test for orthodoxy. I begrudgingly knelt in my pew and tried to commune with the Real Presence, silently speaking to God and begging for a response. Eventually I came to enjoy the spiced scent of the incense and used the silent time to meditate, clearing my head of thought and anxiety. Thinking about nothing felt refreshing, in a sense, transcendent.

After Evening Prayer, the dress code ended and dinner was served. Shorts, sweats, and jeans prevailed. After eating, I'd spend about fifteen minutes singing along to CDs in my room. Pat observed that when I was stressed I sang louder and more aggressive songs. One night, he, another fellow, and I blasted different Disney musicals from our rooms while I ran from door to door singing and acting out the lyrics. On weeknights, we did homework and gathered in one another's rooms for our favorite TV shows: *The West Wing*, *Deep Space Nine*, *Friends*, and *Will and Grace*. We didn't have cable in our rooms—too much late night temptation—so we watched *South Park* in the lounge with our church history professor, a seventy-year-old Missionary of the Sacred Heart. Friday nights, Mick rented movies for everyone to watch on the Donnelly Lounge's big screen. The first weekend, he rented Baltimore films, including John Waters's *Pecker*. Pat, Mick, and the Baltimoreans laughed their asses off. I didn't understand the humor. They claimed that after a few years in "Balmer, Merlin" I would. Some guys were offended and tried to ban R-rated movies and *South Park* from the lounge. Father Lowell denied their protest.

After my TV breaks, I talked on the phone to stay connected to friends and family in the lagging time zones, but things were rough. My family was struggling because my sister Maria had fallen in love with an atheist. One friend's marriage was buckling under the weight of his wife's addictions. When another friend discovered her almost-fiancé had a wife and family, he assaulted her. Another friend had been raped by the leader of her scripture study group. I listened. I cried with them. Into the late hours, I tried to help.

During the day, I fell asleep at my desk or in the library. When I spoke to Father Quinn about it, he said, "You worry too much, Rastrelli." My fatigue was "a normal adjustment" to the new routine and the large amount of reading required by graduate school. When I nodded off in his theological anthropology class, it was another issue. The connections between Greek philosophy, Christian history, and spirituality captivated me; still, I struggled to remain awake. The coffee refills became frequent, especially before the classes I thought would be my favorites—scripture and liturgy—but which bored me. They seemed to be nothing more than a rehash of prescribed rubrics and acceptable canons of scholarship.

"You can't ask that," I heard from my classmates after I questioned professors about the absence of purgatory in scripture, the justification for denying women priestly ordination, historical massacres in the name of the papacy and God, and other "scandalous" topics.

"Someone in the pew is going to ask me. So if we don't discuss it here, then where?" I responded. I thought about the real-life shit my friends were facing.

In my mentor meetings with Quinn, I inquired about Father Stout and the others from the Ocean City fiasco. He shared only that the rector had spoken to the bishops of those involved. They'd handled things as they'd seen appropriate. But seminarian Ben and Naylor seemed unscathed. By the end of our first semester, Luke had become Naylor's best friend. When VD Ben came for his official seminary visits, he fluttered about them. I wanted an apology. From them. From Father Stout. From Doctor Lauz.

Near midnight on an autumn night, I paced about my room on the phone with Father Scott. One of my close St. Stephen's friends, suffering from an undiagnosed condition that caused chronic, excruciating pain throughout her body, had been in the hospital for more than a week, possibly dying. Father Scott hadn't visited her, even to perform the anointing of the sick. I'd observed how he'd called her things like "saddlebags," despite knowing she struggled with anorexia. When I confronted Father, he scolded me: it was none of my business; I had no understanding of what it meant to be a priest. I shouted back, not caring if I jostled Pat from his snoring. But Father Scott knew how to silence me. I hung up. Hating him. But hating myself more.

The next morning, I apologized to Pat. I pushed through my midterms. I enlisted in a program that delivered soup and sandwiches on the streets to Baltimore's destitute. I volunteered at a homeless shelter. Monthly, I met with Counselor Number Nine, the seminary's smiley old psychologist. We "worked though" my transition into seminary life and the adjustment "beyond the stress" of the abuse lawsuit. I tutored struggling classmates and lagged after class to engage professors with questions. I never missed a spiritual direction session. I jacked off to gay fantasies. I confessed jacking off to gay fantasies. I scoured the stacks for research. I tried to compose perfect papers. The organist developed a scheduling preference for me. I sang for Alumni Day and special Masses involving visiting bishops: candidacy, lector, and acolyte—the hierarchical steps on the way to priesthood known as the minor orders before Vatican II. I aced my finals. When I saw Father Scott over Christmas break, I had no desire to sleep with him; I ordered him to therapy. I preached the Church's teachings on premarital sex to my little sister. I gave up masturbation for Lent—the first few days of Lent. I performed in the seminary talent show: parodies of popular hymns and spoofing seminary procedures with inside jokes. Whenever someone asked for volunteers, I offered. I was known as "a nice guy." Felix christened me "Golden Boy." He teased, "You're so golden that light shines from your ass."

I stood at the bar, waiting to order a drink in the seminary's basement pub. We newbies had thrown the fourth-year guys a party celebrating the completion of their comprehensive exams. We'd prepared and served them a special dinner, which included wine enough for the wedding feast at Cana. I'd just finished the dishes and figured I'd join in the postprandial spirits. Guys slapped down bills, buying for their buddies. We treated one another all the time. Beers were a buck; hard drinks a couple. Those who had money from their previous lives sometimes slapped a twenty on the Formica, "Drinks for everyone!"

Caden from Louisville, the graduating class's golden boy, squeezed up next to me. At six-five, with a cleft chin and an athletic build, he looked like Ben Affleck's better-looking twin. I was only a couple years younger, but he was already a deacon—the final step before priesthood. He'd made his promises of obedience and celibacy. I wondered what my life would have been like without Lauz. I could have gone to seminary right out of high school. I could have been mere months from priesthood.

"You want a beer?" Caden asked, with a smile my grandma would trust. "A thank you for the great meal."

"Thanks." I was taken aback. Other than "hellos" in the hallway, Caden had never spoken to me. I assumed it was because he was uninterested in making friends with new guys or conservative. Or stuck-up. But he was just shy. Maybe he needed a good buzz to engage socially. I didn't like beer but felt obligated to accept. I raised my bottle, "To surviving seminary." We clinked our Coronas and swigged. We exchanged small talk. He finished his beer and rolled the empty bottle between his palms. "You're cool. I wish we'd talked sooner."

"Me too," I said. "But it's a big house." The crowd at the bar roared. Over Caden's shoulder, a gray-haired guy slammed flaming shots of sambuca.

"You're really nice," he smiled again. "I wish I'd have gotten to know you better." His brown eyes betrayed regret. I knew about his eyes. He'd preached about them at adoration. When he was a kid, a friend challenged him to see who could stare at the sun for the longest. Caden won with a permanent blind spot seared into his retina. In his homily, he'd compared that experience to looking at God, knowing the divine will, and forever having God's presence burned into one's soul. I hoped that in three years I could preach like him.

"We've got a few more months. Plenty of time to get to know each other," I said.

"Another beer?" he asked.

"I was planning on watching the second movie."

"Great! Get us a few spots." He rushed to the bar.

Even though the anti-R-rated contingency had vacated the lounge, the couches around the television were full. I sat behind them in a small armchair. *There's Something about Mary* filled the big screen. Ben Stiller's character had just zipped his genitals into his fly. Caden returned and handed me another beer.

"Thanks," I said, before laughing at the film. He chuckled.

After a few minutes, I noticed that he only laughed when I laughed. Out of the corner of my eyes, I could see that he was sitting on the edge of his seat, watching me.

I looked directly at him. He leaned toward me with a giddy smile. I turned back to the screen. Not moving. I faked a snicker at a lame joke. He unleashed a piercing cackle. I stopped laughing. I stopped drinking my beer. When he finished his, he offered me another.

"I'm good."

"Come on! Celebrate some more."

"I still have some left." I sloshed my half bottle.

"Well, finish it. I'm getting you a fresh one."

He turned for the bar. When he put his money down, I sped through the shadows, exited the lounge, hopped on the elevator, and sprinted down the empty hallway into my room. I turned the deadbolt and wrapped myself tightly in the bed's covers. My heart beat wildly. He'd wanted to have sex.

And so had I.

A few gentle raps shook the door. I froze. If the bed creaked, if he heard me breathing, he'd wait me out. The blood swished through my ears. I silently begged God for help, to make me strong enough to resist. A louder knock. What if he woke the neighbors? I shifted my weight. The bedsprings squeaked. The doorknob rattled. Father Scott warned me about this. In seminary, he'd fucked a guy who had followed him to his room after a shower. No, I wasn't Father Scott. I watched the crack along the bottom of the door. Caden's shadow. I wanted that shadow to sear its image into me. *God save me from myself,* I beseeched. The shadow disappeared. I remained in bed, blaming myself for leading Caden on and regretting the missed opportunity.

The phone rang. I got up to answer, to tell him to leave me the fuck alone, but I feared I couldn't resist. I waited until the red message light blinked and dialed my voicemail. It was Caden: "Hello, um, Doctor Rastrelli." A sudsy giggle. "I'd like to finish our, um, appointment." Another giggle. "So come on up for a nightcap, Doctor."

I forwarded the message directly to Father Quinn's voicemail and went to sleep.

I sat in Father Lowell's office. Caden was Father Quinn's spiritual directee. Again, Quinn had to recuse himself from his disciplinary role. Lowell handled it just as he had the Father Stout case. He listened and commended me for coming forward, but I sensed a subtext. He probably knew the reason the gays were drawn to me. Dogs run in packs, and they eat their own shit.

A few days later, as I sat at my desk reading, Caden ducked into in my doorway. With downcast eyes, he apologized and begged forgiveness. Afterward, when we passed each other in the hallway, we said nothing. His other deacon friends stopped greeting me as well. Word was out. I didn't tolerate homos.

Father Quinn greeted me with his usual "Butthead! How the hell are ya?" I wondered how he could remain so kind after I'd outed two of his star pupils. He invited me into the sitting room adjacent to his smoking office. He asked how I was doing with the fallout. I told him I was fine. Quinn assured me I'd done the right thing and expounded on my coming first-theology evaluation.

As my mentor, he would compose my official faculty evaluation and sign off on my written self-evaluation. He said that I was doing great. I'd integrated into community life. I was kicking academic ass. But the formation faculty members were concerned about my inability to say no, which indicated a minor lack of personal boundaries that might have been a sign that I was running from some deeper, unresolved issue, perhaps perfectionism, which was a form a narcissism, the need to be God, or it might have been that I was a workaholic, like my dad, Father Scott and Father Hunter, which could ultimately lead to burnout in a parish and result in a boundary violation with a parishioner or the collapse of my prayer life or, God forbid, celibacy . . . and salvation. I had what every seminarian dreaded: a formation issue.

"So what?" I said. "I'm supposed to let my grades fall or sleep through Morning Prayer?"

"And you should skip Lowell's systematics class for the next two weeks." Quinn shook his head. "Smart ass." He challenged me to slow down, to learn to say no.

"Can you do that?" he asked.

"No."

He chuckled and then shot me a serious stare.

"Sure." But I was pissed. "Doesn't the faculty realize that I said no to Stout and Caden?"

"Of course they do, Butthead." He smiled. "You need to think in larger terms."

The faculty wanted me to find the Holy Grail of seminary formation: balance.

We brainstormed ways I could adjust my schedule: taking more time to relax and exercise, limiting my cantor gigs, and spending less time on the phone trying to solve everyone else's problems. I needed to include these strategies in my self-evaluation to illustrate personal growth. Parish life would have an endless number of demands to meet and crises to solve. I couldn't do everything. Be strong for everyone. Fix everyone. Save everyone. Quinn warned that if I didn't learn to depend on God and others, if I couldn't ask for help or make an effort to care for myself first, I was bound to fail. I thought of Father Scott sitting at his computer sixteen hours a day, how he'd told me I was the only one who really knew him, who really cared. I wrote down Quinn's prescriptions.

"You're a gifted guy, Rastrelli. So many strengths," Quinn said. I set aside my pen, feeling I had a direction. His eyes narrowed as if he were looking through the façade of my accomplishments, peering into my darkest fear, "But are you weak enough to be a priest?"

I didn't know.

CODEPENDENT NO MORE

The director of our summer-long hospital placement, a German expatriate chaplain named Jürgen, asked his standard question of the group: "In one word, how do you feel?" Another intern had just recounted being with a patient who died in excruciating pain. Through the window, the harsh California light unmasked our blemishes. Of course, that was the goal of Clinical Pastoral Education (CPE), the official formation program for seminarians' hospital ministry: tear us down and build us back up.

One by one, the others answered Jürgen's question: "Unhappy." "Sad." "Anxious." "Devastated." "I'm curious," someone answered.

"Curiosity is not an emotion," Jürgen said, like the Terminator. "You have mad, sad, glad, or anxious. Choose one."

"Well, now I'm anxious."

The group's eyes moved to me. I felt so many things. I was sad for the person who died and her family. I was frightened and worried—anxious—about experiencing my first death. I was frustrated—no, mad—that I couldn't stop people's suffering. In philosophy, I'd studied the problem of evil—rationalizations of why an omnibenevolent, omnipotent God allowed innocent people to die excruciating deaths while rapists and sexual abusers lived. God seemed deficient. Created in God's image, I was deficient too. Was this what Quinn had meant by "Are you weak enough to be a priest?"

"Anxious," I said.

Later, in my one-on-one with Jürgen, we unpacked my emotions. Chaplains couldn't stop suffering. We were deficient by virtue of our humanity. If we tried to be God, we'd hurt our patients. The cardinal sin of chaplains—saying, "It's OK"—was the fastest way to undermine patients' trust and invalidate their feelings. We were to practice "helping skills" for a "ministry of presence" by listening and utilizing "understanding statements" that gently nudged patients to claim their emotions. We were to "be" with them in whatever they experienced. To my surprise, I was good at it. When my first patient died, I sat with the family.

"I absorbed their pain and they seemed to find some peace," I said to Jürgen.

He informed me of a "growth edge"—CPE-speak for "formation issue." I was "codependent." I needed to be needed by people and perceived as lovable at all costs. This need fueled my empathy, but I could get lost in others.

"But even God is codependent." I spouted what I'd learned at St. Mary's: the "economic" versus the "imminent" Trinity; how the Father, Son, and Holy Spirit are interrelated but separate—a paradox; and how humans were created in the image of this relational God. "It's in our God-given nature to be dependent. It's what brings us into communion. How can that be bad?"

"Our greatest strengths can be our greatest weaknesses," Jürgen said. He told me to read *Codependent No More* and to do the Enneagram, a personality index that would explain how my "gifts" were also "shadows." "Ministers interact with people at their most vulnerable," he warned. "You must protect those you serve by confronting your weaknesses."

Jürgen's words resonated with something my pastoral counseling professor had said: week after week, year after year, as parishioners unmask their deepest needs for God's love and Communion at Mass, it was common for them fall in love with their priests. Celibates were vulnerable. To maintain celibacy, you had to protect your promise. It started with "Can I see you after Mass again Father?" and ended with a love-struck parishioner's seducing an overworked, lonely priest.

In the months since, I'd blamed myself more for what happened with Father Scott. Maybe he was right: I'd seduced him. My professor's warning to protect myself from seductive parishioners clashed with Jürgen's caveat to protect them from me.

Had Father Scott failed to protect me? Was it normal that I'd fallen in love with him? Everything between us was so messy.

I couldn't let Jürgen be present to that part of me. My superior from Dubuque, Father Dixon, had informed him that I'd just been through painful sexual abuse litigation, was currently undergoing extensive therapy, and didn't need to rehash these things in my CPE group. I had to fix my codependency on my own.

After work, I rummaged through Borders's psychology section, gathering Jürgen's prescribed readings. An additional book caught my eye, *Men in Love: Men's Sexual Fantasies; The Triumph of Love over Rage* by Nancy Friday. With chapters on homosexuals, virgins, and even animals, maybe someone else had fantasized about his priest.

When I got back to my sister Jenny's house in the Inland Empire, where I was living, I hurried to my room and devoured the chapters: "Straight Men, Gay Fantasies," "Bisexuals," and "Homosexuals." Besides sexually aroused, I felt relieved. Other men, even heterosexual men, fantasized about making love to men. I wasn't alone. The author analyzed same-sex fantasies, concluding that most of the men who "labeled" themselves homosexuals were in their teens or early twenties. She stated: "My own feeling is that in another five or ten years, several of the men in this chapter may well have changed their minds." As I hid the book at the bottom of my underwear drawer, the final sentence of the chapter haunted me: "Life is all about choices."

As I watched the fireworks over Disneyland from the hospital's rooftop, I was sure of my choice. Aware of my psychological sins, I'd worked hard with Jürgen to exorcise my ministry of countertransference, triangulation, and codependent tendencies. Father Quinn had been right when he'd asked, "Are you weak enough to be a priest?" I was exposing my weaknesses and crushing them. And I was being strong for the vulnerable people I served. I'd just held a bedpan in the ER while a patient vomited into it. The lone chaplain on call, I was ready for anything.

My pager buzzed.

Minutes later, I stood in the doorway of a darkened room. Inside, monitors wreathed the bed and cast a green wash over the tiled floor. A dapper man sat by a toddler, whose nose, mouth, neck, and arms sprouted tubes. Machines bellowed his chest. The nurses informed me he'd drowned in a neighbor's pool. Braindead. The parents had to decide when to remove him from life support. I had nothing to say, nothing that could make this better. I listened. We recited rote prayers. We were silent.

After a few minutes, the father asked, "Where's God, Padre?"

I flipped through the theology texts in my mind and spoke what I'd learned, what I hoped was true. "On the cross, Jesus joined himself to the world's pain. Your boy isn't alone. Neither are you. Here and now, God is suffering with you."

"Are you fucking kidding me?" said a young woman in the doorway. "Where was God this afternoon?"

She ran off. I moved to follow, but her husband grabbed my hand. "Don't. Please, Padre," his voice was gentle. "She'll come around." He caressed his son's loose curls. "Right now, he needs you more."

I set my briefcase by the front door. Jenny entered the vestibule dazed. Dad's oldest brother, Uncle Bob, was dead from a stroke. I'd grown closer to him since he told me that he'd been sexually abused, and that if he'd known Lauz had abused me, he would have "nailed his balls to a log and pushed him over backwards."

"There's more," Jenny said. Someone from Cedar Falls had called. A student who'd gone on the Antioch retreat I'd led died after being thrown against a wall by an angry customer. And there was still more. Pat called from Baltimore. A classmate who I'd tutored had died of a heart attack.

When I was alone in my room, I crumbled to my knees and prayed: "Are you fucking kidding me?"

I sat in the conference room's circle of padded chairs. "I'm beyond sad and mad. I'm devastated. Disoriented. Exhausted. I need to be with my family. Not as a priest. Not to fix. Just to be with them. As a nephew. A son."

"You're too weak to be trusted with others' grief," Jürgen said. He commended my growth—being able to acknowledge my weakness—and told me to go home.

When I returned, I worked long days to make up my clinical hours. Exhausted, my loneliness increased, but my patients never noticed. Jürgen gave me a fine evaluation and reiterated my need to work on developing stronger emotional boundaries.

I drove eastward. As canyons and mountains turned to plains and cornfields, the summer's deaths clung to me. I envied Jürgen and my married patients, who had flesh and blood to hold them at night in their pain. God wasn't going to embrace me and wipe my tears. I consoled myself by replaying fantasies I'd read in *Men in Love*. As I passed through Iowa, I stopped at Father Foley's to say hi and to thank him for his letters. Within an hour, we'd blown each other.

Immediately after we'd finished, I wanted to get as far away as possible. In the next town, I stopped at a gas station, ripped apart *Men in Love*, and slammed it into the trash. Something had to change. Looking in the rearview mirror, I stared at a man who was too weak to be a celibate priest.

THE ROAD LESS TRAVELED

I ripped the claws and legs from the Maryland blue crab and tossed them into the pile of empty shells and worthless appendages in the center of the table. Each year at St. Mary's began with the crab feast, the new brood's initiation into Chesapeake life. Gathered around a secluded courtyard, my brothers ate, drank, and bantered, seemingly unaware of the fellows who hadn't returned, some by choice, one by death. Thankfully, Abdel, Pat, Felix, and Mick were back. After what I'd done with Father Foley, I wondered whether I'd be back in another year. I ripped the lungs from my shell, scraped out the "mustard," and tweezed the tiny pieces of meat.

"This isn't worth the work," I said.

"Beer helps." Abdel slid me another Corona.

When the crabs and free booze ran out, we retrieved our mail from the post-office boxes lining the wall outside the basement's pub.

"You get more mail than anyone," Pat said.

"Everyone wants a piece of Tom," Felix said.

Waiting for the elevator, I separated my letters from the junk. A familiar blue calligraphy marked the last envelope. I let the others lead the way onto the crowded elevator as I slid Father Foley's letter between the others. Why had I let him back into my life? Jürgen had been right. I had no "emotional boundaries." This wasn't a "growth edge." It was a chasm.

When we reached the third floor, I followed Mick into the hallway.

"Where're you going?" Pat giggled. His scalp and nose flushed a darker shade of rose.

"Shit." I stumbled back onto the elevator.

"Lightweights," Mick's voice trailed off as the doors closed.

Pat and I had moved into 4A. After first theology, everyone was offered an optional upgrade to two small rooms or one of the few prized double-sized rooms—a benefit of the vocations shortage. We opted for the two-room plan so we could separate our offices from our bedrooms, which would look good on our evaluations—strong boundaries between one's work and private life nurtured healthy celibacy. We remained next-door-neighbors. His office/TV room split our bedrooms. My headboard no longer jiggled with his snore. I wished the guys goodnight, entered my office, locked the door behind me, and read Father Foley's letter.

He swore never to act out with me again. We could just limit ourselves to backrubs in the future. He wrote, *I pray for you at the altar, Thomas, always at the altar.* I thought of his lips kissing babies and his hands anointing elders. He invited me to come again and concluded, *Love and prayers, Pete.*

From the severed envelope, I plucked his hundred dollar check. I yanked my orange-handled sewing shears from my desk and carved my name from the check.

On an unsullied envelope, I scribbled Father Foley's address and slapped a stamp. No return address. I wrapped the mutilated check, with an open window where my name had been, in a piece of loose leaf, stuffed it into the envelope, and delivered it to the mailbox, sure that I could resist him in the future.

In my Pauline epistles class the next week, I learned a new word, "cruciformity": conforming one's life to the crucifixion. St. Paul's spirituality revolved around Jesus's sacrifice on the cross, the ultimate act of love. Paul called Christians to imitate this sacrifice and extirpate whatever they placed before God. I read in Galatians: "Now those who belong to Christ have crucified their flesh with its passions and desires" (5:24). But my sin had kept me from doing so. I was out of control. Jürgen had been right about my poor personal boundaries, but it was more than that. It was pride. I believed I could defeat my worst sins, my flesh, on my own.

In the back of the chapel, a few feet from where the pope had prayed, I pushed aside the weighty maroon curtain of an ornate wooden box and stepped into the darkness. A notice on the liturgy bulletin board indicated that the Franciscan priest who'd completed the psychological intake for my CPE application was in the confessional. Preferring face-to-face, I'd never gone to confession in the box. The wooden kneeler creaked under my weight. My sweaty elbows slid on the smooth ledge at the foot of the waffled screen that reminded me of a theatre scrim. On the mustard-colored fabric, the silhouette of a head, which looked like a limbless crab, invited me into the sacrament. The Franciscan wasn't on the seminary faculty. I wouldn't have to face him in the classroom. Maybe the traditionalists were right: anonymity in the confessional *was* more pastoral. I rested my chin on folded hands and stripped the shell of shame and pride from my sin. The dusty mildew scent of old timber gave way to the salty taste of my sweat as I nailed my past with Father Scott and Father Foley to the cross.

"That was a brave confession," the Franciscan said. "It sounds like you really needed to get that out."

"It doesn't feel like there's anything left."

He spoke with an East Coast accent that I couldn't place. He didn't condemn; he offered hope. He suggested that I speak to a counselor about my celibate, homosexual struggles.

"I'm Tom Rastrelli. I saw you last spring for my CPE interview."

"I thought it was you." The shadow of his hand gestured. "But I couldn't be sure through the screen."

"I'm not fan of blind confessions," I said.

"Neither am I."

"And it's hot as hell in here." I'd said it without thinking.

He laughed, "Ain't that the truth?"

I wiped the sweat from my brow and rubbed it on my black slacks. "Would you be willing to be my therapist?"

"I'd be honored."

And with that, he granted me absolution.

I rushed to my truck, eager to make the forty-five minute drive to my first session with the Franciscan. When I turned the ignition, the radio blasted a gay love song from *Rent*. The day before, Abdel and I had belted tunes the entire way back from Sunday Mass at a progressive downtown parish, the knobby steeple of which popped up at the end of the Jones Falls Expressway like a "big white phallus." At least, that's what Felix had observed. I flipped off the music and drove in the opposite direction.

Beyond the urban sprawl, the countryside looked like Iowa except for interspersed swatches of shady woods and sodden McMansions. When I turned onto Folly Quarter Road, the monastery—or "provincial house" as the Franciscan had clarified on the phone—sat atop a gradual hill. A grove of trees framed the limestone structure and its simple arcade. The provincial house probably contained a few hundred monks' cells. I parked the truck and passed through one of the arches into the central courtyard. A hot breeze rustled my hair. Water tinkled in a large stone fountain. A blackbird cawed overhead, but not a hooded soul was in sight. Monastic orders had been harder hit by the shortage of vocations than dioceses. I wondered how many remained in this community and how much longer these walls would house holy men.

Under the central arch at the back of the courtyard, I halted before two bulky dark wooden doors. I thwacked the intimidating metal knocker against the warped wooden face. Some small birds flapped and chattered at the blackbird. Staring at the splits in the door's weathered grain, I thought of my celibate failures. When the Franciscan had agreed to counsel me, I hadn't told him he'd be Counselor Number Ten. In another year, there would probably be an Eleven. The bolt turned with a metallic snap. The door opened inward.

"Welcome, Tom," Number Ten said.

He wore charcoal slacks, an oxford, and a burgundy button-down sweater. I'd expected his black habit—Conventual Franciscans didn't wear brown—but he looked like a regular guy. A few strands of his thinning gray hair flopped over his forehead. I followed him through the dim vestibule into a large study with weathered shag carpeting, bookshelves, couches, armchairs, and a few small windows.

"Please sit. Make yourself comfortable." Ten extended a hand toward a couch upholstered in crisscrossed shades of beige. He moved to a matching armchair. I sat at the end of the couch nearest him. It smelled of dirt, sweat, and incense: the story of my life.

Starting with Jimmy Engel's penis in the basement during kindergarten, I told him everything: Lauz, how I'd tried to be perfect to cover the fact I'd been abused, Tobey, leaving the Church, the theatre, Father Scott, my priestly calling, fucking Father Scott, and my failure to stop Lauz. As I spoke, the Franciscan's eyes barely blinked behind his glasses. When I cried, his thin lips retracted into a grimace. When I laughed, he smiled. His interlocked fingers rested peacefully on his slight belly. He didn't take a single written note. I waited for him to scorn me. He didn't.

Then I revealed the details of the drive back from CPE, how I'd used

Father Foley for sex. I described our sixty-nine and how his scent had made me gag. "You must think I'm disgusting," I said with my eyes downcast.

"Look at me, Tom." I reluctantly did. He peered into me. "I don't think you're disgusting. I think you're finally being honest."

For the first time in my life—correction, for the first time since confessing Tobey and the doctor to Father Scott—I'd trusted someone with my entire darkness. And he'd simply passed me tissues and offered to get me water.

He checked his watch. Four-thirty. I'd been talking since two. Normally, our sessions would be fifty minutes, but he'd let me continue because it seemed as if I needed to get it all out. The catharsis had drained me. I wasn't sure I could drive, and it was rush hour. I'd miss Evening Prayer and dinner. I had tons of homework and had to prepare for my new pastoral placement. "I gotta get it together." I shook like a drenched puppy. "All right. I'm good."

"You are good." He gently waited for my reaction.

"I'm *fine*." I needed to get out before I lost it again. I gathered my clumped tissues from the end table.

He watched. "It's OK if you need to stay in the chapel for a while or walk the driveway until you feel like driving."

"Thanks." I balled up the tissues like a damp snowball and wrapped a fresh one around it.

"What do you do for fun?" he asked.

"What?"

"You did some incredible work today. So I want you to do something nice for yourself. Something fun that won't hurt you physically or emotionally." He scooped the small trashcan next to his chair and extended it to me.

I tossed in the proof of my tears, my shit. "OK," I lied. The last thing I needed was a reward. Sackcloth and ashes were more like it.

"I'm serious, Tom. Starting tonight when you get home, and each day until our next meeting, you have to do something fun."

"I'll try."

We stood and shook hands. I was relieved he didn't hug me. His hand didn't linger. He maintained strong professional boundaries, just what a seductive, homo priest-sucker like me needed.

"And be gentle with yourself," he added, as if he'd just read my mind.

Fuck that, I thought. *I deserve it.* He led me over the snarled carpeting to the door. I halted. He was right. "Being hard on myself hasn't worked."

He turned back to me with a morose grin. "It hasn't."

"Wow." I felt myself tense up. I'd been emotionally beating myself since the doctor. "I don't know how to stop."

"Don't worry about it. We'll get there."

I ground my heels into the weathered carpet and picked at my fingernails. If being hard on myself hadn't worked, what would?

"You did great today," he said, and escorted me through the vestibule to the exit. I tried to believe him but couldn't. My mind twisted like a moth in sap.

Before I stepped outside, Number Ten's eyebrows arched. His eyes grew severe. "This week," he said, "every time you aren't gentle with yourself, I want you slap yourself three times in honor of the Trinity."

The stones of the vestibule cried out with our laughter. My body hadn't forgotten how to howl, how to feel joy. We shook hands again. But this time, he grasped my right hand with both of his, to which I responded by adding my left. The handshake seemed to last for a minute. His smile and eyes channeled ferocity and pride. He'd really meant it when he'd said I'd done great. I wanted to pull him into a hug, but instead I stepped into September's furnace.

The beltway moved slower than the Vatican's forthcoming apology to Galileo. As I fell into the hypnotic cycle of depressing and releasing the brakes, I replayed the session in my mind. The two handshakes, his smile—he had to be gay too. I wondered if he had sex with his Franciscan brothers.

When I got back to my room, I was too tired to sing or get out my recently purchased guitar and beginner's book to plunk though "Home on the Range" or "I've Been Working on the Railroad." Too exhausted for anything fun, I collapsed onto my bed, my mind fixed in the past.

Someone knocked. I crossed to the sink and splashed my face. "Come in."

Pat's shiny head and grin peeked around the doorframe. "Hello, neighbor," he said in a stretched singsongy tenor, an entrance worthy of *Seinfeld*'s Kramer. Then he saw my face. His eyes tightened. "You OK?"

"I don't know." I sat on the edge of my bed; he, on the smoky loveseat—there wasn't enough room for a bed and a full-size couch in the tiny room.

I explained that I'd been to a new counselor and was emotionally beat. He told me he'd started with one as well, a Trinitarian psychologist, who happened to be Father Quinn's longtime housemate and closest friend. We laughed because I was seeing Ten, who was a Franciscan, best friend, and housemate of Pat's mentor, the seminary's history professor. How nice for our monastic mentors to have company when they returned home every night. I wouldn't have that in a rural cluster of five or six Iowa parishes, the only priest in the county.

Pat also felt "stripped raw" after his last therapeutic session. "Growth hurts," he said.

"Damn right." I hopped up. "I need to do something for myself—something fun—doctor's orders."

We went to Pat's office and renewed our subscriptions for the coming season at Baltimore's Center Stage. I tried to convince him that he'd love the coming production of the feminist masterwork *For Colored Girls Who Have Considered Suicide When the Rainbow Is Enuf.* Then we slipped down to the Donnelly so I could have some food, a drink, and fun.

"Drinking doesn't qualify as fun. Not in and of itself, anyway," Number Ten said. "How many did you have?"

The couch's upholstery felt like a cheese grater. I set aside my pen and legal pad, where I'd jotted notes on my past week's daily attempts at fun. The shadowed monastery seemed exceedingly humid. "I don't know. One or two."

He looked less like a psychologist this time, wearing not a button-down sweater but a knit short-sleeved shirt, much like my own.

"One is all right, but more than that and judgment wanes. Boundaries blur," he readjusted his weight in the chair. His hairy forearms looked much like my own. I wondered if we shared other Italian traits. I explained how my Italian father taught me to respect alcohol by serving wine at our weekly family meal. The only times I'd been kind of drunk were at Father Hunter's parties, but I'd never had a hangover, never thrown up. I was a lightweight, buzzed after a drink or two. Plus, I had reason to remain sober. The closet demanded focus. Being drunk would lead to letting down my guard, doing something stupid like hitting on someone the way Caden had with me. Others might discover I liked men. My being a seminarian living in a school maligned by conservatives as "The Pink Palace" didn't figure into the equation.

"Even so," Ten said, "When having fun, stay away from alcohol."

Apparently our Italian childhoods were different.

I recounted the other things I'd done for fun: walks with Pat, seeing *American Beauty* at the old Senator Theatre with Mick, guitar lessons from Abdel, and playing in the rain when Hurricane Floyd came through. Felix and I had braved the high wind and razor-like downpour to run, leap, and splash about the giant lake that had formed over the seminary's vast front lawn. We slid headfirst through the soup of rainwater, grass cuttings, and mud. "I was just present."

"Fantastic," Ten said. He asked to use my pen and paper and moved from his chair to the couch, inches separating our thighs. He spoke excitedly as he scrawled PLAY, PRAY, and WORK on my pad: "The point of play, or fun, is to get you in the present moment; to be who you really are and share this with those close to you." A true Italian, he talked with his arms. His forearm nicked mine. "You also experience who you are when you pray." And he didn't flinch. "You come to know yourself as God does. You are affirmed and loved."

He circled the words and scratched lines connecting PRAY and PLAY to WORK. Again, his forearm hair brushed mine. My skin tingled. "Only after being affirmed for who you are, finding yourself in your prayer and play, can you go into the workplace to add your value to the world." Yet again, his arm hair swept over mine. "Work is cooperating with the Holy Spirit to renew the face of the earth."

He handed me the pen and paper, rose, and returned to his chair. As we spoke, I snuck a few peeks of his crotch, checking for a bulge. Nothing. I castigated myself and tried to refocus on the task at hand, fixing my defective sexual boundaries.

Over the months that followed, I exposed every detail of what happened between Father Scott and me. Ten never judged. He commended my courage and told me not to be so hard on myself. When I echoed Father Scott, calling myself seductive, needy, self-centered, and sinful, Ten reminded me that I was lovable. I wanted to believe him. If I'd have been lovable, then the doctor wouldn't have hurt me and Father Scott wouldn't have berated me. Whenever I said that I should be different or should have behaved in a more holy way, Ten redirected me to substitute "Wouldn't it be nice if" for "should." But I protested. The past had already happened.

"It's my fault. I *shouldn't* have had sex with Scott."

"Well, it takes two to tango," Ten said. "Besides, I'm not convinced it was really love."

He told me to read the section on love in M. Scott Peck's *The Road Less Traveled*. Lifting his hands, he said, "These are two people. Separate. Individual. But when they fall in love," he slammed his hands together, interlocking his fingers, "they lose all sense of boundaries and individuality. It's not love. It's infatuation. An ecstatic confusion. A projection of one's own desires for love onto the other." He pulled his hands apart, made fists, and slowly moved them away from his chest, holding them side by side. "But true love involves separating from that enmeshment. Moving forward cooperatively and separately. Allowing the other to be other. Wanting—and doing—for the other what is best for him in the eyes of God. You and Scott never shared that."

I recalled the retreat house in Dubuque, when Father Scott wouldn't talk until after I'd sucked him off. Ten was right. It hadn't been love.

I purchased Peck's book and devoured it. In addition to his explanations of love and infatuation, Peck claimed that to be a good therapist, one must truly love his or her patients. Ten had used a masculine pronoun when describing love. Was he telling me something?

I lived from appointment to appointment. My studies, pastoral placement, and friendships at the seminary were stimulating and confirmed my vocation, but Ten affirmed my lovability. In his presence, I felt fully alive. Everything he said or did seemed veiled with unspoken attraction. I started having wet dreams about him. To stop them, I jacked off every night before bed, but I was unable to keep myself from imaging sexual scenarios involving his hairy forearms, the prickly couch, and the physical enmeshment of our love.

At our last meeting before Christmas break, while discussing my desire to completely embrace celibacy and stop masturbating, Ten, wearing a sweater and sports jacket, asked about my sexual fantasies. "If you're brave enough, I'll help you analyze them." He claimed that I fantasized for a reason: to fulfill an unmet need. All semester, my pastoral counseling professor had been saying, *All behavior is a manifestation of need.* Ten claimed this about my fantasies. People didn't die from not having sex. Unlike food, water, and air, which the body needed to survive, genital behavior wasn't required. It was just a desire. If naming these fantasy-veiled longings would help me be celibate, I would.

"I'll try."

"I admire your courage." He straightened the wrinkles in his sweater and rested his folded hands in his lap, hands that I'd pictured massaging me, stroking me.

I tried to speak but couldn't. He tilted his eyes and smiled lovingly. I looked away. Frozen, I gasped for breath. My chest heaved as I sobbed for what seemed like minutes. He said, "Take as long as you need. I won't leave you." I pulled my knees to my chest and cradled myself, but I couldn't stop the swell of lament and humiliation.

He said, "Are you OK?" I'd asked Father Scott the same question, which had moved him to "love" me and then fuck me. I stopped crying. Stopped moving.

I stared at the frayed carpeting between Ten's black leather shoes until my vision blurred. An attraction/revulsion burned in me. Was I destined to fuck priests until I finally destroyed everything? I wanted him to quietly undress me, caress every inch of my skin, and swaddle me with his nakedness until there was no more isolation. No more pain. But I needed him to fix me. I needed to speak.

"Where'd you go?" he asked. "Tom, tell me what's going on."

My jaw clenched. "I can't."

"Just say it," he said softly, as if he already knew.

I didn't dare look at him. But I forced myself to. I needed to see his reaction: "I'm afraid you're going to take me to bed."

His chin lifted; his lips pinched together. I looked away. He was repulsed. I yanked a tissue from the box on the end table and blew my nose, awaiting his judgment.

His chair rustled. His shoes shifted. From the edge of his seat, he reached for me.

I jerked away.

"I'm not going to hurt you, Tom." His hands tenderly wrapped around mine. "I need you to look at me when I say this." His voice sounded flat. Through the reflection of my face in his glasses, I saw his dark, grave eyes. "I'm not the doctor. I'm not Father Scott." He took a breath. "Do you hear me?"

I shook my head.

"That was then. This is now," he said, still clasping my hands. "You're my client. I promise to care for you, even to love you, and because of that, I will never sleep with you."

THE THEOLOGY OF THE BODY

HUMAN LOVE IN THE DIVINE PLAN

From the open window in the bathroom, I watched gusts of snow curling over the drifts in the seminary's parking lot below. I had almost forgotten about the weather. At St. Mary's, classes, meals, gym, Mass, alcohol, library, bookstore, and confession were all under one roof. Those in pretheology and first theology who didn't have weekly pastoral placements could remain in the building the entire semester. I'd never make it to my placement or to see Ten this week. I slammed the window. Even seminarians' shit stank, but it was no reason to open a window in the middle of a nor'easter. Halfway to my room, a portly fellow from Atlanta with a gift for public speaking called me into his room.

"You're not gonna show me something nasty," I said from the doorway.

"Naw." He waved me in with a grin.

I stepped in and flinched. He howled. On his computer screen, a disembodied, cartoon erection equipped with balls moved back and forth across the bottom of the screen while upwardly shooting loads of sperm at *Space Invaders* that looked like floating vaginas.

"The look on your face," he laughed. "Priceless."

"Lowell can monitor our internet."

"Whatever, man. It's just a joke."

In our human sexuality, marriage, and celibacy class, we were learning that sexuality was more than our dicks; it consisted of our entire relational being. Sexuality was the power that drove us to interact with the world. It was our capacity to love. Our sexualities were a gift from God and in the image of a God who related to the world as a communion of Father, Son, and Holy Spirit. But I felt like the floating penis on the computer, oriented toward one thing only: release. I needed fresh air.

Trudging through the snowdrifts Pat, Abdel, and my doppelganger, Ryan Boyle of Syracuse, bitched about the bizarre seminarians who were diluting the priesthood. One fellow, a redhead from Shreveport, clipped his finger and toenails in the hallway. Another, an ultraconservative Baltimorean with a PhD, the posture of a swan, and a repression problem, had been heard screaming in the grotto; he'd defended himself to the faculty, claiming he'd been doing his prescribed anger-release therapy.

"Imagine his future staff hearing that screech every morning," Ryan said. Using his soccer skills, he body-checked Abdel into a snow bank. The seminary grounds and Northern Parkway were deserted. Besides the wind, only our laughter pierced the silence. Crowned in snow, the building looked like the palace of an ice princess.

We bitched on. The student body president, who looked and drank like David Hasselhoff, had stumbled into his doorframe and split open his forehead. The house's inside joke was that he'd written *The Idiot's Guide to Catholicism*. Rumor had it that he'd been gloating about smuggling women into his room.

"The cream of the crop," I said, before shoving Abdel back into the drift. Pat laughed.

"You bastard," Abdel said, as he lunged at me. He missed and wrestled down Pat.

As we walked on, I told them what had happened when I'd delivered Mass music to the cantor with the cinnamon toupee. Because of health problems, he had a room with a private bath where he could soak and do what he called, in a thick Appalachian accent, "my aromatherapy." When I'd arrived, his door was ajar. I knocked. It swung open. The musky spice of scented candles emanated through the cracked bathroom door, where I could hear water gently sloshing. A husky, supple drawl invited, "I'm waitin' in here, Stephen."

"Holy shit! What did you do?" Abdel asked from the ground, where he was making a snow angel.

"I told him it was me, tossed the music on his desk, and got the hell out." I fell into the snow next to Abdel and flapped my arms and legs.

"That's just wrong," said Pat, joining us on our backs.

"I knew they were fucking," Ryan said, and kicked snow in our faces.

Even more wrong was the sweaty guy from Grand Rapids, who spoke in deep grunts, was obsessed with bodily functions, and looked like

Sasquatch—that's what the Old Testament professor called him. Before he arrived, the common windows had remained closed during winter. I hadn't caught him in the act, but his time was limited. In the Donnelly the previous weekend, he'd walked from the bar to the couches by the TV, pressed his ass against Mick's shoulder, and ripped a fart. As Mick chewed him out, the flatulent fellow laughed, repeating in his lethargic, deep voice, "That's funny."

"Fantastic boundaries," Abdel said.

"Imagine that at Mass," Ryan said, extending his hand to Pat. "Peace be with you." He lifted his leg and made a fart noise. Abdel and I whipped clumps of snow at his ass. The snowball fight swallowed the conversation. As we tossed and tackled, I silently commended myself. Ten would be so proud of my "play" time. Before going inside, we buried Mick's car with snow and built a trinity of snowmen on its hood, top, and trunk.

After a few snowed-in days, I was anxious to resume therapy and my pastoral placement as a chaplain at an institution for adults with developmental disabilities and traumatic brain injuries. The clients and residents of Gallagher Services lived in apartments with eight or ten others and a rotating twenty-four-hour staff. My supervisor, Diana, a petite and pretty brunette with a cotton-candy southern accent, referred to them never as patients but as "the folks." During the day, another couple hundred folks were bused in from group homes or dropped off by family members for a day program. On my first day, I'd been eager to broaden my ministry experience and engage the folks. I followed Diana into the main room. Littered with toys, craft supplies, walkers, and wheelchairs, it looked like a cross between a childcare facility and nursing home. A short, skinny man in his twenties, who looked as normal as my brothers preparing for ordination, approached me with a stoic stare and an outstretched hand. We shook. Firm grip. When I released, he glared at me as he lifted his open palm to his nose and sniffed his fingers.

I froze, unsure of how to respond.

"He does that," Diana said. "You'll get used to it."

But I couldn't get used to the smell of the place: body odor, urine, and soiled diapers.

The folks who were capable worked half of each day, stuffing cheap prizes into plastic bubbles for the twenty-five-cent machines that tempt children at grocery store exits. The staff assured me they earned a just wage as Catholic social teachings required, but I doubted the folks made even the measly hourly wage of the resident staffers.

A woman with Down syndrome batted eyelashes at me and demanded hugs, which were forbidden and pastorally inappropriate. I tried to explain that I was studying to be a priest, but she responded, "Priest, will you marry me?" Another fellow, six-four, had a face and arms like Sylvester Stallone. "Tom, can I ask you a question?" he said. If I answered affirmatively, he'd repeat the question. When I answered negatively or said, "You just asked me one," he'd laugh and smack me on the back, saying, "You're crazy." Another fellow, with a square jaw and a perfect smile, repeatedly asked with singsongy stretched words, "We still friends, Tom?," as he trailed me. At first, they all frightened me. They were like children in adults' bodies, with the power to assault staff members and the sex drive to drop their pants and masturbate at any moment. Both happened. Regularly.

"How'd you respond?" Ten asked from the plaid armchair.

"I told him to stop and pull up his pants. When he didn't, I asked the staff for help and they handled it." I explained that Diana was teaching me to send clear messages and to protect my personal boundaries.

He smiled.

When I wasn't leading a song group or a spiritual crafts exercise, I assisted Gallagher's occupational therapist and worked with those suffering from the most severe disabilities. These adults were borderline catatonic and had bodies contorted like bristlecone pines. After we moved them from their wheelchairs onto a mat, the occupational therapist and I put them through a regimen of physical exercises in which we stretched and massaged them while ethereal music fluttered and vanilla candles burned. They were modern-day lepers, trapped in deformed, unclean bodies and shipped off to walled sanctuaries: forgotten, neglected, and discarded by the physical aristocracy. They were deaf-mutes longing to be opened, and we touched them. Even the most incapacitated folks responded to tactile stimuli. They moaned and giggled. Some cracked distorted grins. Others just drooled, but for a few moments, they seemed to experience a connection, something holy, beyond their corporeal prisons.

Late into the night, I contemplated why I'd been spared mental and physical deformity. But I hadn't. Staring at the black wooden cross with a golden corpus hanging over the foot of my bed, the one Father Scott had given me for graduation, I prayed for the strength to resist my flesh. Then I imagined being stuck in a snowstorm while driving somewhere with Ten or one of my seminarian brothers. We'd have to snuggle together naked in a sleeping bag to survive. I offered up my stiff appendage and was left in a pool of loneliness. Blaise Pascal called it the "God-shaped vacuum in the human heart," and C. S. Lewis, the "God-shaped hole." What I couldn't understand was why a loving God created us with such painful deficiencies.

"Filling that hole with sex or masturbation is futile," Ten said. "Did you know that the English word 'sex' comes from the Latin word *secare*, meaning to divide or sever?"

This made sense to me, for each time I experienced orgasm, my communion turned to guilt and loathing. I finished feeling more divorced from God, trapped in my disordered body like one of the folks at Gallagher. Sex was a false promise. Part of being human was being lonely, separate, even for married couples. As I learned in human sexuality class, all were called to chastity. What I needed were intimate, chaste friendships that provided spiritual companionship, the true love and intimacy that my bodily desires couldn't provide.

"That's right," Ten said. "Build on your friendships at St. Mary's."

One night, I returned from the Donnelly to find a hundred phone books, snatched from the mailroom, stacked in front of my door. After we'd buried Mick's car with snow, a practical joke war had ensued. Suspecting Ryan, I placed the phone books in his laundry bag, dresser drawers, and between his mattress and box spring. He suspected Mick, swiped extra hangers from storage rooms, and filled Mick's room with them. All the while, it had been the newbie with an innocent puglike face named Nicky Pazzo.

In late winter, some newbies used a mannequin in their presentation on the history of the Franciscan habit. After class, they stored the unclothed dummy in one of the confessionals. Ryan kidnapped the mannequin, which quickly migrated through urinal stalls and showers. Its severed arms terrorized from under beds and pillows. When Nicky forgot to lock his bedroom while praying with some guys in the adjacent room, I hauled the mannequin into his room, opened the window and screen, and placed the armless torso on an outer ledge. When Nicky returned to his room, he shrieked at the bare-chested, bald man with crystal blue eyes peering into his fourth-story bedroom.

I shuffled against a hard vinyl chair in Father Quinn's office—not his smoking office, but the vice-rector's putative one. Quinn hunkered behind a massive desk littered with piles of books, papers, and folders, rummaging through the seminary's *Rule of Life*, probably scanning for a paragraph banning practical jokes. Before I reported to Quinn's office, Pat had said, "This is what you get for messing around." I picked at my fingernails, golden boy no more.

Quinn sighed as if he hadn't had a cigarette since breakfast. "Rastrelli, what the hell is going on up there?"

"I'm not sure."

He strutted around his desk like a TV cop in a poorly written interrogation scene. "Don't play dumb with me." He leaned back against the front of his desk and glowered down at me. His voice softened, as if focusing his anger. "I know about the mannequin."

"We're just blowing off steam."

"Bring it to me. Now."

Sweat rolled down the back of my neck. I hadn't seen the damn thing or its disjointed arms in over a day. "I don't know where it is."

"Well find it, damn it. I wanna scare the hell outta Lowell." It took more than a week to find the mannequin and its arms, but my quest to integrate the disparate appendages of my sexuality continued. One afternoon, while reading for human sexuality class, I read a sentence, reread it, reread it again, wrote it on a note card, and pinned it to the bulletin board over my desk: *Desire is not an emptiness longing to be fulfilled, but a fullness longing to be in relation. Desire is love trying to happen.* Pascal and Lewis were wrong. There wasn't a God-shaped hole in my heart. I wasn't empty. There wasn't anything lacking in me. All of me was created by God, even the shit and sexual attractions. Needing others, needing love, and desiring sex were a sign not of weakness but of wholeness and holiness. My entire being was a God-given gift.

"Fantastic," Ten said. As the spring months passed, he affirmed my realization and put it to work in our analysis of my sexual fantasies.

The sucking fantasies were really about my desire to be nurtured and fed. The fucking fantasies were about wanting to deposit a part of myself in another or to receive him into me. Ultimately, all the fantasies were about my desire to be connected, to know others and be known by them, and to merge the fullness of my being with God. Ten called me to move beyond the practical joker and drinking buddy by opening up to my friends. He challenged me to follow my natural instincts and deepen my relationship with God by incorporating music, poetry, and hiking into my prayer.

I prayed as I wandered through the woods, not the rote orations of old but by clearing my mind and meditating on the rhythm of my footsteps. Located on the forested bluffs of the wide Potomac River, the Jesuit spiritual center had been the perfect choice for my weeklong private retreat. As I hiked, I focused on the unapologetically vivid green of newly unfurled leaves, the spongy give of the earth, the delicate dewdrop clinging to a veined blade of grass, the fungal aroma of life sprouting from death, and the invigorating sting of the downpour on my upturned face. I felt larger than myself, as if my body were an illusion, something to transcend until I disappeared into God's presence. But it wasn't enough. I needed to make the communion that I felt real. I threw my arms around a tree and embraced it.

After nightfall, I ventured into the darkness, seeking serenity in the unseen. When the light from the retreat house faded, I found a marble bench and listened to the gentle sloshing of earthworms moving in the soil. It sounded as if God had a heartbeat in the earth. I wanted to offer my entire being to that God who had made me holy and loving, full of blessed desire. I stripped. Mud bubbled between my toes. My skin tingled in the breeze. I lifted my hands to the stars: naked but no longer ashamed.

"I love you, Lord. Take me. All of me. Penetrate my body, my darkest places. Use me to do your will."

"Am I crazy?" I asked. "For stripping naked in prayer. For hugging a tree?"

"Not at all," Ten smiled. "It sounds like a beautiful experience of God. And I bet the tree enjoyed it."

He was a Franciscan after all.

"This sounds like an incredible communal experience for you. I'm not discounting that. But you need to reach out to your friends too. You have to come down from the mountain and trust flesh-and-blood people at some point."

In the cool May darkness, Pat and I circled the track tucked behind the prep school across from the seminary. As we walked, I told him about my prayer experience on retreat and how Ten prescribed reading the mystics. Pat and I shared how much we'd learned in our therapy, spiritual direction, classes, and friendships. We laughed about the afternoons we'd spent crying alone in our rooms after therapy and agreed that the pain had been worth the growth. But neither of us spoke about our orientation. That was irrelevant, for we were celibate, and our entire sexual-relational energy was to be channeled into loving God and serving the common good.

When the track curved, our elbows inadvertently knocked. We knew it might be our last walk for quite some time. After finals, Pat was headed to pastoral year—a yearlong parish placement between second and third theology required by some dioceses.

"I'm not good at maintaining friendships," he said. Our white tennis shoes glowed lavender as we passed through a circle of muted light. "You have so many close friends from before seminary, but I don't." I wanted to tell him it would be okay, but a lot could happen in a year. His voice sounded like it was wilting as he said, "I've never been as close to anyone as I am to you and Abdel."

On the backside of the track, we sat on some metal bleachers just outside the pools of light dotting the way. As he unmasked his fears of going into the parish and losing touch with us, memories of our time together funneled like seeds into a combine, gathered together so they could be cast apart: how we'd spent Thanksgiving with his family, how we'd laughed and cried together at the theatre, how we'd watched a lunar eclipse from the seminary roof, how we'd traveled to California with Abdel and walked the beaches, how he and Abdel had taken me to his sister's rental near Ocean City for my birthday, how they'd humored me and gone to the beach in winter coats so I could touch the ocean, how we'd stayed up each night playing guitar and singing songs that had deep spiritual meaning for us, and how I knew his routine, recognized the scent of his soap, the rhythm of his snore, and the nuances of his moods. I'd never known anyone better.

"I love you guys," he said, sounding like he might cry.

"I love you too."

"I don't want to lose you."

"You won't," I said.

We started walking. We didn't speak. I wanted to reach out and take his hand in mine.

But I couldn't.

We walked forward through the darkness.

SPIRITUAL EXERCISES

I ripped off my T-shirt, eager to toss myself into the warm Atlantic waters off Assateague Island National Seashore just south of Ocean City. The summer in Iowa had been great. At my eight-week parish placement, I'd preached, presided over wake services, and brought Communion to shut-ins. I'd avoided Father Scott and Father Foley and maintained my celibacy. I'd missed the ocean and my brother seminarians.

With his Caribbean tan, Abdel darted for the water, while Irish-skinned Mick and I smudged sunblock across our chests.

"You're so white I need welding glasses," Mick said. "You're, like, Father Weiss white." Weiss was our canon law professor and an albino.

I handed him the sunblock. "Will you get my back, please?"

As he slicked down my spine, I felt no attraction, no discomfort. I'd come so far since my first trip to Ocean City.

"With your Robin Williams forearms, I thought you'd have a hairy back," he said.

"Just shut up and finish."

In spite of an offshore storm, we ran toward the rough water. The waves weren't huge, maybe three feet high. They broke not in orderly pipelines but in choppy segments like an oncoming stampede of Assateague's miniature horses. As I sloshed into the water, a current ripped my feet from under me. The breakers pummeled and rolled me along the shore. Mick reeled me in and steadied me on the foamy sand.

Abdel floated by, clapping. "Buen trabajo, Tommy. A divinely inspired wipeout."

I bowed. "Gracias, Papacito."

A few weeks earlier, Abdel had visited me in Iowa. We'd hiked the bluffs of the Mississippi, wandered through corn mazes, and relaxed with my family and friends. We'd developed a playful banter, in which we often made shit of each other as a sign of respect and humility. Mutually effacing humor wasn't in my familial repertoire, but it flowed naturally with Abdel and Mick.

Since swimming and bodysurfing were too risky, we settled on our towels and watched the seabirds whip along the current. Pat had invited us to his sister's beach house for a few days to reconnect before our classes and his pastoral year began, but he'd refused to come to the beach, preferring to mope alone. Whatever. The rest of us could bond.

"What's the worst thing you've ever done?" I asked, hoping to build some intimacy.

Abdel grabbed some Coronas from the cooler. Mick ran his fingers through his slick black hair streaked with silver, "Why?"

"We're going to hear everyone's worst in the confessional. So let's see what it feels like. It all stays here. Under the seal."

They agreed. Over the breeze, Mick's rough voice rippled with gentle vulnerability as he spun a remorseful tale of sleeping with a married woman years ago. As his eyes softened, I noticed Abdel's brown eyes tighten with something that looked like anger, intimidation, or guilt.

When Mick finished, I knew exactly what to share. Plus, my story would loosen Abdel. When I was thirteen, I'd hatched a plan to get back at a neighborhood girl, who'd sicced her dog—the same Cujo that attacked my sister—on my guy friends. I'd gleaned the revenge plot from Fred Savage's character in the family film *The Boy Who Could Fly*. To get back at the girl, we boys took turns pissing into a rapid-fire squirt gun and then ambushed her.

The mist from the waves pelted my sunglasses. Abdel's sullen gaze had intensified.

"Seriously?" Mick snapped, and tossed his empty bottle into the cooler. "I confess adultery and you a childhood prank?"

"Have you ever pissed on someone?" I retorted.

"Shit," Mick rolled his eyes. "I'm done confessing. Abdel?"

Abdel's generous smile and dimple were gone. "Guys," he shook his head, "I can't do this." He hurried off, skirting the tempestuous shore.

Mick expelled a toxic sigh. "Fuck you guys." He twisted open another beer, took a long swig, and pulled his towel over his face.

I recalled how our human sexuality professor had described the challenge of celibates to build and maintain intimate relationships. She'd called us "porcupines squeezing together for warmth."

"She was right," I said to Ten.

He grinned painfully. "So what are you going to do about it?"

At a loss, I babbled. This wasn't how I wanted to start the year. I'd be ordained a deacon in March and promise lifelong celibacy and obedience to my bishop and his successors. I had the support of my family, my archdiocese, and the seminary staff, which had just awarded me the Cardinal Shehan Scholarship. Newly pregnant Jenny called the scholarship the Most Valuable Seminarian Award. Many at school thought of it as the Brownnoser Award. I liked to think of it as the Future Bishops of America Award. Not that I wanted that. First, I had to get ordained a deacon and then a priest, which meant I had to master celibacy. I hadn't acted out with anyone in over a year, but I was still masturbating. The Church taught that masturbation was a self-centered sin, gratuitous pleasure, and against natural law, for nature revealed that every orgasm had to take place inside a vagina and be open to procreation. Masturbatory fantasies were an affront to the dignity of the human person because they reduced God's holy people to sex objects.

"An erection is just an erection, a normal physical reaction to attraction or physical stimulus," Ten said. "It has no power over you."

I lifted my forearm from the dusty upholstery and scratched. "Then why can't I stop?"

"If you have an itch, you scratch it. Right?"

I stopped working my arm. "But this is different." Without thinking, I glanced at his crotch for any signs of arousal. None. He was incredible.

"It's not different." His legs maintained their relaxed, wide stance. If he'd noticed my downward peek, he indicated nothing. He calmly continued, "Your body's wired for sex. When you focus on an erection, hormones and physical discomfort build until you have to relieve the pressure. You can't fight bodily urges head on. So you need to—"

"I don't want to repress my sexuality. Why would I repress something that's supposed to be a gift from God?"

"I'm not saying that." He tapped his fingers on the arm of the chair. "Repression only makes things worse. It leads to acting out, sometimes with tragic consequences. What you need to do is sidestep the urges."

When I got an erection or caught myself fantasizing, I was to imagine an Internet Explorer–like window containing my sexual thoughts. Then

I was to click on my list of Favorites, which he and I were going to fill with more "life-giving" activities than self-gratification. By opening up one of these alternate "favorite websites," I could distract myself and engage in a celibate and no-less-intimate, activity.

We brainstormed options. The prescriptions of the pre–Vatican II Church, before the development of sexual psychology, we scorned. Cold showers were a joke, as was the old seminary maxim, *Keep your hands above the sheets.* Physical mortification, by way of whipping or puncturing the skin with a barbed belt or garter, was way too medieval and Opus Dei for me and made little sense because the body was "the temple of the Holy Spirit." Ten conjured more psychologically evolved practices.

One "Favorite" was to go to the gym, but only if no one attractive was exercising. I could also practice my guitar, which would leave my uncallused fingers stinging, in no mood for groping. Another option was to watch TV in my bedroom or study in my office *with the door open.* I could refocus on work and fill my day with so many priestly tasks that when I collapsed into bed at night I was too tired to jerk off. There were plenty of class lectures to prep for the adults preparing to become Catholics at my new placement, St. Louis Parish in Clarksville, Maryland.

I stood on the goldenrod carpet of St. Louis's sanctuary dressed in my white alb for my first weekend of service. Behind me, a forty-foot-tall, pastel mosaic shimmered: St. Louis the King, leader of the Second Crusade, offering his golden diadem to an Anglicized Christ wearing a bloody crown of thorns. Behind the warrior saint's outstretched arms, the skyline of Mecca loomed, with its dark-skinned pagans begging conquest. When Monsignor Anthony Gallo, the pastor and my supervisor, had given me a tour of the facilities, he'd repeatedly apologized for the mosaic's political incorrectness. But what could he do? The parishioners would riot if he removed the beloved artwork.

Gathered before the mosaic, we sang the Alleluia. Monsignor Gallo left my side and strode to the ambo. He was olive skinned with groomed silver hair and the body of a tennis player. I'd chosen to intern with him for the next two years because he'd engaged me personally, spiritually, and intellectually. Rumor had it that he'd refused the pope's request to become a bishop because he preferred serving the people, not the corporation. He was secure enough in his beliefs to joke about the absurdity of the institution, including his induction into some secret order like the Knights of Malta. As a "knight," he had the right to enter a church on horseback. "Imagine the cleanup," he jested.

After the Alleluia, he faced the pews of the fan-shaped, 1970s edifice, which on the outside looked like a large brown hubcap. "A reading from the Holy Gospel according to Mark," he announced. "Glory to you, oh Lord," we responded, while making minicrosses on our foreheads, lips, and hearts, a silent prayer for the word of God to reside there always. Not having perused the readings before Mass, I was shocked to hear him proclaim Jesus's healing of the deaf-mute. *Ephphatha!*

Later, over crab cakes and wine, I told Monsignor Gallo and his stoic young associate how I'd heard the same reading six years earlier when God called me to priesthood.

The centerpiece's candle flickered in Monsignor Gallo's obsidian eyes. He said, "As I've come to believe, Tom, there are no coincidences."

I agreed. God had confirmed my vocation, again.

But that night, in the rectory's minuscule attic guestroom, I couldn't stop thinking about the beach with Abdel, Mick, and Pat, porcupines squeezing together for warmth. I worried about being alone the rest of my life. The twin bed seemed suddenly small. I wanted to fill my loneliness, so I began masturbating. *Sidestep it,* Ten's voice reverberated in my mind. I pulled my hands from under the sheets, pictured an Internet window in my mind, moved the cursor to Favorites, and scanned the list. Watch television! I grabbed the remote and surfed. The rectory had premium channels I'd never had. HBO. A documentary series called *Real Sex* was reporting on a group of nudists who practiced group massage and masturbation. I lowered the volume, worried a priest might pass below and hear. The masturbators spoke of the release of tension, spiritual energy, and otherworldly pleasure their gatherings conjured. They claimed finding community, integration, and transcendence. With my eyes on the men's buttocks and glimpses of their limp penises—the title, *Real Sex,* was frustratingly misleading because erections were never shown—I jacked off and fell asleep.

"So turning on the TV is out," I said to Ten.

We expanded my Favorites list. He spoke of the benefits of community. I could seek out a brother seminarian to go for a walk. If it was late, I could call family or friends in an earlier time zone.

Back at St. Mary's, Mick and Abdel weren't interested in walking. They spent more nights drinking at the Donnelly with Ryan, who had become increasingly sarcastic and biting. While I thought it mildly amusing, he always seemed annoyed by the new guys who confused us because we looked alike. But now, while sharing cantor duties, he constantly goaded me. Not feeling welcome around him, I avoided the lounge and wandered through the woods behind the school.

My walks were an exercise in solitude, which Ten claimed was different from loneliness. Solitude was a virtue, a voluntary and sought-after emptiness into which God entered and empowered us, whereas loneliness was an emotional deficit that drained one's energy and resulted in desperateness for attention, companionship, and sex. But even in solitude, I felt the need for something incarnate, to hug the trees. I couldn't resist my desire for family, to return inside and call my sister Maria, who'd just married Gabe, an atheist. She'd found love, but I fretted she'd compromised her faith and wouldn't find work in rural Washington to use her Catholic studies degree. Our relationship was a mess, marred by Jenny's antipathy toward Gabe. She had threatened "in good conscience" to refuse being Maria's matron of honor. Calling my family increased my stress and isolation. I missed Pat, but when we got together and I spoke of seminary happenings, his aloofness perplexed me.

"Ever since we went on that walk together in May, he's been weird around me. Maybe he sensed that I wanted to hold his hand."

"Why didn't you?" Ten asked.

"Because celibacy."

He explained how, in most European cultures, male heterosexual friends walked arm in arm. Hugging and even kissing between men didn't mean sex. He reminded me that I'd shared how I greeted and said goodbye to my dad and Italian uncles with hugs and kisses without making anything sexual of it.

"But if I held Pat's hand, he'd think I was gay."

"You sound frightened."

I realized my arms were crossed, shielding my heart. My knees pressed together shaking. I was terrified of myself, of what I would do if I held Pat's hand. "Holy shit. I'm homophobic."

He looked unfazed. "You sound shocked."

"Well, yeah. I mean—I'm gay."

"Exactly," he said.

I'd never said it out loud before: I'm gay. It had slipped out. I was safe with Ten, but I still trembled. "Why am I so afraid?"

He explained that many homosexuals were the most homophobic. Thanks to our culture's negative stereotypes, AIDS, and religious condemnations, gays were conditioned to be homophobic. My fear fueled my self-loathing and loneliness, making it more difficult to connect with God and friends. If I didn't let this dread go, I was bound to repress my sexuality and compromise my celibacy. He told me to take my homophobia to prayer, to embrace my loneliness, and to see it as an opportunity for solitude.

We added another option to my Favorites menu: pray. If the physical need to masturbate was too strong, I should retreat to the chapel. I couldn't jack off there. But I could still fantasize—about the shadowed spaces behind the recessed side altars lining the nave or the hidden pews in the choir loft—there were so many possibilities. I preferred to pray alone in my room, where my Favorites included writing in my spiritual journal or singing.

After locking my bedroom door, I removed my clothing, so nothing restricted me physically. I turned on music that reminded me of the love I had for God and vice versa: anything from David Haas's contemporary Catholic hymns to Collin Raye's country ballads about sacrificing everything for love. Focused on the lyrics, I cleared my mind of exams and papers, news of Father Scott's latest iteration of "the new Tom," Abdel's drinking, my family's drama, my homophobia, and my gay fantasies. Picturing pure whiteness, I emptied my lungs and inhaled slowly, completely, as I'd learned in my old voice lessons. I stood, swayed, and moved my arms to the beat and rhythm of the music, in intricate gestures reminiscent of the Tai Chi I'd gleaned in my theatre movement courses.

After clearing my tension, I returned to the ground and contemplated, continually clearing my mind to nothingness. Some days, for a change, I'd meditate, constantly refocusing my mind on a word, image, or scripture passage. Before long, this routine brought me peace. I sensed God in the void. I began to desire solitude and realized that being homosexual was a gift that allowed me to encounter the world, experience celibacy, and love in a unique way.

Ten rubbed his hands together, "You sound like King David when he danced with abandon before the Ark of the Covenant."

"So this is OK?"

"It's a gift."

What I was doing was spiritual, sexual, integrated, and normal. My erections were merely a physical sign of my desire to be in communion with God.

Still, I masturbated. The worst was waking up in the middle of an erotic dream, before orgasm. We seminarians called wet dreams "freebies," for we'd learned in moral theology, no conscious decision, no consent, no culpability, and thus, no sin. Finishing off a wet dream after waking was deliberate and not celibacy.

Ten and I assessed my masturbation patterns. We found that I jacked off more frequently during times of stress, especially midterms and finals, and during times of greater loneliness. In these moments, it was imperative to access my Favorites, to schedule time with friends for a movie or dinner. Even if I could only spare an hour or two, a quick trip for gelato could quell my isolation and assuage my loneliness. I needed to fix things with Abdel.

I corralled Abdel, Mick, Nicky, and Pat into an evening of dinner and intimacy in Baltimore's Little Italy. As we discussed how much we missed our friends who'd graduated, I fought the urge to check out the Italian waiters with bodies like ancient Olympians. Abdel seemed annoyed because the babble-filled space made it difficult for the rest of us to understand his Puerto Rican–Boston accent. Our banter turned to an alumnus named Dick Smith, a curmudgeonly widower who was supposedly pleasant if you pushed past his prickliness.

"I never got to see the pastoral side of Dick," I said.

"I don't miss him at all," Mick said. "The bastard."

"Amen," Nicky added.

A nearby table roared with laughter.

"Well, I love Dick," Abdel said.

"What was that?" I calmly asked over the racket.

"I love Dick!" Abdel shouted just as the noise lulled. Faces throughout the dining room turned. Nicky, Mick, and I cackled. Abdel shot me that same needling look of anger, intimidation, or guilt I'd seen at the beach, when he wouldn't confess his worst sin.

"You walked right into that one," I said.

He joined our laughter, but I could tell he was faking. I had recognized his worst sin, the one he'd refused to share at the beach: he loved small *d* dick.

I wanted to talk to him about it, to tell him I was gay too. It was easier to hurt him.

A group of us went to Niagara Falls on a three-day weekend in October. Abdel and I braved the Hurricane Deck, where we got doused by walking under a section of the falls, while the older guys went antiquing or something. The total power of the water, which ripped the pockets from our rented raingear and soaked through our clothing, was like a glimpse of God's grace, or so Abdel and I mused afterward while crouching under hand dryers in a fast-food restaurant.

"Tommy, I need to tell you something," he pulled out a sopping pocket and held it under the stream of hot air. "I've been struggling, doubting my vocation. I'm also seeing Ten."

"OK," I said. "Is he helping?"

"I hope."

On the ride home, we wailed to *Les Mis* and made up parodies about *les misérables* populating the seminary. Everything seemed normal, but after our return, he became distant again, choosing vodka with Ryan over time with me. Rather than talking to him about it, I continued to amuse the others with the account of Abdel's accidental public profession of his love for dick.

Because Ten was also seeing Abdel, I felt uncomfortable discussing our conflict. Instead, Ten and I devised more Favorites. Rather than masturbating, I could hike through the fall foliage. But when I drove into the mountains, I passed numerous rest stops and thought of stories I'd heard about men blowing each other in the surrounding flora.

My weekends at St. Louis seemed more "life giving": post-Mass meals with the priests on Saturdays and theology discussions with Monsignor Gallo over cappuccino between Sunday Masses. Now I understood why Pat preferred the rectory to the seminary's microscopic insularity. Ten affirmed my friendship with Monsignor Gallo but advised me to deepen my intimacy with peers who were going through the same growth pangs. They would be my safety net, my family, after ordination.

I tried to get closer to Nicky. He lived a few doors down. Whenever I left my door open, he lumbered in, expecting a prolonged conversation. This was great for my battle with masturbation but horrible for my studies. I liked him, but our conversations always seemed to focus on him: whether he should switch to a different diocese, his ambivalent friendship with Ryan, his loneliness and drama. After our sessions, I often felt the need to bill him. Then I berated myself: he was reaching out, offering me friendship, and I responded by faulting him.

Late one night, he sat on my stiff loveseat, confessing his latest spiritual growth and peace. Perched on the warm radiator, I listened with my back against the cool window and feet on the bed. We spoke of the spiritual gurus we were reading: Henri Nouwen and Richard Rohr, Catholic men who'd embraced their masculinity and sexuality as a vehicle of God's grace. We'd both come to experience our sexual-relational energy as a gift for deeper communion with God and others.

Nicky's forehead wrinkled like a pug. He clenched his underbite. "I'm homosexual," he said.

I felt the urge to slink against the window, but I didn't. Remaining calm and aware of my homophobia, I responded with the truth, "I thought you were." I just hadn't expected him to admit it and risk being ejected from seminary. "This is great. For you."

He exhaled. "Thanks."

"It doesn't change a thing," I lied. It changed everything. I could tell he was attracted to Ryan and me. Skinny guys were his thing. I wanted to get as far away from my damn bed as possible.

"I'm still the same me," he said. "I'm still celibate."

He was right, but I'd heard that before. "'Celibacy is celibacy even if your thing is goats,'" I quoted Father Scott. What the fuck was wrong with me?

After a short laugh, Nicky said, "I knew you'd be OK. You mean a lot to me."

He was feeling me out. He probably knew I was gay. He waited for me to reciprocate. Instead, I used my pastoral counseling skills, offered an "understanding statement," and turned it back to him: "You sound relieved."

He vented. I listened. After a suitable length of time, I showed him out and gave him a quick loose hug and a few pats on the back.

"I don't feel the need to come out to anyone but God," I told Ten. "As a celibate, my orientation doesn't matter."

Refocusing my sexual energy on God and sidestepping my physical urges mattered. I told him how I'd enjoyed Thanksgiving with Pat's family. Nicky and I were making regular trips to Little Italy for gelato and walking the Inner Harbor. The Favorites list was working. "I haven't masturbated in weeks."

"This is progress, Tom. Nice work," he said. "Now what are you doing for fun before finals?"

Twenty of us squeezed into a long table at an Irish pub. For a stress reliever before exams, Ryan had arranged for us to see *Late Night Catechism*, an interactive theatrical comedy in which the audience played a yardstick-whacking nun's disobedient religion class. I sat nearest Ryan, Abdel, and Mick, who each ordered beer. I got a soda.

"You need to unwind," Abdel said.

"Lightweight," Ryan mumbled.

"Better that than a drunk," I said. Heads turned.

"Don't be such a dick," Abdel said. "Get some boundaries."

"Well at least tomorrow's a Saturday," I unfolded my napkin. "No Morning Prayer to interrupt the hangover."

"Enough, fellows," Mick said. "Don't make me take you outside and beat you."

Abdel and I shared a forced laugh, but I stewed through the remainder of the meal. *Boundaries? Who was he to judge? Let him drink away his vocation. And his celibacy.* I'd noticed how Ryan looked at Abdel and sensed Ryan's desire.

As we walked the mist-slicked sidewalks of Towson after the show, the fellows decided on another bar. Flanked by Mick and Ryan, Abdel turned back to the rest of us and said, "Come, Tommy. Enjoy yourself for once. The faculty won't strip your scholarship." Amid the group's laughter, he turned around and strutted onward. Their frozen giggles dissipated in the darkness.

On any other occasion, jokes about my being such golden boy were standard banter. But Abdel's icy subtext and his suddenly nonendearing use of my name's diminutive devoured my last doubt. I was an outsider.

I yanked the scarf around his neck.

"What the fuck?" he screamed, backpedaling on the frozen pavement, nearly falling.

Jerking the scarf like a leash, I ordered, "We need to talk."

He got in my face. "Not here."

The others kept walking, no longer laughing.

He tugged at his scarf. "Let go, asshole."

"Fuck you." I released him.

He ran to catch up with the others. I fled to the seminary.

Around 2 a.m., I woke with a full bladder and blue balls. I needed to get out of my room or I'd jack off. I'd been celibate for a month, a record stretch. I dragged myself to the bathroom and pissed through the erection until it subsided. On my return, the elevator opened. Abdel stumbled out, looked up, and froze, oozing cigarettes and booze. That dark look of fear, intimidation or guilt hardened on his face.

"I'm not your mother, Abdel," I said. "But I might be your conscience."

I passed him and returned to my room.

A few hours later, I awoke, feeling like such a dick. I'd made a fool of myself. It wasn't my place to fix Abdel, to control him. I had to let him go.

To combat the loneliness, I reached under the covers. I halted and ran through my list of Favorites, but there were no viable options at 4:46 a.m. A fantasy flooded my mind: ten slinking his way onto the itchy couch while admitting celibacy was a front and that the pope really allowed priests to relieve one another of their earthly pressures. He ripped the white tab from my black clerical collar, unzipped my fly, and went down on me. *Stop!* I shouted in my mind and pictured a giant red stop sign, as Ten had instructed me to. This was the last resort when the sidestepping "Favorites" failed. *Stop!* I hopped out of bed and knelt at the mattress's edge. With my fingers interlocked in a stony fold, I begged for strength to persevere.

An hour later, I gave up on the giant stop sign.

"The bottom line is, don't worry about it," Ten said in our postfinals session. "Celibacy's more of a journey than a destination."

He reminded me of the law of gradualism, which I'd studied. Moral conversion took time. As priests, we were supposed to guide those struggling to overcome their sinfulness using incremental steps. When someone failed and sinned, we were to gently refocus them on the righteous path and support their renewed attempt rather than browbeating them. The key was one's "fundamental option"—whether an individual at their core was oriented toward God or sin. Even though I was focused on God, I was still an infinite mystery. No matter how hard I tried to understand and control myself, parts of me would always remain beyond reach.

"Maturity is the ability to live peacefully with ambiguity," Ten said. "That ambiguity makes us vulnerable. Through our vulnerability, God's power emerges."

I thought of the porcupines trying to press against each other for warmth. Abdel and I had been pulling the quills from our own flesh and jabbing each another. In his second letter to the Corinthians, St. Paul spoke of the "thorn in his side," which he repeatedly begged God to remove. I looked at Ten and spoke the words of God's response to Paul: "My grace is sufficient for you, for power is made perfect in weakness."

"Exactly," he relaxed into his chair and smiled. "That, and be gentle with yourself."

Suddenly, everything seemed to make sense. What I'd studied about "cruciformity" in my Pauline epistles class, what I'd learned about the "shadow sides of my gifts" in CPE, what I'd uncovered in therapy, and what I'd been fighting in my friendships: through my wounds, ambiguities, and blessedly depraved sexual orientation, God's grace flowed. God had even used my disordered attraction to Father Scott to lead me to the priesthood. God had transformed my darkness into light and healing for others and would continue to do so if I remained open and vulnerable to God's grace. I thanked God for my sinfulness, for making me weak enough to be a priest.

As the near-solstice sunset faded into night, I zoomed around the beltway back to the seminary. Abdel deserved an apology. How could I have been so presumptuous as to play his conscience? All semester, I'd been badgering him, judging him, because I couldn't accept my own ambiguities. Maybe he wasn't even gay. It didn't matter. That was privileged information belonging to Abdel and God alone. If God loved, supported, used, and forgave me in spite of my sins, I could do the same for Abdel.

The seminary's parking lot was nearly empty. Most guys had fled for the holidays. I didn't see Abdel's rusty Tempo. When I returned to my room, I phoned him. He was already off to any number of parishes in Worchester or home to Puerto Rico. Neither of us had cell phones. He'd stew for the entire break. Our friendship might not recover.

In January, I marched down the endless hallway to Abdel's room. Our bickering seemed a distant mistake. Over the break, I'd spent a week on retreat in the Mojave Desert. My realizations about my sinfulness's being a tool for grace expanded and my desire to live celibately magnified. Afterward, I'd spent Christmas with my family at Jenny and Mike's in Corona. Jenny had welcomed Maria *and* Gabe into her house. We'd taken turns feeling my nephew move in Jenny's belly. My biological family's rifts were healing; so could my spiritual family's.

I knocked on Abdel's door. From around the corner, laughter erupted. I slowly turned the doorknob and pressed inward to see whether he'd returned yet. Locked. Amid the distant merriment, I heard a voice say "Rastrelli." I slipped around the corner into the empty wing. A few feet from an open door, I heard, "Mister Not-So-Straight As." I froze and held my breath. "He's so far up Quinn's ass." "Abdel's too." I discerned the voices: a couple of my classmates, a caustic artist from Ocean City's diocese and the impish student body president from Abdel's. Their rancorous litany cycled onward through my group of friends.

I bolted to my room and punched the mattress. No matter how much sexual integration work I did, no matter how much I tried to appear straight, and no matter how much loneliness I endured for the sake of the Kingdom, some people would always dismiss me as a sinfully active fag.

LETTING GO

THE SPIRITUALITY OF SUBTRACTION

Seated in one of the conference room's plush swivel chairs, I nibbled on the plastic cap of the pen that I'd been instructed to bring. Black. Blue was unacceptable. Around the massive table, the twenty of us to be ordained deacons loosened our clerical collars and bitched. We were in the midst of midterms. For those of us being ordained at St. Mary's, the event was weeks away, at the end of March. Between classes, ordination planning, and parish placements, we were working seven days a week. The last thing we needed was an unexpected meeting called by Father Quinn.

He entered with an apologetic smile and explained the purpose of the meeting: "No big deal. Just a formality." Before ordination, we needed to write—in cursive, not print, to prove the documents were in our own handwriting—a letter and a duplicate to our bishop stating our intention to be ordained. The exact wording of the text, something about entering ordination of our own volition and without stipulation, had been predetermined by Vatican clerics. We had merely to copy their prescriptive phrases onto blank sheets of paper. We'd completed similar letters when we'd passed previous milestones: lector, acolyte, and candidacy. This was an exercise in humility and futility. If even a single error were made, the draft had to be discarded. I hadn't written in cursive since eighth grade, so it usually took me four or five attempts to get two error-free drafts.

As Quinn passed the prepared text and blank sheets of paper around the table, Abdel's DB who'd badmouthed us mumbled, "Another time-wasting hoop."

"Just get it over with," Quinn said in a smoky growl.

No matter. Despite my stress and sinus headache, I was ready for ordination. I'd even patched things up with Abdel. When I'd told him about his DB talking behind our backs, Abdel revealed that his DB warned him to keep his "belt notched tight" because I was going to try to rape him up the ass as he slept. We agreed to stick together and work through our differences.

As Abdel's DB passed me blank sheets of paper, I realized something was different. In previous iterations, we'd been free to compose such letters in the privacy of our rooms. Quinn must have read the puzzlement on my face, for just as I raised my hand, he revealed a second letter for us to copy and passed it around. Again, "No biggie." This text promised that we wouldn't preach, teach, or confess anything that defected from the magisterial teachings of the Catholic Church. "Just a reiteration of the promises you'll make at ordination," Quinn said. "Don't worry. Your penmanship won't be judged by your fourth-grade teacher, Sister Mary Sunshine, patron saint of head smackers."

Most of the guys laughed and scribbled away, but a few of us were more concerned with the legalese. It read as if we were signing away our canonical rights. If we were ever to publicly challenge the Vatican or our bishops' interpretation and/or application of Scripture and Tradition, even in good conscience, the letter might be interpreted to justify the Church's throwing us out. I wanted to get my canon law professor's take, but we were instructed to leave all copies of the letter behind.

"What happens if I don't?" I said.

Quinn swallowed. His Adam's apple bobbed between the open black tabs of his clerical collar. "Don't be a pill, Rastrelli," he jested, before castigating me with an icy gaze. He knew exactly what the letter meant. He knew it was autocratic bullshit and didn't want to defend it. "We all did it, Rastrelli. Just write the stupid thing."

I reread the prescribed text. It contradicted the Church's sacramental theology: people had to enter a sacrament of their own free will, without coercion or condition, or the sacrament was invalid. But if I didn't sign the letter, I wouldn't be ordained. I shouldn't have been surprised. I'd learned in canon law of marriage class that couples seeking to enter a "mixed marriage"—one Catholic and the other a non-Catholic—had to make written promises to raise their children Catholic or they couldn't be married in the Church. Why would those to be ordained be treated differently?

Quinn peered at me and mouthed, "Write the damn letter." In three years as my mentor and then spiritual director, he'd never mentioned the secret, last-minute oath. No one had. But why was I hesitating? I knew obedience meant giving up control of my life, career, and public persona to the archbishop and his successors. I had no problem swearing my life to God, but a fallible intermediary was another thing.

On retreat over Christmas break, I'd reflected each day on one of the five promises I'd make at diaconate ordination: to live celibately, to proclaim the Catholic faith, to pray the Liturgy of the Hours for the salvation of the Church, to shape my life according to Christ's example, and to obey. Ironically, the day I'd spent focused on obedience was the only day I diverged from my schedule of spiritual exercises. Over the break, I'd had my first private meeting with Archbishop Haggis. And I had to request it. My superior, Father Dixon, had been shocked, as if I were asking the archbishop to give me a pedicure. Nevertheless, I was granted fifteen minutes of pleasantries with the man who would determine my future and had never answered my question about his calling to the priesthood. I knew more about Father Quinn's secretary than I did about Archbishop Haggis.

So far, obedience had been easy; the archbishop had granted my requests to study Spanish in Miami, to go to St. Mary's, and to complete CPE in California. But larger issues were at stake. What if he ordered me to do something wrong? After canon law class, I would argue with Father Weiss about how pastorally and morally harmful it was for bishops to enforce the rule of law at the expense of its spirit. For example, a man who'd been made impotent in an accident couldn't be validly married in the Church no matter how much he loved his fiancé and served the greater good of the community, simply because he couldn't get an erection and have intercourse to produce children. The Church deemed his relationship unworthy, not "life-giving." But an elderly couple could marry, even though they were past childbearing age and might have been married, divorced, and received their Church-sanctioned annulments three or four times over.

Across the conference table, Father Quinn yawned audibly. Everyone else had finished their letters and left. I imagined what Quinn's reaction would be if I stabbed the pen into my finger and signed the letter with blood. Would he furiously hurl his book across the table? No. He'd offer me a drink. We'd get wasted and commiserate over the failure of the Church to live up to its ideals. I copied the words.

I scanned the foreign-looking loops, crosses, and swirls of smudged ink that had flowed from my pen. I had been praying for years to be led by God, for my commitment to deepen, and to be a vessel of healing for those in need. I thought of what Father Weiss had said after he couldn't defend the logic of the marriage canons concerning impotence: "It's what the Church teaches. I was ordained to represent the Church." I wasn't promising obedience to the Church of Thomas Patrick Rastrelli of Modern Day Saints but to a divinely inspired yet humanly flawed institution. My options were dying as my commitment deepened. Moreover, the eunuchs and mixed couples needed priests like me who understood their struggles with Church teachings.

I signed the letters.

"It's official," I said to Quinn. "This document states that I can no longer defect from the Catholic faith." I handed him the signed oaths. "So, whatever I say goes."

"God help us all," he chuckled. "I need a cigarette."

St. Mary's neo-Gothic chapel was packed. Adorned in the seminary's choicest liturgical garments, white with gold and periwinkle embroidery, Archbishop Haggis sat enthroned in the presider's chair. Father Lowell, a few other bishops, and an assortment of acolytes flanked him. In the nave, the first choir of pews brimmed with priests and deacons in white. In the adjoining stalls that followed, those of us to be ordained deacons sat with our families, friends, and brother seminarians. Clouds of bittersweet incense streaked in stained-glass light hovered over the pews. The Gospel reading had just concluded. Absorbed by the silence and pure anticipation that followed, I'd already forgotten every word. I'd started crying the moment I'd processed into the chapel and seen my parents and family waiting for me to join them in the pew, which I'd done after bowing to the altar, as I'd been instructed on my first day of seminary.

From the sanctuary, Father Lowell began calling the names of the *ordinandi*. Each man responded by standing, answering "present," and stepping into the nave's aisle. "Thomas Patrick Rastrelli." Mom squeezed my hand. Dad placed his hand on ours. I looked into his eyes. He whispered, "Go to God." Mom handed me a half-used tissue from her purse. I stood to the sound of my name and stepped into my future.

After the archbishop's homily, he asked those of us being ordained a series of questions to which we were to answer affirmatively and thus make our promises of prayer, service, and celibacy. "Are you resolved, as a sign of your interior dedication to Christ, to remain celibate for the sake of the Kingdom and in lifelong service to God and mankind?" All the years of sexual sin, shame, confusion, and doubt dissolved with a simple: "I am."

We took turns kneeling before the archbishop as he placed his hands over our folded hands and asked, "Do you promise respect and obedience to me and my successors?" This was it: the moment of my previous life's passing, the moment I trusted God to always work through my archbishop and lead my life into the greatest possible future. As John the Baptist had said of Jesus, "He must increase; I must decrease." Every choice that I'd ever made and every choice that I would never make were sacrificed as I swore: "I do."

Moments later, I prostrated myself, with my palms, forearms, chest, abdomen, and legs pressed against the floor of the nave. My forehead rested on my fingers, my dripping nose smashed to the side by the chilled marble. Father Hunter had joked that this was the true moment of celibacy, when an old monk with a scissors reached up from a hidden trapdoor and snipped off one's genitalia. I evicted the humorous thought by opening my eyes and staring at the bruised-purple marble pooled with my salty tears. "The salt of the earth," Jesus had called me to be. I listened to the Litany of the Saints chanted by the kneeling congregation. "Pray for us. Pray for us. Pray for us," they repeated, calling the Holy Spirit to remake the six of us into deacons. I closed my eyes and lost myself in the lengthy chant's rhythm. It felt like my entire life, every event of my past, my failures, my successes, my struggles, my gifts, my joys, and my sorrows merged together like a supernova and then exploded, vacating my soul. The saints of old reached forward from the past and down from heaven. The whole of salvation history surged through me. As I inhaled to incant each "Pray for us," a tingling sensation started in my chest and gradually spread throughout my extremities. I shut my eyes. Faces passed in and out of my consciousness: my parents and grandparents, who had baptized me into the faith; my siblings and friends, who'd grown with me; the doctor, whom I prayed to forgive; Father Scott, who knelt in the pews among the priests and whom I could never forgive; Pat, Abdel, and my brother seminarians, who despite our theological differences and personality conflicts were bound to one another in service of a greater good; Father Quinn, who was apologetically absent, placing his ailing parents in a nursing home; and Number Ten, who taught me I was lovable and in our last session confessed he thought that I'd someday become a bishop. I'd been taught that during ordination—the sacrament of holy orders—a man was ontologically changed, meaning his entire being was restructured or reordered toward God and the community of baptized believers as their servant. As faces, memories, and emotions passed through my consciousness, I felt purged yet overflowing, disintegrated but unified, isolated while connected to everything. I let go of it all, and I was filled.

Later, at the reception in the seminary dining hall, Dad asked, "What did it feel like when you were prostrate on the floor?"

I answered, "Pure communion."

I felt the same, a week later, when I returned to St. Stephen's as Reverend Mister Rastrelli—my diaconal title—to assist Father Scott and the deacon with the Triduum celebration. At the Good Friday service, four students balanced a full-sized cross made from railroad ties over their heads, hauling it to the front of the chapel. As they processed, hidden students in the transepts pounded nails with steel mallets. After proclaiming John's account of the passion, Jesus's arrest, torture, and execution, I stood before the wooden cross and preached the shortest homily of my life.

"A self-assured seminarian wanted to stump his elderly priest-professor and asked, 'Father, after fifty-something years of ministry, can you summarize the Gospel in one word?' The wrinkled priest's milky eyes didn't blink. He stared the young man down and said, 'Surrender.'"

I looked at the college students and adults crammed into the pews, some of whom had been there at the start of my calling: the deacon and his wife; my old cleaning partner, Josie; and others who'd settled in Cedar Falls. "Surrender," I commanded them. I turned around and looked at the cross. Behind it, Father Scott sat in the presider's chair draped in blood red vestments. I thought of everything I once was, how God had saved me from and loved me in spite of my sin. I thought of my fears and struggles concerning obedience, loneliness, and celibacy. Again, I said, "Surrender."

A few days later, in California, I held my nine-day-old nephew, Titus, for the first time. Brushing my fingers through his downy black hair and gazing into his cobalt eyes, anything seemed possible: celibacy, obedience, not having my own children and family. I had Titus, whom I would baptize over the summer into the peace and love of Christ. I had my friends and their children. I had my brother seminarians, deacons, and priests. I had the people of God. I would surrender it all for them.

Shortly after returning to St. Mary's for my final year of studies, I turned on the television after my early class to discover two towering smokestacks over Lower Manhattan. That weekend at my parish placement, Monsignor Gallo had speakers placed on the roof because the Mass crowds extended into the parking lot. Parishioners wore buttons with pictures of friends, family, and colleagues who were missing at Ground Zero and the Pentagon. Some threw themselves against me, crying, and begged God to help.

After I proclaimed the Gospel, Monsignor Gallo stood at the ambo and verbalized the pain, confusion, fear, and anger that he and every person squeezed into and around the church were suffering. No one fidgeted or spoke a word. Out of their despair, he drew hope. The peace of Christ, which according to scripture, "the world cannot give," was nearly tangible as his words echoed over the shell-shocked crowd. When he finished, he returned to the presider's chair at my side. I clasped my folded hands, knowing that no matter what happened, no matter how hard the demands, no matter how painful the sacrifice, I was ordained to bring people healing and would obey God and Archbishop Haggis by laying down everything to succeed in that calling.

THE CHANGING FACE OF PRIESTHOOD

In the predawn darkness, a chartered bus chugged at the foot of St. Mary's façade. Dressed in my finest collar, I stumbled aboard with a few dozen of my brothers. Father Lowell had charged us with a mission: hobnob over breakfast with members of the United States Catholic Conference of Bishops, who were in Washington, DC, for their annual November meeting, and get them to send more meat to the seminary.

As the bus rolled to a stop in front of the bishops' hotel, my chest tightened. Openly gay Catholics wrapped in coats and scarves lined the dimly lit sidewalk. Candles flickered before their frozen faces as they maintained their silent, twenty-four-hour protest of the Church's teachings on homosexuality. I rushed past them with the herd of soon-to-be-priests into the warm hotel.

In the safety of the conference room, which smelled of coffee, dry cleaning, and musk, we waited for the guests of honor to arrive. We bitched about the ungodly hour and planned our ecclesial courting: "What's he looking for?" "He's into Opus Dei, so you stay away from him." "Thank goodness mine's a liberal." "Liberal with the altar boys!" "Is my collar straight?"

We knew that the number of men entering seminary had been dwindling for decades. Seminary rectors were desperate for bishops who would commit seminarians. Each of us was worth roughly $100,000 to $150,000 in tuition.

Father Lowell understood that the way to a bishop's heart was surrounding him with free food. And strapping young men, flitting about, drunk on the Church's salvific mission. He catered the annual breakfast, hoping our guests would see the superb pedigree of St. Mary's seminarians. According to Lowell, we were the true "changing face of priesthood": intelligent, articulate, pastoral, spiritual, and psychologically integrated holy men who would lead the American Church into the new millennium.

Attendees were plucked from the student body according to certain parameters. First selected were the sole seminarians from a diocese. The last best hopes for continuing their bishop's ontological line at the seminary, these orphans were burdened with the highest stakes. No one wanted to be known as the doofus whose idiosyncrasies convinced his bishop to sever historical ties with the oldest seminary in the nation. These fellows had to sell their bishops on the school at all costs. Recruit a diocesan brother.

Next chosen were the handsomest twenty-something seminarians. We were charged with winning new bishops to the fold. Nothing impressed a crusty bishop more than a beautiful boy hungry for holy father's attention. After four straight years of attending, I knew the unspoken drill. Conservatives targeted the right-wing bishops; liberals, the left. Theological crossbreeding was forbidden.

Finally, most of the African Americans, Latinos, Asians, and Africans were conscripted. The whitewashed conference needed to see that St. Mary's reflected the diverse and "small *c* catholic" Church that the bishops represented. Those of us who'd been to El Salvador as part of a class on the Church in the Third World or spoke Spanish were equally invaluable.

As for those lacking in physical blessings and from dioceses with multiple diocesan brothers, they were left behind at the seminary, full of rejection and resentment.

Our collared sentry dashed in, proclaiming, "The bishops are coming!" We leapt to attention, straightened our jackets, yanked at our cuffs to display our gold crucifix cufflinks, and dusted flakes from one another's shoulders. Father Lowell barked last-second talking points: "The new library expansion houses the archives of the Archdiocese of Baltimore. This year's graduating class is the largest in years. The preeminent expert on Mark's Gospel has joined our faculty."

The bishops descended. Their break, a mélange of fruit Danishes and seminary statistics, rushed past. We preached the wonders of St. Mary's. They nodded benevolently. We admired their jeweled pectoral crosses; they, our enthusiasm. Some conversed in close proximity with their hands on our elbows or biceps. Others maintained a respectable distance.

I excused myself from the genial gaze of the Bishop of Springfield, who always attended but never committed seminarians. Archbishop Haggis had arrived. He was cordial but brief, always a pressing committee meeting to attend. After he departed, I rejoined the fellows working Springfield and the bishops that weren't using the seminary. We laughed at their stale jokes and offered coffee refills. They struggled with our names, while we calculated their levels of interest. Savvy seminarians teased out common ecclesial acquaintances, hoping for the opportune connection: a St. Mary's alumnus. The active bishops hustled off to deliberate the fate of the American Catholic Church, while a smattering of retired guys dallied, collecting smiles and sweet rolls.

After the courting concluded, Lowell congratulated us on a job well done, and we exited the hotel. As we waited in line to enter the bus, I felt the gaze of the gay protesters. Fear whipped through me like the bitter wind scouring the Capitol. My diocesan brother Matthew, who I'd studied with at Loras, had come out of the closet and dropped out of seminary at Catholic University in Washington, DC. Before my diaconate ordination, he'd detailed his reasons for quitting: he was angry about the Church's harmful teachings and treatment of homosexuals; he couldn't separate his private and public selves. While Matthew was right about the injury caused by the Church's teachings, I believed that things would evolve. Progressive people were needed both outside and inside the priesthood to effect change. Still, I prayed not to see his frosty face among the protesters. As our line meandered past them, I wasn't the only seminarian averting my gaze, frightened that if I looked a gay in the eye, he would know. His glare would strip away my shield of celibacy and proclaim me a known homosexual.

The bus seemed to take forever to pull away. Slouched behind the safety of the reflective windows, I watched the protesters' frozen exhalations rise through beams of low morning light like incense at the altar. No one on board spoke of them. We silently accepted their judgment until we were whisked back to the safety of the seminary and the corresponding compartments of our collective clerical closet.

I sat among my classmates, sipping coffee and taking notes in my favorite class, Theology of Ministry and Ordained Priesthood. A new faculty member, a candidate for joining the Sulpicians, taught it. Physically fit, young, and socially adept, Father Turner was the only ordained faculty member who lacked obvious idiosyncrasies. He didn't have the wobbly Barney the Dinosaur giggle and penchant for Twinkies of the Old Testament professor. He didn't randomly stick his tongue out like the new canon law professor. He lacked the moral theologian's Kermit the Frog voice, the director of liturgy's extensive Lladró figurine collection, and the history professor's lingering goggle-eyed stare. When I observed Father Turner, I could imagine myself a fulfilled priest.

He lectured on the "question" of women's ordination. There was actually no question because Pope John Paul II had made a definitive statement that the teaching was immutable. Some conservatives even argued that his statement was infallible. Simply put, women couldn't be ordained because Jesus hadn't chosen any women for his twelve apostles. Many theologians and scripture scholars had amassed counterarguments, but as Father Turner reminded us, our job as priests would be to help the people make sense of the teaching, not to feed dissent. The worst sin a priest could commit was to "scandalize the faithful" by doing something that might lead them to question the authority of the Church or lose their faith. A priest's job was to find an argument that convinced him so he could teach others with authentic conviction. I had yet to discover such an argument for denying women holy orders.

Father Turner described a new supporting argument set forth by a female theologian named Sara Butler. According to Butler, the Church's "nuptial symbolism"—Jesus Christ was the bridegroom; the Church, his bride—explained why women couldn't be ordained. Christ offered himself in an act of "active self-donation" to the Church, who received him in an act of "active receptivity." Therefore, Christ and the Church were like a husband and wife having sex: the man/Christ emptied himself, while the woman/Church received him. Because priests stood "in the person of Christ" and embodied his sacrifice for the Church at the altar, priests were required to be men because only they were capable of sexually "donating" themselves.

As my classmates verbalized agreement with Butler's argument, I scribbled in my notes: *It seems to me that she's making active self-donation and active receptivity mutually exclusive.* Father Turner explained that a new school of thought in the Vatican led by Cardinal Ratzinger—the head of the Congregation for the Doctrine of the Faith (known as the Congregation of the Holy Office of the Inquisition before 1908)—was using this argument to justify denying homosexuals ordination. Father Turner's face blushed and his brow creased as he continued. Because homosexual acts were "intrinsically disordered," a gay man was incapable of "active self-donation" and therefore couldn't stand "in the person of Christ" at the altar. In other words, because homosexuals gave up "an evil" to be celibate, this wasn't a real sacrifice, like Jesus's on the cross. While it wasn't yet official Church teaching, Cardinal Ratzinger, the most powerful man in the Church after the ailing pope, believed the ordination of homosexual priests was by definition invalid.

"So what do you think of that?" Father Turner asked with a grave smile.

I stopped writing. No one moved. The room's radiators sizzled.

I felt rejected. My orientation didn't matter as long as I was celibate. That was the deal—what I'd been taught before I'd promised obedience and sworn my life away. "Screw Ratzinger," I wanted to respond, but I couldn't verbalize my disagreement or show emotion. If I did, my classmates would know I was gay. Slowly, I raised my eyes from my notes. Everyone's faces were vacant, as if we were all bluffing in a poker game while holding the same hand.

"It won't happen," Ten assured me in our next meeting. "Who'd be left?"

"Even if it does, there's no way to enforce such rule," Quinn assured me in spiritual direction.

Besides, I was getting ordained to serve the people of Iowa, not some faraway, disconnected homophobe in Rome. I refocused on preparing for my comprehensive exams. Over winter break, I helped my parents move from my childhood home in Clinton to a suburb of Des Moines. I planned the ordination festivities with Father Dixon and the two to be ordained with me in June. Everything was coming together. But I couldn't stop thinking of what Matthew had said about not being able to separate his private and public selves when it came to the Church's teachings on homosexuality.

On the drive from Des Moines to Baltimore, I occupied my mind by listening to the NFL playoffs and singing show tunes. Around midnight,

I rolled over the last pass in western Maryland, pulled into a rest stop, parked, skidded down the icy walkway, and entered the men's room just in time. Two toilet stalls offered options: an empty one and another in which a fiery-haired man sat, door ajar, thighs apart, stroking his cock. I froze confounded and intrigued. His iceberg-blue eyes implored me to enter. Part of me wanted to. I panicked and scanned the space, hoping for additional stalls I might have missed when I'd rushed in. Two men stood abreast at the urinals with their backs to me. Their plush winter coats touched as they masturbated each other. I stood aghast. I'd heard the rumors about rest stops and gays, even priests, getting busted blowing men in the bushes, but I didn't actually believe them. Sex really was this easy to find.

I considered grabbing toilet paper and using the woods, but if someone—an undercover cop—found me, he'd misunderstand. I'd be arrested and outed. I zoomed into the empty stall, locked it, and sat. A boot from the adjoining stall slid under the metal wall and nudged my ankle. He thought my ambivalent stare had been an invitation. I whipped up my pants and sprinted to the truck. Fucking assholes! They gave homosexuals who were living chaste lives a bad name. We weren't all deviants.

Squeezed into the sluggish seminary elevator, my brothers complained about the frigid January weather. A few of us discussed our comps that were just a week away.

"Has anyone heard about the sexual abuse in Boston?" Pat said, as he scanned a newspaper. "It sounds like Cardinal Law was involved."

"Well that can't be true," someone snapped.

"Just the anti-Catholic media at it again," another said.

I rushed to my office and drowned myself in studies. But each day more priests, bishops, and dioceses were exposed. Everywhere I went, I heard talk of priests sexually abusing children and, even worse, being defended and enabled by bishops, who'd bullied victims and silenced them with money.

"Why can't these victims just let it go?" I heard in the lounge. "For the survivors of sexual abuse, that they will find healing and the grace of forgiveness for their perpetrators," I heard during the intercessions. "The alleged abuse happened decades ago. Move on," I heard in the gym. "Their statute of limitations has expired," I heard in the classroom. "They're just suing for the money," I heard at meals. "It's because the gays have infiltrated the seminaries and usurped the priesthood," I heard from the conservative Catholic media. "It's because John Paul II killed Vatican II, and clerical celibacy breeds abuse," I heard from the Catholic left. I got an A– on my comps. And I was full of wrath.

At the bishops, who calculatingly sent serial abusers into unsuspecting parishes and classrooms for decades. At the reporters, not for breaking the stories but for implying that all priests were perverts. At the conservatives, not for being angry but for equating homosexuality with pedophilia. At the liberals, not for challenging the systemic abuse of power but for their disregard for harrowing sacrifices made by sincere celibates. At the legal system, not for empowering victims to speak the truth but for allowing them to have been silenced in the first place. But most intensely, I was furious with myself for dropping my case against Lauz.

The tsunami of accusations proved that abusers didn't change. How many more children had been sacrificed because I'd been too weak to come out of the closet, too self-concerned to risk getting kicked out of seminary? I should have exposed Lauz and ended his career.

And what of Father Scott? That high school boy he'd told me about, the one who'd gotten hard when they'd hugged, what if Scott had lied? What if he'd done more? We hadn't had sex since I moved to Baltimore, but had he really changed? I should have confronted him more fiercely.

"Let's watch all the *shoulds*," Ten gently reminded me in our next session. "You did the best you could under the circumstances."

"But I could never forgive myself. If—" Hunched over my knees, I clenched my hands between my thighs.

"If what?" his voice nudged. "If there were more victims after you?"

"Yeah, but it's more." I tried not to cry as I told him about the previous weekend at St. Louis. While I greeted parishioners after Mass, a towheaded child darted across the tile, plowed into me, wrapped his arms around my thighs, and planted his face directly in my crotch. This was nothing new. Kids loved to hug priests. But his parents' faces had said it all.

"They were afraid. Of *me*," I said. "And so was I."

"You're worried that you'll abuse a child?"

I stared at my blue jeans, my knees grinding together, and sobbed. "Yeah."

"Look in my eyes, Tom." His voice was tight. He leaned forward in his chair. "Are you sexually attracted to children?"

"No," I gasped, as if I'd been punched in the nuts.

"Then why would you fear such a thing?"

"Since I was abused, I'm bound to abuse others."

"That's bullshit!" The crackle in his eyes left me petrified. "Listen to me. It's very important you hear me. Maybe if you hadn't gotten therapy, if you'd grown into adulthood believing sex with kids was normal, then that might have been the case. But you've gotten help. You're less likely to harm a child than the average guy on the street. You hear me?"

I pried my hands from my thighs, grabbed a tissue from the coffee table, and blew my nose. "I hear you."

"You're more qualified to be a priest than ninety percent of the yahoos wearing collars."

My resentment toward Father Scott intensified. I spoke to him only to discuss the planning of my Mass of Thanksgiving, which would be at St. Stephen's the day after my ordination. Local tradition dictated that a newly ordained priest didn't preach at his Mass of Thanksgiving, but the pastor of his home parish or a priest who inspired his vocation did. The St. Stephen's community expected golden-tongued Father Scott to preach. But he hadn't gotten help. I worried about the guy my friends had called "the new Tom" and the musician who'd become Father's "new Tom" after the previous one abruptly disappeared. I needed to expose him to the archbishop, but if I did, the archbishop might cancel my ordination.

"I don't know what to do," I said to Ten. "I don't want him anywhere near me."

"I hear your anger and confusion, but Scott's behavior is out of your control."

Ten told me to "let it go" and suggested I view Father Scott's preaching at my Mass as "an opportunity to embody God's forgiveness" so

I could begin anew and focus on more "life-giving" things. "It's more important that you focus on God's plan for you to serve others through your priesthood."

I did as Ten prescribed. I emailed Father Scott and asked him to preach. I prayed for the strength to forgive and move on. I refocused from what I couldn't change onto my prayer life, intimacy needs, friendships, and "having fun" during my final months in Baltimore.

Since returning from his pastoral year in August, Pat had been prickly. I feared our friendship was dying. Over February break, I invited him to my sister's in California. We needed to reconnect and have fun, but abuse headlines ruled our conversations. We tried to reconcile how the bishops were the continued line of the Twelve Apostles, the Holy Spirit, and Jesus, but so many had been accused, especially the conservative East Coast guys. I tried to find hope in Haggis and the progressives. He'd turned Father Tim Divenny, a close friend of Father Scott and Father Hunter, over to the police when he was accused of abusing eighth-grade boys on camping trips. Tim went to jail. It devastated Father Hunter. Father Scott wouldn't discuss it. Over time, I'd focused not on the abuser's crime but Haggis's actions. I could trust him. He and the progressives would make things right.

Then one morning, I picked up the newspaper to find Cardinal Mahony of Los Angeles, one of the most progressive American bishops, accused of mishandling sexual predators and intimidating victims. I'd defended Mahony's liturgical reforms in class. I'd wanted to lead as he had, but he was just as bad as the rest. For the first time since I'd heard my calling in the pew at St. Stephen's seven and half years earlier, I doubted. It wasn't hesitation: How can I be a priest if I don't stop masturbating? It was disbelief: What if God isn't working at all through the bishops that I've sworn my life to obey?

The next week, I moseyed down to St. Mary's library to research a paper. As I passed a classroom, a bombastic voice yanked my attention. Through the door's hatched windows stood Father Stout. The asshole who'd hit on me in Ocean City three and half years earlier had been invited to lecture about parish management. I darted up to Pat's office and vented my incredulity. The deceit was everywhere.

"I'm coming out of the closet," I told Quinn in our next spiritual direction meeting as we walked the quiet blacktop road that followed the woods behind the seminary.

He reached in the pocket of his spring jacket, pulled out a cigarette, and lit up. "Where's this coming from?"

I backtracked through the months. Starting from the media's sexual abuse blitzkrieg, I spoke of Father Stout and the men having sex in rest stops and how their actions gave conservatives more fuel to blame homosexuals for sexual abuse. At the bishop's breakfast, I'd hobnobbed with supposedly holy men, some of whom had now been exposed for harboring pedophiles. A few had done the deed themselves. The silent stares of the gay protestors seared my conscience. I knew the ecclesiology, how the bishops' authority stemmed from a direct line to Jesus, but they were criminals. Who were they to question the validity of a gay man's ability to image Jesus Christ and to be ordained? Matthew's words explaining his decision to leave seminary became my own: "I don't know if I can separate my private and public selves. Isn't the goal of formation integration?"

"Of course it is," Quinn said, more gravelly than usual. He stopped and turned to me. A tree cast a web of shadows over his face. He lifted his hands to chin level, leaned into me, and went into lecture mode. "Here's the thing, Thomas. You have to ask yourself: Am I going to be a gay priest, or a priest—," he paused and rolled his fingers and cigarette through the air like a barrel, "—who happens to be gay?"

"What's the difference?" I turned my head to inhale, trying to avoid his secondhand smoke. "Either way, I'm gay. It's a part of me."

"But are you gay first and then a priest? Or a priest first—and then gay?" He smiled, satisfied with the distinction.

"Both. And." I hit him with what he'd taught me in class. *Both/and* was the paradoxical answer for every ultimate question in Catholic theology: scripture or tradition, faith or works, Jesus's divinity or humanity, are we sinful or good, is faith a solo experience or communal.

“Touché, Butthead,” he said, smiling. Over our heads, a canopy of newborn leaves rustled in a sunny breeze. “You’re a smart guy, Rastrelli. Just give it some thought.”

I kicked a pebble onto the grass. “I have. I don’t want to lie about my sexuality anymore.”

“It’s not lying if those asking don’t have a right to the information.”

I wanted to shake the nicotine from his bones, to scream, *It was that kind of thinking that landed the bishops in the papers!* Still, part of me wanted him to be right. Silence was simpler, easier, and maybe my need to come out was just my pride at work. *It’s all about Tom*, as Father Scott used to say. My promise of obedience demanded that I surrender my ego. But couldn’t Quinn and I at least be honest with each other?

“Gay Catholics don’t have positive role models. I don’t know of a single gay priest who’s healthy. Do you?” I stopped. He kept walking. This was the closest I’d come to asking him whether he was gay. He’d been housing with another Trinitarian, Fin, for decades. They vacationed and picked out carpeting together. They spoke about their golden retriever as if she were their child. Even if Quinn and Fin weren’t having sex, they were a couple. I stepped in stride with him and asked, “How am I supposed to be an integrated gay priest when I have no one to look up to? How does celibacy actually work?” I stopped again. “I’m asking you.”

He turned to me. His face became whiter than a funeral pall. “I’m sorry, Rastrelli. But that’s not a conversation I’m comfortable having with a student.”

We returned to the building in silence.

When I asked Ten how celibacy worked for him, I got the same answer almost verbatim. He was uncomfortable discussing his personal life with a client. That would be a breach of “professional boundaries.”

But how could anyone who’d sworn obedience to pedophile-protecting bishops claim the cover of professional boundaries? I felt like a sinking ship among a fleet that had wandered into a minefield. After laying the mines himself, the fleet commander had ordered radio silence.

I didn’t want to drown alone.

THE WILD MAN'S JOURNEY

As I trod down a bike path between a narrow canal and lake in Princeton, New Jersey, I looked back over my shoulder. I turned for the meandering middle-aged man who nibbled on a cheese steak with a delicacy that begged notice. I rubbernecked for the Latino runner with skin like freshly baked bread and a chest that demanded worship. I lingered while feigning interest in a historical marker, hoping that the smiley professor, with a sparkle of the infinite in his weathered eyes, would offer me a supplication. But none did. If they had, I probably would have zoomed back to the Vincentian retreat house and locked myself in a confessional. In three months, I'd be a priest.

I was on my final seminary retreat, my last chance to muster some focus, to locate the calm before a straight-line wind rushed me into priesthood. But each morning in the cleric's private dining room, the front pages of the *New York Times*, the *Philadelphia Inquirer*, and the *Times of Trenton* whipped up fresh accusations. I flipped through them, frightened I might find stories about Dubuque or Baltimore. I mulled over every sexual sin that I'd committed. Were my sins made public, I'd find myself on page 3A. I went to reconciliation and reconfessed all my sexual failings. I knew that I'd already been forgiven, but I needed to hear it again. I needed to feel flesh-and-blood hands on my bowed head as I heard the words "I absolve you of your sins." I needed to sense God. But I couldn't.

My final night in Princeton, I went for a walk around the retreat center's grounds. An impenetrable fog masked the spring moon and streetlights. A soggy chill soaked through my boots as I stumbled upon a stone shrine in a grass clearing hidden among the foliage. I raised my arms to the inky heavens and quoted Isaiah: "Here I am, Lord." I stripped. "You have me. You see me. Now show yourself."

Behind me, before me, above me, and within me there was only the vaporous void.

Back in my monastic cell, I shed my sopping layers. I wanted to sing and dance, to rediscover God's presence, to pray with abandon as I'd done before the advent of the sexual abuse headlines. Something had to fill the emptiness. I couldn't make noise with retreating nuns in the neighboring rooms, so I reclined in an armchair, closed my eyes, and tried to empty my mind, to make room for God by picturing whiteness. My skin felt as numb as my soul. I began to massage my arms, legs, and chest, imagining God loving me, touching me. Then I was touching myself, picturing the men on the bike path, Ten, the archbishop. I knew it was sinful, but I couldn't stop. As climax approached, I felt loved again. I began to pray, offering each fantasy until only God remained in my shuddering body.

Afterward, I felt guilty. Seeking God by means of spiritual orgasm—how often did priests get that one in the confessional? But I also felt cleansed, as if God had penetrated the deepest fog of my shame. Even the most sinful part of me had become sacred for a moment.

"So am I," Pat said, after I shared that I might be having mystical experiences in my prayer. He spun away from his desk and leaned toward me. Pressing against a tucked-in, burgundy oxford, his moderate belly hung over the beltline of his khakis. Below his fly, he sported a slight bulge to the left. All year, he'd seemed consumed with frustration regarding all things seminary. Including me. He hadn't wanted to renew our theatre tickets. He'd quit singing in the choir. He'd sworn off performing in the talent show. In December, he'd opened up to me about his struggle to stop masturbating and be wholly celibate. I'd been preoccupied with a pressing deadline for a paper on the necessity of suffering and kept turning back to the computer. He'd left in a huff. After that, our friendship seemed on the verge of collapse. We'd bickered the entire February break in California. I'd decided never to travel with him again. As I sat on his cozy couch, listening to tales of his body, abdomen, and genitals tingling in ecstasy when he prayed before the Blessed Sacrament, our discord dissipated like vapor in the wind.

"Incredible." I shifted and propped my foot on my knee. "And you had an orgasm?"

"Yeah." His fingers tapped his thighs.

"Without masturbating?"

"I know!" His hazel eyes widened. His bookish face split a grin. "It's crazy, right?"

But it wasn't. We were supposed to channel our love and sexual energy into God. That was celibacy. As Pat described his prayer life and his love for God, it sounded as if God were wooing him, hunting him down as a husband did his wife, until they consummated their relationship. Pat hadn't masturbated in months; he was saving himself for God. As a reward, God had blessed him with spontaneous ejaculations. To get to that next step, I needed to quit jacking off, to pour my *eros* into God.

We pondered the mystics—Teresa of Avila, John of the Cross, Francis of Assisi—how they'd recorded their ecstatic prayer experiences. Pat of Baltimore turned to his desk. Next to his laptop, a dog-eared copy of St. Teresa's *Interior Castle* sat atop a pile of books. He punched something into a Google search. "Check this out."

I knelt on the thin carpeting and rested my elbows on his desk. He smelled of Irish Spring and fabric softener. His forearm hair was thinner than mine. I wanted to run a finger through it, to see whether it was coarse or silky.

A photograph of Bernini's sculpture, *Saint Teresa in Ecstasy*, filled the computer screen. Sprawled out on a boulder, the chiseled Teresa's head was whipped back, her mouth agape, and eyes rolled upward in abandon. One of her hands sprouted from the sleeve of her tunic and dangled over the stone's edge. Were it not for the religious nature of the artwork, I would have concluded her other hand was underneath her vestment, manipulating her lady parts. A boyish angel with a mischievous grin stood over her, clasping an outstretched arrow ready to pierce her heart. Her legs stretched wide; her toes clenched like a porn star. I knew her desire. I longed to have God penetrate me with divine love, to fill me with that same rapture.

"It's beautiful," Pat said before closing the internet window.

I moved back to the couch. Since Pat was channeling his sexuality into God, I had nothing to fear.

"I'm gay," I said.

He relaxed into his chair and smiled. "I know."

"How?"

"We're in seminary. We're gay until proven straight."

I laughed, and the world didn't end.

"I'm gay too," he said.

Still, he didn't want to be labeled. He was also attracted to women and, years ago, had been jacked off by his only serious girlfriend. Once. But nearly all his attractions were homosexual. I told him about Tobey, Father Scott, and Father Foley, how difficult it had been for me to become celibate. He told me about a former colleague, a married man. They'd wrestled around on hotel beds, gotten hard, but never did anything naked. He confessed that before seminary, he'd run up huge bills calling 1-900 numbers. One phone sex guy had told him to cinch his balls with a necktie while jacking off and to use cornstarch instead of Vaseline.

"Did it feel good?"

"Incredible. But it was sinful." He lowered his head. "I paid strangers for phone sex." The skin on his smooth head was afire with shame. I wanted to press my cold palms against it.

I told him about Doctor Lauz and the failed lawsuit.

We disclosed everything we'd been holding back: our therapy sessions, how our counselors had helped us combat our sexual fantasies and live our callings; the sexual abuse headlines, how the attacks on the seminaries, priesthood, and homosexuals had left us angry, wounded, and vulnerable. When I confessed seeing the man jacking off in the rest stop, Pat didn't know whether he'd have been strong enough to resist. We vowed to be there for each other. The world didn't support celibacy. It didn't understand us. Accountability and honesty would carry us through the difficult times. So would love. Real love. Not the lust that the gay community packaged as love. The rest stops. The neckties. The cornstarch. We shared the platonic love of friendship—*philia*—and the pure love of Christ—*agápe*. Working together, we would succeed in celibacy.

He covered his mouth and yawned. "I have to get to bed."

"I wish we'd had this conversation years ago."

"Me too."

We hugged. Tightly. Unrushed. His warmth against mine. I didn't care that he could feel all of me against him. He didn't flinch. They were just erections, after all, a physical sign of our love. We didn't have to act on it.

Pat knew when I rose in the morning. Through the wall, he could hear me brushing my teeth, gargling, and blowing my nose. I could pick out his frail, tenor vibrato from the chants in the chapel. He recognized my moods and forgave my evening singing outbursts. When I rounded the corner of the endless hallway, I could recognize his snore. His parents, siblings, and extended family had welcomed me into their clan on holidays. I could identify him by the freckles on the back of his hand. He knew me, all of gay me.

"I love you," I said.

His embrace tightened. "You too."

We released and stepped apart, no more than a foot separating our faces. With his rectangular glasses, round cheeks, and drooping nose, it had always been easy to picture him in his former life as a banker. But now, something had changed. He was beautiful. In his eyes, I recognized a familiar quiver of vulnerability. And desire. He was in love with me too.

We didn't act out. His diaconate ordination was a month away; my priesthood, two. We did everything our formation had prepped us for in case of the most dreaded emergency in celibate life: falling in love. We talked and prayed about it. At diaconate, I'd promised to model my life according to Christ's; Pat was about to do the same. Jesus hadn't had sex with Mary Magdalene or with "the (male) disciple whom he loved," so we offered our "gift" of being in love back to God as a "sacrifice."

"So you've admitted to each other that you're in love?" Ten said.

"Yes. But we're offering it to God," I said.

Ten wondered if my "infatuation" with Pat was a reaction to my impending move, combined with the rush of having a peer accept me for being gay. I disagreed, for in the days after telling Pat, I'd also come out to Nicky and Felix. "I feel accepted and loved by them, but I'm not in love with them."

I explained how Pat was having spontaneous orgasms in prayer and how I was having similar experiences. Finally, I'd stopped masturbating and was offering my entire sexuality to God. As I prayed, powerful images were filling my mind. In one, God was a whiteness swirling about me like a tornado. As I focused my love into God, the whiteness entered my body through every pore. I edged toward physical orgasm, feeling communion with God. In another image, I was crucified on a cross. Thirsty. Pat lifted a large grape to my mouth. I bit into it and the Blood of Christ shot out, filling me with more love, oozing down my cheeks, and dripping onto the parched soil. A vine sprouted from the drops, coiled up the cross, branched apart, and encircled my body. Each branch pierced the wounds on my hands and feet, filling me with God's presence and ecstasy despite the pain. In yet another image, Pat and I were beaten, bloody, and hanging in place of the thieves on the crosses flanking Jesus. We realized that by falling in love we'd stolen from him. In our crucifixions, we were offering that love back.

Ten shook his head and squirmed in his armchair. "Tom, you have to be extremely cautious here. I'm not questioning the power of these prayer experiences or your focus on God. But, you're messing with fire." He stretched his hands apart and opened them. "Love is the most powerful force in the universe. More so than gravity. If you fight it head on—" He smacked his hands together. "This love you have for Pat is dangerous."

But my love for Pat had intensified my love for God. With Pat, everything seemed possible, even celibacy in rural Iowa. Still, Ten insisted that I sidestep my "infatuation stage love" for Pat rather than "channeling" it into my prayer. Ten refreshed my old Favorites list, adding ways to build solid boundaries around Pat. We could spend time together in groups. When we were alone together, we might stay in public places like the Donnelly or go on walks. Alcohol was to be avoided completely. If we had to speak privately in one of our rooms, the door needed to be wide open, and we were never to sit on the same piece of furniture.

Pat sat next to me on my bed. The door was closed. After the graduation ceremony we'd hit the Donnelly. My alcohol-enhanced joy had just morphed into grief. My time at St. Mary's was finished. Pat held my head against his shoulder.

The only hesitation the faculty had expressed on my final evaluation was my transition from the diverse, intellectual, and artistic big-city life back to rural, Middle American monotony. I assured them that Iowa had culture; I could always drive into Chicago or hop a plane to New York. In our final session, Ten had reaffirmed my skills for maintaining celibate intimacy and my gifts for ministry. "You're already an incredible priest," he'd said. "Just keep doing what you've been doing." For months in spiritual direction, Quinn had listened to my doubts about ordination and obedience. He'd quoted St. Ignatius's tenet that one shouldn't make life-changing decisions while in a state of spiritual desolation. Everything that pointed away from ordination was a godless temptation. But I didn't feel like I was "in desolation." I loved God more than ever. Was it possible to be called to seminary and not to priesthood? I wanted to ask Pat.

Cradled by him, I squeezed tightly. "I wish we'd have fallen in love sooner." My lips brushed against his cotton shirt and collarbone. "If this had happened before diaconate ordination, we could have been together."

He recoiled to the foot of the bed. "We can't think about that." The inches between us seemed insurmountable. "Those fantasies are temptations," he spat. "They'll undermine our focus on God, our vocations." His head shook.

"You're right." I pulled my feet onto the bed and slid against my pillow and the rigid wall. I told him what he needed to hear. "It's selfish to think that all our years of discernment, formation, and tuition were meant to lead us to each other and not the priesthood."

He crossed his arms, securing his heart. "It's sinful."

But I wasn't sure I believed that anymore.

His hands, jaw, and eyebrows clenched in fear. Of what? Of love? Of us? Of being gay? I didn't feel it: the tension in my heart, the abused child in my gut, the homophobia, the shame. I felt complete. I gently touched his shoulder.

"That's enough," he stood. "We promised celibacy. God chose us to be priests."

"I know."

The loading dock was abandoned. I had stalled my East Coast departure by going to the beach for a week with Nicky and Mick before relaxing with Pat at his parish placement until his deaconate ordination. When I could no longer delay, Pat and I returned to St. Mary's to retrieve my boxes. Our voices echoed down the hollow silence of the endless corridors. As we worked, we recalled how he had welcomed me on my first day, how he'd safeguarded the cherry dresser bequeathed to me.

My furniture, bookshelves, TV, and minifridge, stripped of everything Tom, would collect dust until the fall semester when another Dubuquer claimed them.

"Do you think he'll sing show tunes?" I said.

"Definitely." Pat giggled.

"Promise me, Pat. No duets."

He scolded me with his eyes.

Hoping to keep the mood festive, I'd worn a silky Hawaiian shirt, but as I stood in the doorway of my room, watching Pat roll the cart away, I wanted to say, "We'll never be able to knock on each other's door again. To walk together. To hug before bedtime. Won't you miss that? This is where we fell in love." But he had already shoved the cart onto the elevator. I shut the door and locked it for the last time.

After we loaded the pickup, we circled to the front of the building to drop off my key. Pat snapped a picture of me smiling before the façade. "You'll be back before you know it," he said. On the drive back to his rectory, he added, "We still have Felix's ordination in a few weeks and then yours. It's not over yet." Between gearshifts, we held hands.

After Felix's ordination, we seminarians returned to a retreat house overlooking Lake Erie, where we were spending the night. Most of the guys left for a bar, but Pat was beat and remained. So did I. We had a lot of catching up to do. During my two weeks in Iowa, my dad had lost the management job for which he'd moved to Des Moines and was downplaying the financial implications. Mom, having left her position as a music teacher for Dad's career, was frantically applying for jobs that provided health insurance. When I stopped by St. Stephen's to go over the plans for my Mass of Thanksgiving, Father Scott had greeted me with an overly tight hug and orders "not to worry" about the cost of the Mass festivities. My prayer life continued to be ecstatic. Watching Pat hang his alb in the closet, I kicked off my wingtips and debated where to start.

"I jacked off with cornstarch," I said.

"How was it?"

"Messy. And strangely hot. Temperature hot." I unbuttoned my sweaty clerical shirt and asked him, "Did you like it?"

"Too much clean up, if you ask me."

We turned off the lights, stripped down to our underwear, and got into our twin beds. I sweltered in the June humidity under the starchy, bleached sheet. I kicked it to my feet and rolled onto my side, wondering if the light penetrating the blinds was enough for Pat to see the outline of the erection pressing against my briefs. His sheet was pulled up to his waist. Our voices lowered into whispers as we spoke of the last night we'd spent together in Baltimore. We'd given each other backrubs—fully clothed in jeans and button-down shirts. I'd lain with my chest against his back. His butt and my denim-swaddled erection had tensed on contact. When I stood up, his shirt had migrated upward. The crimson imprints of my shirt's buttons dotted his back. After he'd moved to the couch, I knelt between his thighs and pressed my ear to his chest. I'd wanted to hear the sound of a heart that beat love for me. Now, as I studied him from across the tiny room, his chest hair absorbed the light, a void longing to be filled. I needed to hear that sound again.

"How's your back?" I asked.

"Kind of sore."

My skin tightened in anticipation. "Do you want a backrub?"

He tossed off his sheet and rolled over. "If you must."

I climbed onto the side of his bed, afraid that the slightest nick of my legs or dick against his skin would result in excommunication. He silently guided me to the knotted areas. Slowly and rhythmically, I spread my fingers and pressed my palms against his back. As his muscles relaxed and his breathing deepened, I inched in from the edge of the mattress. I straddled his legs. The hair on our thighs enmeshed. He didn't protest. I pressed my chest against his back. His perspiration enhanced the peppered scent of his deodorant. My skin felt like it would molt. He rolled over and pulled my ear to his chest and embraced me. His heart beat loudly. I slid over him, nothing separating us but the thin cotton of our underwear. Our bodies nudged, trying to merge. Our arms squeezed frantically, as if at any moment an archangel might tear through the ceiling, rip us apart, and cast us into the opposite reaches of hell.

I had to know all of him, to let him know I loved him completely. I reached under the elastic and stroked him. His head rolled back in an exhalation worthy of Bernini. We shed our last layers of celibacy, kicking our useless briefs to the floor. We thrust against each other with the ferocity of mystics and the passion of the zealots, and I felt a communion I'd never known, an incarnate, flesh-and-blood love.

After climaxing together, we remained intertwined. Something had changed. I didn't feel guilt. I didn't feel shame. I felt complete, full of life and love for Pat, for everything. Silently, I thanked God for making me lovable, making me gay, and blessing me with Pat. The Church was wrong. There was nothing wrong with being gay. Our love was holy.

"I didn't want that," he said in a tinny quiver. I squeezed him tightly, hoping to wring another drop of ecstasy, to channel my bliss into his fear. He pushed me away. "We need to sleep. Separately."

From my bed, I watched his chest billow as he slept. Fantasies flooded my mind: after a hard workday at the nonprofit, I entered our flat to find him in the kitchen, red wine in hand, something Chesapeake on the stove, wearing only an apron. I made love to him against the tile counter as the toppled wine cascaded along the grouting and spotted his apron. Then I sat next to him at a funeral—someone close to him, something very tragic. I held him and kissed the crown of his head. Then we were at Fort McHenry, navigating a rainbow dragon kite with our adopted children. Two girls, one boy. Then we were priests, patiently awaiting the end of Lent and our next getaway. We could make it work. Somehow.

When he rose in the morning, I smiled from my bed. He turned his back and pulled up his jeans, "That can never happen again."

"I know." I didn't believe him.

We caravanned to an emaciated steel town in the mountains. Pat and I assisted Father Felix as deacons during his Mass of Thanksgiving. Everyone celebrated at a reception, singing karaoke and drinking hard. Pat didn't smile at me the entire day.

We settled into an unused faculty dormitory at a Catholic school for the night. Unfortunately, there were a plethora of rooms; we'd each have our own. I followed Pat down the institutional hallway and waited for him to select a room. He chose the one at the end. Smart thinking. Secluded. I claimed the one next door. It would make a good sound barrier. "Neighbors," I said, "Just like old times."

“Good night, Tom.” He smiled at me and entered his room.

After everyone settled, I tiptoed to his room. A strip of light beckoned under his door. I knocked.

“Pat it’s me,” I whispered. “Can we talk?”

Silence. He was probably waiting for me to instigate. Maybe that allowed him to feel less guilty. I turned the doorknob. Locked.

As I inched back to my cell, I looked back but saw only darkness.

GAUDIUM ET SPES

I stared at the burnt parmesan halo on my empty soup bowl. An exodus of grannies and businessmen brushed past our booth. Across the table, the wife of the deacon from St. Stephen's apprised me of the final preparations for my Mass of Thanksgiving and reception in Cedar Falls.

"I know things have been difficult between you and Scott. I don't need to know why. And I'm not taking sides," she said. "He's really pouring himself into this. He's working hard on his homily. Even if he won't say it, he still thinks of you as his son."

I picked at the sauerkraut remnants of my Reuben. "I know."

She'd come to Des Moines to check on her elderly mother, but her relaxed shoulders, open arms, and calculated pauses indicated her spiritual director mode. She'd hardly touched her salad. She'd come to appraise me.

"So how are you?" she asked.

"Things are fine." I pinched my straw into half-inch zigzags. "Mom and Dad are excited. With Dad's job situation, they need the distraction. The chalice they gave me is incredible. Everything's rolling." I crimped the straw inside my fist. "It'll all be over in less than two weeks."

She leaned in, reached out, and gripped my fist. "No, Tom. How are *you*?"

Her face was like a full moon, gleaming but tinged with melancholy. Her spiritual direction practicum had taught her well; she was reflecting my state of being. She knew something was amiss and squeezed my hand. She wasn't going to let go until I confessed.

Through the cracks of the dust-coated blinds, I watched an enormous American flag flapping. It was tiny compared to the one at Fort McHenry in Baltimore. Why hadn't Pat and I gone there together? There were so many things we hadn't done.

"What is it Tom?"

Shit. She knew. She could see it: my conflicted, broken heart. My eyes filled. "I'm just scared."

She released my hand. "You can still walk away."

She'd said it easily, as if she were changing her order from Caesar to chef salad. For the past six years, she and her husband had sent me fifty dollars a month, an endless stream of letters and prayers, and more vocational affirmation than anyone outside my family. She'd taken me to A. J. August on Main Street in Cedar Falls and purchased the black suit that I'd worn at diaconate ordination, where her husband had vested me in the deacon's stole. I would wear that suit and that stole in nine days at my priesthood ordination. He would proclaim the Gospel at my Mass of Thanksgiving; she, the Old Testament reading. Thousands of dollars had already been spent on the reception she was helping coordinate. And just like that, I could walk away.

"No. I can't." Something pressed against my grief, something safer, easier. Anger. "Eight years of discernment, the money, the people. All the nonrefundable plane tickets. The seminary, hell, the entire local church of Dubuque has affirmed my vocation. I already made my promises. I can't just walk away."

"You still have a choice, Tom." She took my clenched hand again and pried her thumb under my grip. God, how I wanted Pat to be the one touching me, telling me this. "I wouldn't love you any less."

"I know that."

I felt tears warming my cheeks. Fuck. I was tired of crying.

I pulled it together long enough to survive a conversation with Mom, who sat at the kitchen table combing through scrapbooks for pictures to display at my reception. Dad was at a sales call, trying to salvage the loss of his management income. I sunk into my temporary room in the basement. With my feet hanging over the end of the twin bed that had seen Dad and then me into adulthood, I phoned Ten. It was the first time he'd been free for a session since Pat and I had made love. With a hushed voice, I confessed everything.

"I'm weak." I curled around my body pillow. "A despicable sinner."

"Welcome to the human race," he said. Pat and I had been inevitable;

compassionate men like us were bound to fall in love and act out. Our love was a gift, but our actions weren't consistent with our state in life, our celibate commitments. We needed to pull back, to reestablish boundaries.

"But it hurts so bad."

"That will subside in time." He explained that "patience" was based on the Latin word *pati*, which means "to suffer." "Part of maturity is learning patience, learning to suffer well. Be patient with yourself. Don't take yourself so seriously."

How could I not? This was the rest of my life.

"I fucked everything up. I'm too weak, too depraved to be a priest. I want to call it off."

"Stop, Tom," his voice smacked me. He ordered me to stop the fantasies, to picture the giant red stop sign in my head, and yell at myself: STOP! Whereas the deacon's wife's compassion had angered me, Ten's reaction soothed me. Finally, someone was sticking up for God's will. Someone was treating me like the letch I was. "Jesus needs you to be a priest. The people of the Church need your gifts, Tom. Jesus needs you."

How could I turn my back on Jesus? The choice set before me was obvious: the Church or the world, chastity or gay sex, life or death. When Pat and I had spoken earlier on the phone, he'd said, "Our vocations are bigger than our love." He didn't want a sexual relationship. He didn't even want a "dry marriage"—two promised celibates who talk every day, vacation together, have joint ownership of a home like husband and wife even if they aren't having sex. He'd moved on.

"I don't believe him," I said to Ten. "He still told me that he loved me."

Ten informed me of an unnamed client, a priest who'd left because he'd fallen in love with a man. When the couple's infatuation wore off, their "illusion of love" died. Gay men couldn't sustain lifelong, loving, and committed relationships. Psychology and experience proved this. Ultimately, all they wanted was sex. Eight minutes of pleasure. What Pat and I had was a passing, faux intimacy. What God offered was eternal. "Pat isn't even a possibility. You have to stop the fantasies."

But I couldn't. Pat said that he loved me with his lips and his body. God only used a mediator, a Church in scandal.

The annual convocation of Dubuque's priests had concluded. Clerics trickled out of the Loras College ballroom. Ordination was three days away. Morale was low, for the sexual abuse crisis had engulfed the Midwest. Accused priests were being removed from their parishes. Archbishop Haggis had presided over "healing Masses" at these parishes. My brother priests fretted that Haggis was about to be transferred to clean up in Wisconsin. Liberal Archbishop Rembert Weakland of Milwaukee, my ecclesial role model, had just resigned after being accused of sexually exploiting a seminarian. While he was the seminarian's superior, Weakland used his position of power and betrayed the seminarian's trust by having ongoing sexual relations with him. The victim had been thirty at the time of the scandalous "relationship"—a decade older than I'd been when Father Scott grabbed me in the confessional. I realized that Father Scott had done the same when I was his student, spiritual directee, penitent, parishioner, and employee. He had abused his power and my trust. I wanted nothing to do with him, but he had been everywhere at the convocation: playing piano during liturgy, flitting about the receptions, and telling everyone how proud he was of me. As we walked out of the ballroom, the three of us to be ordained received words of affirmation, handshakes, hugs, and even a few kisses on the cheek from our brother priests. We were the future of the priesthood, the hope struggling clerics needed to justify their commitments. Superstars. I had to get the hell out.

I escaped to the cathedral. I needed to smell the dusty frankincense of the air, to hear my prayers rise up to the ribbed vaults, and to feel the steadfast pew that would ground me during the ordination. I found a television reporter and her crew. At the foot of the sanctuary, they filmed a take on the scandal. I ducked into the rear stairway and zigzagged through the bowels of the cathedral that Father Scott had taught me to navigate when I was in college.

The crypt was deserted. My footsteps echoed off the floors, walls, ceiling, and altar. Backlit stained-glass windows lined the walls, conjuring the illusion of sunlight. Indigo and amethyst washed over the creamy marble floor, streaked with grayish veins. Two rows of inscribed rectangles lined the floor. They identified Dubuque's deceased bishops, decomposing in peace, a peace I longed for. For 165 years, these holy men led the faithful of the local church; they'd received the obedience of eager priests. But were they worthy of it? I'd served the funeral Mass of Archbishop Burne just before I'd started at Loras, a grand honor. I could have reached out and touched his coffin as it was lowered into the vault. He'd been sainted by the masses, but the decades of his term as archbishop, 1962–1983, etched into his tombstone, indicated otherwise. How many pedophile priests had he shuffled?

I turned off the lights and collapsed into a kneeler at the side of the altar. Throughout seminary, I'd desired to be a vessel of God's love. In my pride, I'd prayed to know the cross, to be tested, and for the strength to pass that test. My pleas had been answered, but it was too much. I bowed my head and begged, "I love you, Lord, but please take this vocation away from me. I don't want to be a scandal, to hurt people. Set me free." But thoughts of Christ in the garden of Gethsemane emerged, how he'd sweated blood. They dwarfed my doubt. I quoted him: "Not what I will, but what you will."

The electrocuted squirrel that formed a bridge between the Church and the world lay smoldering outside the cathedral. Inside the stifling edifice, on the very spot where the newscaster had reported on the sexual abuse scandal, I prostrated myself for the Litany of the Saints. Resting my forehead on my hands, I tried not to let my nose touch the carpet that smelled like an old leather shoe. From the packed pews, family, friends, parishioners, priests, seminarians, and strangers knelt, chanted, and prayed with the saints for God to remake my classmates and me into priests. I dredged through the sludge of sound, hoping to pinpoint Pat's frail vibrato less than twenty feet away in the first two pews with my family. A year earlier, at diaconate ordination, I'd felt united with the saints throughout salvation history; my tears had been blissful and sure. But now the streaks smearing my temples scalded me with pain, weakness, and grief. Pat and I were lost among the masses.

I clenched my eyelids, joined in the cyclical "Pray for us. Pray for us. Pray for us," and filled my mind with a numb white void. After a few verses, an image materialized. Naked, I lay prostrate at the foot of Christ's cross. The gritty, dusty ground caked my body hair and crunched between my grinding teeth. I wailed for my sins and disregard for God's gifts. Lunging at the base of the cross, I wrapped my arms about the jagged wood. Splinters pierced my skin. Warm crimson dripped from the crucified Christ, sprinkling and streaking my upper body. He leapt down from the cross and lifted me to my feet. Blood streamed from holes in my hands, feet, and side. He took my hands into his, lifted my wounded palms to his lips and kissed them. Holding them tightly in his own mutilated hands, he gazed into my eyes and said, "I love your wounds. I will love others through your wounds." He embraced and caressed me. Our soiled flesh became one. I felt peace.

When the litany ended, I knelt at the foot of the altar with folded hands and bowed head. The congregation chanted "Veni Sancte Spiritus," as the archbishop and nearly one hundred priests took turns laying their hands on my head. "A priest is a man first," my deceased grandpa Rastrelli had said to my dad, and he to me on the day I left for St. Mary's. The consecrated clerics who were touching me, blessing me, were wounded men. Just like me. God had worked through them in spite of their sinfulness. God would work through me, too.

As the seemingly endless succession of priests pressed their palms against my gelled hair, my vertebrae compressed. Spasms shot down my spine into my knees. Rather than fighting it, I welcomed the physical anguish. The higher voices of the Latin chant faded, until the buzzing bass remained. The music echoed over the pews. The twinging in my back remained. Intoxicating. No one had warned me that the rite was so agonizing, so ecstatic.

I opened my eyes. Behind the wooden altar and in front of the braided spires of the wooden sanctuary screen, the priests stood staring at me with folded hands. Their shadowed faces loomed over their white vestments. Some smiled. Others had the constipated gaze of forced piety. They had passed Jesus's priesthood onto me. I wiped the tears from my face, closed my eyes, and listened to the archbishop's frantic vibrato intoning the Prayer of Consecration. I rose and turned toward the congregation. One of my brother priests, a local fellow and alumnus of St. Mary's, lifted the deacon's stole from my shoulder and replaced it with a white priest's stole. I met my family's proud gaze in the front pew. Behind them, Pat fought back tears.

"Let me smell them again," Pat said from behind the steering wheel of my truck.

From the passenger's seat, I extended my consecrated hands, still slippery with chrism from the archbishop's blessing. Pat pressed his nose into my palms and inhaled the balsam bouquet, "I love that smell."

A twinge of pain bolted through my upper back into my fingers. The nearly three-hour rite and two-hour reception had left me dehydrated. My right arm and hand throbbed with handshake fatigue. My upper back knotted in exhaustion. My cheeks continued to smile, even though hours of grinning had left me feeling like I'd blown up a thousand balloons. I had never felt so loved, so exhausted. I retracted my hands, thankful that Pat had agreed to drive me to Cedar Falls for the Mass of Thanksgiving rehearsal at St. Stephen's. I sniffed their scent.

"My hands are anointed and holy," I said. "What does it mean?"

"It means, Father Tom, that you are a priest."

"Holy shit!"

I filled him in on every detail of the ordination: the surprising back pain during the laying on of hands, the archbishop's intense gaze as he anointed me, the communal buzz of praying the eucharistic prayer while channeling Christ with all the priests, the sudden moment of panic when I noticed Grandpa teetering with heat exhaustion in the front row during Communion, and the relief that followed when he was fine. Neither one of us had heard an explanation from anyone as to how the cantor, who lead the music in spite of the peach pirate patch on her face, had lost one of her eyes.

"Some things are just meant to remain mysteries," he said.

It felt incredible to laugh with him again. The past two weeks since we'd slept together had been all regret, confusion, and desolation, but now, in the ripples of the most affirmation I'd received in my life, anything seemed possible.

"I love you, Pat."

"I love you too."

"Give me your hand," I said. He placed it in mine.

We vowed to support each, to be honest about everything, to be there for each other come what may, to build up each other's priesthood, and to love each other always. Even if at some future day we failed in our celibacy again, we would help each other rebuild God's calling.

Communion concluded. Standing in the sanctuary of St. Stephen's dressed in new, forest green vestments, I thanked everyone who had influenced my vocation over the years and worked to make the Mass of Thanksgiving perfect. In the pews, people from each scene and act of my life awaited my next line. Aunts who had changed my diapers and uncles who had tickled me until I nearly pissed myself now respected me. My siblings and old friends from Clinton, who had shared the stage with Tobey and me, finally understood me. My acting professor, who hadn't set foot in a Catholic church in decades, sat in the back pew applauding me. Josie, my failed attempt at a girlfriend, sat with her husband and the choir, crying tears of joy for me. The deacon's wife, who had enabled me to embrace my choice to become a priest one last time, winked at me. My brothers from St. Mary's—Felix, Nicky, Mick, Pat, and even Abdel, who'd offered our strained friendship another chance by coming—chuckled at me, for my thank-yous had lasted over twenty minutes. They hadn't seen anything yet.

I strutted down the stairs into the nave toward the tabernacle and the windows that opened to the lush lawn and brick buildings of the university. My vestments swung about as if they might lift me into the air. I pointed at the pew in which I'd once sat. "This is where it started. This is where an angry lost kid listened to a homily about a deaf-mute and was opened to God. This is where I heard my calling to be a priest."

I marched up into the sanctuary and gazed at the upturned faces. They were the *real* Church, full of longing and trust. They deserved more than what scandalous priests and bishops had shat on them. My voice thundered through the speakers: "No matter what you're hearing in the press—there's a lot of misinformation out there. Go to the source. Call seminary faculties. Talk to seminarians. The good men are still in the seminaries. And we are radically committed—radically meaning we're gonna give our all to our vows, to our promises, and we are going to be the best priests that we can be. And live the mystery that we celebrate, which is the Lord's cross. We will turn over our weaknesses to the Lord so that he can make them into strengths."

The crowd leapt to their feet. My bones reverberated with an electric buzz that could only be the Holy Spirit. The foundation of St. Stephen's had never rumbled with such hope.

I returned to the presider's chair and stood next to Pat, who had been at my side while I consecrated the bread and wine, as both deacon and beloved.

"Bow your heads and pray for God's blessing," he ordered.

I imparted the blessing and announced the recessional song. Over my shoulder, Father Scott, who had eloquently preached the homily, opened his worship aid. At the piano, his new protégé, a blonde undergraduate, pounded away. We went forth singing, "The heavens are telling the glory of God and all creation is shouting for joy."

PART IV

ST. JUDE, THE APOSTLE

Patron Saint of
Lost Causes
2002–3

Judas, not the Iscariot, said to him, "Master, what happened that you will reveal yourself to us and not to the world?"—John 14:22

THE HOLY LONGING

I scurried through a terminal at the Baltimore-Washington International Airport. A priest for nine days, I'd celebrated Masses in Cedar Falls, Clinton, State Center (Mom's hometown), and my parents' living room. Exhausted, I had eight days of freedom before reporting to St. Jude's and sixty-hour work weeks until I retired at seventy or whatever age the bishops deemed appropriate. My plan had been to relax at home, but Pat's sister offered me her vacant house near Ocean City. He was dropping off the key.

Over bobbing heads, I spotted him standing among the folks beyond the security line. He wore a short-sleeved, burgundy shirt with a St. Mary's logo and khaki pants. His elbow rested on a railing by the escalators to baggage claim. His hand dangled. One of his loafers was propped on its toe. I'd never seen him so relaxed, so playful. We rushed together and embraced, unconcerned with the crowd.

As the escalator descended to the luggage carousals, I filled him in on the past few weeks. He grinned like a kid with a secret. I scanned for the car rental booth. "Where's Alamo?"

"That's unnecessary," he said. "My pastor told me to go with you, to enjoy one last week of freedom before priesthood swallows you."

I wanted to press my lips against his. But I held back. The night we'd acted out, he'd avoided my mouth, refusing to betray Christ with a kiss.

As we drove to the beach, my mind tripped on fantasies that I wanted to confess. Still, I didn't want him to stop smiling, to stop holding my hand. If I said too much, he'd do a U-turn and follow the streaking headlights back to Baltimore. I focused on non–"us" things. No, I hadn't heard a confession yet. Yes, I was nervous about the first one. No, Father Scott hadn't hit on me. Yes, consecrating the bread and wine was a spiritual rush. During a few Masses, my body had even become warm and tingly, almost like the ecstasies we'd experienced.

He pulled his hand from mine and wiped it on his khakis. On my palm, our sweat chilled. In the dashboard's light, I couldn't read his face. He might as well have been behind a confessional screen. I kept talking, hiding my fear that he was freaking out, that he'd never touch me again, that mine was the only erection in the car.

"Are you all right?" I asked and touched his hand.

"My hand was just sweaty." He turned his palm over, squeezed my fingers, and asked, "Are you hungry?"

"Starving."

We pulled into a McDonald's. As I opened the restaurant door for him, the bulge in his pants confessed everything.

Minutes after arriving at the vacation house, we stood in the great room, bodies and bulges pressed together.

"This feels so good," he said, kneading my shoulder blades with his fingers.

I nuzzled into his neck. My lips brushed his skin, "I missed you so much."

"You too," his breath sent a tickle over the nape of my neck.

Our fingers migrated down each other's backs. "So, what do you want to do?" I asked, as my hands reached his beltline.

"I don't know." His pelvis gently rolled against mine. His fingers passed my belt. Our heads turned. Our lips met, then our tongues. And there was no Doctor Lauz, no Father Scott, no Father Foley. No priesthood. Only Pat.

When we finished making love for the second time, Pat kissed me and said, "We should really go to sleep." I wanted to remain as we were, to dream in his arms, listening to the beat of a heart that loved me. But his arm kept falling asleep, and our dicks kept getting hard. I returned to my bedroom and slept.

Midmorning, we made love in the shower. We skipped the beach, preferring to remain unclothed and entwined. He slept through most of

A Beautiful Mind. When his snoring startled him into consciousness, I stroked him back to sleep.

Midafternoon, as a thunderstorm passed, we curled up on the back porch swing, naked and unashamed. I recalled stripping in the rain on retreat and demanding that God reveal God's self to me bodily. I thanked God and snuggled into Pat.

We finally dressed for supper. He steamed shrimp seasoned with Old Bay, while I set the table, singing and dancing to *Fosse*. As the wine enhanced our buzz, we shared our fantasies. Since middle school, I'd always wanted to slow dance with a man. After eating, we embraced while swaying in circles. As we shared more fantasies, he blushed. He'd imagined squeezing into the same pair of underwear with a man. We undressed each other, and I stepped into his briefs, which surprisingly stretched to accommodate us. His blessed fullness against mine, we shuffled in slow circles.

He lay in bed on his back. Wrapped around him, I softly serenaded him with a ballad from *Rent*: "With a thousand sweet kisses, I'll cover you." Starting from his toes, I worked my way up, blessing every inch of his skin with pecks. When my whiskers nicked the arches of his feet, he giggled. When I kissed the inside of his thighs, he quivered. When I kissed his hairy pecs, he curled his fingers through my hair. I wanted to baptize him with passion, to change him ontologically, to brand him with the indelible mark of my love so that he would never again know loneliness. Last, I kissed him on the eyelids. When he opened them, I studied his irises, their spatter of chocolate, sunflower, silver, and jade. I stared into the infinite black of his pupils and said, "I wish I could kiss your soul."

He smiled. "You already have."

On the Fourth of July, after three nights of lovemaking, I loaded Pat's duffle into the car. He rushed about the house checking lights, unplugging appliances, and turning off the water. Before leaving, we embraced in the great room. He pulled away refusing my tongue. "When we get back to Baltimore," he said, "we're going to behave."

After two days of celibacy at Pat's rectory, I cornered him on the leather couch in his sitting room. Outside on the sidewalk below, parishioners gathered for Saturday evening Mass. I unbuttoned his clerical shirt and unzipped his slacks. If I could pleasure him just right, he'd lose his inhibitions and touch me again. He'd hug me and tell me he loved me, that I kissed his soul.

After he came, I pressed against him and kissed his neck. He pushed me aside and pulled up his underwear and slacks, "I didn't want that." I shrunk into the couch. "We have to stop, Tom." His voice sounded hollow like a penny dropped on cold steel. "This is just your pattern. You slept with Tobey when high school ended, with Father Scott when college ended, with me when seminary ended. You don't do transitions well."

He was right. I had injured him, was injuring him, his faith, and his vocation. I had to become the priest God ordained me to be.

"I'm sorry, Pat." I remained on the couch, frightened my words might crush him. "The last thing I want to do is to hurt you. And I don't want to live a double life."

He buttoned his collar and reinserted his white tab. "Then you have to move on."

I returned to the guest room and brushed my teeth. An hour or so later, at Mass, he fed me the Body of Christ. After dinner, we went to our separate rooms. On the plane the next morning, I closed my eyes and replayed every detail of our honeymoon at the beach.

"I wish I could kiss your soul."

"You already have."

I landed and moved into St. Jude's.

THE FIRST FIVE YEARS OF PRIESTHOOD

I stumbled through the dark unfamiliar bedroom and caught my shin on the lower corner of the bedframe. "Shit." I swiped at the dresser and knocked the chirping alarm to the floor. "Fuck. Sorry, Lord." 5:30. After the excitement of my first weekend in the parish, I'd been unable to fall asleep until after two. The pastor had left for a weeklong vacation. As the newly assigned associate pastor of St. Jude Parish, Cedar Rapids, Iowa, I was in charge.

My bedroom and adjoining bathroom beamed bleach white. Everything had been painted a year earlier, when parishioners renovated the associate's new quarters. I emptied the bedroom's dehumidifier into the shower. A few days earlier, when I moved in and turned on the shower for the first time, inch-long insects with C-shaped pinchers on their butts shot out of the nozzle. That night, when I pulled back the bedcovers, more bugs wriggled between the sheets. "Earwigs," Father Frank, my pastor, had called them. There wasn't money for an exterminator, he said. "You're not afraid of few harmless bugs, are ya?" When I called the previous associate to inquire about the infestation, he'd said, "Yup. I made friends with the bugs." After flushing the earwigs, I made the bed, tightly folding the white sheets, stained with my predecessor's sweat, under the mattress. I had no desire to make friends or sleep with the bugs.

Ducking a forehead-clipping doorframe, I passed through my tiny sitting room and ascended the stairway into the kitchen. I'd shower and shave after unlocking the church. Weekday Mass was at seven, but a handful of elderly women arrived for their morning rosaries shortly after six. I flipped on the coffee maker and slipped out the back door into the muggy twilight.

St. Jude's was a block east of the rectory. If not for its Protestant-like white steeple and cross over the brown bricked carport, the structure could have doubled as a drive-through bank. Over the low-pitched rooftop, a rising wedge of peach bled into the sooty night. Pat and I had never shared a sunrise. I added that to my mental to-do list and unlocked the front doors.

Throughout Mass, I thought of Pat. As I preached, I contemplated his words. As I elevated the bread and wine, I offered up my love for him. As I shook hands in the lobby, I longed for his grip. The aged Mass-goers pelted me with enthusiasm, as if they'd never seen a priest without a receding hairline. They extended meal and movie invitations. "We look forward to having you on the social concerns committee, Father." "An athletic fellow like you must love baseball. How about a game sometime?" "You're going to be our Knights of Columbus chaplain. Right, Father?" "Father, I bet a lot of girls cried the day you were ordained."

I thanked them and did as seminary had trained me: don't accept an invitation on the spot. Never say no. Say, "I'd love to, but I don't have my calendar right now. Call me at the office. We'll schedule something." This was how a priest maintained his schedule and personal boundaries. Saying yes to everything led to burnout, but saying no made one an antisocial asshole. By putting responsibility on parishioners to follow up, most of invitations never materialized.

After hanging my vestments in the sacristy, I returned to the rectory. I had barely an hour to eat and do Morning Prayer before the parish office opened. While downing Raisin Bran, a banana, coffee and orange juice, I flipped through the *Cedar Rapids Gazette.* I needed to keep informed so that my preaching would remain relevant. Father Frank's dishes from the weekend lined the counter. I loaded them into the dishwasher.

In my basement bedroom, I sat on a pillow in my personal prayer space. Between the bed and the closet, a narrow coffee table ran the length of the wall. On the table, I arranged my journal, pens, breviary, Bible, prayer cards, books, and candles. Over the space hung Father Scott's crucifix from college and five icons, ordination gifts: Christ calling Peter to be a fisher of men, Christ washing his disciples' feet, the transfiguration, Christ commissioning the disciples to heal and preach, and a blasé Christ Pantocrator holding the scriptures and sporting "the Rachel" haircut from *Friends*, season one. I prayed through the Office of Readings and Morning Prayer. I asked for strength to get through my first solo week in the parish, to be a vessel of grace. I prayed for Pat's peace and vocation to deepen. There wasn't time to meditate or dance as I had in seminary.

When I returned to the church at nine, the secretary, Lizz, was at her desk in the central office, which adjoined the others. She had bangs like a cinnamon roll and a voice sweet as icing. Phone in one hand, she scribbled on a pink notepad. Fresh coffee wafted through the air. The copy machine chugged out flyers. The typewriter sprouted a form. Lizz mouthed, "Good morning, Father," and handed me a pile of messages.

I'd spent the previous week bringing my office up to seminary code. My desk pressed against the wall with the door so I could see those entering. My computer monitor had its back to the door. This served a double purpose: to protect onscreen information from the gaze of passing folks and to provide cover for the work on my desk. Ideally, the door should have been windowed to protect a priest from false sexual abuse accusations, but mine wasn't. Thankfully, a window opened to the driveway and sidewalk. The blinds had to remain open at all times. The books I'd acquired in seminary lined the built-in shelves opposite the desk. The waist-high counter under the shelves was decorated with my gold-leafed Bible, *Book of the Gospels*, a white stone statue of Jesus teaching the little children, a crucifix carved from Gethsemane olive wood, and a *Sedes Sapientiae* the size of a bowling pin. Under the counter were the files left by my predecessor. I'd ordered them: *Marriage Prep*, *Annulments*, *Weddings*, *Funerals*, *Wakes*, *Sunday Homilies*, *Daily Homilies*, *Holiday Homilies*, *Schools*, *Social Justice Committee*, *Liturgy Committee*, *Adult Education*, *Hospital Visits*, *Continuing Formation*, and so on. At angles, I arranged three identical chairs, two for guests and one for me. A priest's guests—my pastoral counseling professor had said—deserved equal furniture.

The office was perfect except for the previous associate's pride and joy: a gargantuan swivel chair. It could have been the captain's chair from the bridge of the *Enterprise*: the original chair, from the *Star Trek* pilot. The first pilot. Every time I sat in it, itchy crumbs leaked out of the cracked vinyl upholstery.

As I waited for the computer to boot up, I flipped through my pink messages and returned calls. Most of them had to do with wedding preparations. St. Jude's had more than two thousand registered families, many of them young. I had weddings twelve of the next fifteen Saturdays. Many priests secretly preferred funerals and hated weddings: picky brides, drunken groomsmen, and intrusive mothers. I found holy matrimony romantic, full of possibilities for evangelizing and catechizing.

I scanned my email for a message from Pat. He hadn't responded since Father Frank had given me permission to go to Ireland in August with Felix, Mick, Nicky, and him. I was starting to worry. Abdel had written. A classmate from St. Mary's, Michael Walsh, a silver-haired Bostonian with a disposition as sweet as his pipe tobacco, had been removed from ministry. For sexual abuse. I had heard in seminary that the largest percentage of priests who would leave did so during the first five years of priesthood. A few weeks had to be a record.

I searched the internet. Forty years ago, Michael coached hockey and allegedly molested boys. I looked at his smiling face in our class photograph hanging over my desk. I'd eaten with him, lent him my notes, and hugged him at the sign of peace. I'd encouraged him to stick it out when the academics overloaded his sixty-something brain. I recalled a discussion during St. Mary's "Internet and Cybersex" workshop. Michael had ranted that sexuality shouldn't be judged, that it evolved over a lifetime. Is that how perpetrators justified their crimes?

"Excuse me, Father," Lizz said from the door.

I realized she'd been buzzing me on the phone for the past twenty seconds. Her concerned look reminded me of my mother's, "Everything OK, Father?"

"I'm fine."

She looked unconvinced. "There's a man waiting for you in the confessional."

I grabbed my palm-sized *Rite of Penance* and left to hear my first confession.

Sitting in the closet-sized reconciliation room, I struggled to remain focused on the penitent. All I could think about was Michael and the boys he'd abused. Who would fall next? The words of absolution I'd been practicing daily for months eluded me. Relying on the rite book, I got through the confession and sent the man on his way.

I rushed back to the office to call Baltimore. A lanky man with a stain-streaked shirt and a missing front tooth waited in the vestibule. "Hey, Father, my van is out of gas. I have to get to Minneapolis for work tomorrow. Can you help me out?" The scent of whiskey filled the air. Panic overwhelmed me, for Father Frank, who had promised to instruct me on handling drop-ins, left without doing so. Through the windows, I noticed my next appointment, a future bride and her mother, approaching.

"Welcome to St. Jude's. I'm Father Tom." I smiled and shook the man's hand. "Would you mind waiting a few minutes? I just returned from another appointment."

"No problem, Father. Thank you, Father."

I sped into the office. Lizz's eyes bulged with apology. I whispered, "What's the protocol when people ask for money?"

"I'm sorry, but I don't know. Father Frank handles that."

I asked her to tell my wedding appointment that I'd be with them shortly and ducked into Father Frank's office. I rummaged through his desk until I found grocery vouchers. I hurried to my office and wrote on a legal pad: *To Do (1) Prepare staff for drop-ins asking for money, (2) Shelters and soup kitchens? (3) Call Catholic Charities, (4) Ask social concerns committee for leads, (5) Write weekend homily.* The phone rang. Lizz buzzed, "Do you want me to take a message, Father?"

"That'd be great." I looked at the picture of Michael. What the hell had he done? I added *(6) Call Baltimore* to my list.

I invited the man into my office. As instructed in seminary, I left the door open. While most needy folks were harmless, there was always the chance someone could get violent and pull a weapon. This fellow looked hungover or high. He sat in one of my guest chairs, his eyes to the ceiling, and repeated his need for gas money. No matter what he said, I wasn't to give him money. It could be used for drugs or worse. I apologized that I had no cash—even though volunteers were counting the weekend's collection in the conference room—but that I could give him a twenty-dollar grocery voucher. On the legal pad, I jotted his name and wrote *(7) Gas vouchers.*

"Thank you, Father. God bless you." I showed him out and wished him well.

Lizz handed me more pink phone messages. As I scribbled *(8) Return calls* on my pad. My stomach growled. I checked my watch—11:45—and stepped into the lobby to apologize to the future bride and mother for making them wait. A new arrival, a skinny, depressed-looking man asked, "Do you have a minute, Father?"

After the bride-to-be and her mom left—*(9) Check wedding party size limits, (10) Alcohol policy? Onsite school—Aren't we a drug-free zone? (11) Wedding homily*—I got a voucher ready for the skinny fellow who'd been waiting. I scooped up a few more phone messages from Lizz, who asked whether I wanted her to fetch some lunch. "Thanks, but I'll sneak out after this next one."

Twenty minutes later, the skinny fellow remained in my office. He was living with his parents, had seen me Sunday at Mass, and wanted to talk about his financial disarray and inability to hold a job because of depression. A few of my older priest friends had warned me that the town's "crazies" would drop in to pump the baby priest for money. My stomach groaned. I wanted him to leave. I wanted to scream. At Michael. At the bishops. None of the pink messages was from Pat. I chastised myself for not being attentive to my guest. His clean clothing, gelled hair, and soapy scent didn't suggest homelessness. I responded with statements that sounded patient and understanding but were meant to nudge him to his point.

"Would you mind shutting the door, Father?"

I hesitated, but he hadn't asked for money. Maybe he was seeking spiritual direction or confession. "Sure." I closed it. He slumped into the chair like a wire hanger draped with too heavy a coat and sobbed. As gently as I could, I said, "You seem to be in a lot of pain. Like something awful happened."

"It was awful, Father. A priest molested me. Like twenty years ago. It started my freshman year, when I went to high school here." He gestured in the parish school's direction. The priest had lived in the school and lured boys to his quarters. Another victim thought that the perpetrator had moved to Colorado. Over the past six months, news of the abuse scandal had dragged my parishioner-victim into depression. He wasn't suicidal anymore, but he couldn't live without knowing that he'd done what he could to protect other children.

I thought of Lauz and Father Scott still out there. But this moment wasn't about me. I focused on the man and passed him tissues. The Church had failed him for two decades; I couldn't.

After he calmed down, I provided him my office number, the number for free counseling at Catholic Charities, and the number for the archdiocese's episcopal vicar—the archbishop's second-in-command, who handled all abuse cases. The man gave me his number but asked that I only leave the message: *Father Tom called.* I explained that the archdiocese required me to provide the vicar with the details of the case; he'd call to follow up. He said that was okay. I asked him whether we could schedule a visit for later in the week. He said he'd have to check his calendar when he got home.

I walked him to the front door, expecting him to dissolve in the humid breeze. He drove off without looking back.

My watch read 1:39. Lizz was back from lunch. My head pounded. "Can I get you anything?" she asked.

The first flight to Baltimore. "No thanks," I smiled. "I just have to make a call. Then I'll grab lunch."

As I waited for the vicar to answer, I prayed he wouldn't ask how I was. He responded, "Not another one." He told me to email the details—*(12) Email vicar, (13) Get new counselor.* I wasn't to contact the "alleged victim" again. The vicar would take care of him. "You have enough to worry about as a new priest."

When I opened my door, Lizz whispered, "I'm sorry," discreetly pointing to the lobby.

A woman waited. "Can I help you?" I said. She slunk into her chair like a discarded doll.

(14) Pack sack lunch.

In spite of my hunger, I refocused on the woman. Her fiancé had dumped her. Her friends and family, who never liked him, mocked her grief. Her life was "worthless," a "bad joke." She had passing thoughts of hurting herself but never would. Years ago, she'd attempted suicide but would never do so today. She'd been thinking about it, but not seriously. She didn't have a plan.

"You're the only one who understands me, Father," she said, dabbing tears.

I needed to assess her suicide risk with some follow-up questions—*(16) Suicide hotlines*—but I also needed to affirm her experience and her feeling that I accepted her. She hadn't admitted imminent suicidal thoughts. In fact, her "would never hurt myself," "just passing thoughts," and "no plan," sounded like a textbook example of someone who knew what not to say. If she'd indicated that she was an immediate danger to herself, I was bound to call 911. Something seemed off. I took the other route: "You sound relieved or surprised by my reaction."

"So do you," she said.

I felt lightheaded. God, I needed her to be okay, to get out of my office. Without moving, I glanced at my watch. 3:05. When I looked up, she was slinking toward me. I froze, unable to comprehend her actions. They weren't in the seminary playbook. She touched my shoulders and started massaging them.

"Stop this." I pushed past her and moved to the door. "That was inappropriate."

She stood, arms dangling like an abandoned marionette. "I just wanted a hug."

"I apologize. I didn't mean to snap."

She extended her arms, trapping me against the door. "Please, Father. Just hold me."

"No. I'm not comfortable with that." I wedged open the door and extended a hand, "Let's continue in the lobby." She stepped back, wrinkled her lips, and shook her head. "I'm not mad. Please, let's step outside."

I picked up her purse and handed it to her. She cradled it like a stillborn infant. I waited until she exited my office. She refused to sit in the lobby. I explained that I could meet with her again, but only in the lobby.

"You're mean," she howled. She stuck out her tongue and tore out the front doors.

I trudged back into my office. Lizz was on the phone. The second line rang. Lizz buzzed. "I'm sorry, Father. Funeral home on line two."

I shifted in an angular chair in an unfamiliar living room, listening to the family reminisce about the deceased. She had been in her nineties. Her suffering was over. Her daughter and grandchildren were relieved. They seemed more concerned with the rattled young priest who'd come to minister to them.

"How's life with Father Frank?" "How's the staff situation?" the granddaughters asked. Father Frank had mentioned parishioners were disgruntled but hadn't given details. He wanted me to minister to all parishioners in spite of their issues with him. But the question about the staff caught me off guard.

The deceased's daughter leaned forward on the couch, "Enough girls. Let him be. Tell him about Grandma."

As I drove back to the office, I brainstormed wake and funeral homilies.

An evening haze stippled the nearby cornfields. I feared what awaited me, what messages had been left, whether Pat would call again.

The staff had left for the night. On my desk, Lizz had placed more phone messages and a note apologizing for the crazy day.

I wrote on the legal pad: *(17) Staff situation? (18) Wake homily*, and *(19) Funeral homily*. I called the bereavement committee coordinator to initiate the funeral planning. I composed and sent the vicar an email detailing the allegation of sexual abuse, ~~*(12) Email vicar*~~. I worked through the pile of messages, ~~*(8) Return calls*~~, scheduled appointments, and created new marriage files.

The rectory's clock read 8:56. The Chinese takeout tasted as stale as the kitchen's browning brocade wallpaper, but I masticated onward. Scoop fork into chicken, rice, and broccoli. Lift fork to mouth. Open. Insert food. Chew. Swallow. Repeat. This was the life of a priest.

I cracked open the fortune cookie and read: *You are soon going to change your present line of work.*

The table rocked with my laughter, and then my sobs.

I descended into my basement suite and collapsed in my sitting room's oversized recliner. It was past eleven on the East Coast; Pat had fallen asleep long before I ate. The last thing he needed to hear was me breaking down, and I didn't need another lecture about sacrifice.

A feeble voice answered, "St. Augustine's, Father Felix speaking."

"Felix. It's Tommy."

"Oh, thank God. I thought it was another death. You won't believe the day I just had."

Our professors had lied. After ordination, there wasn't a learning curve. There was a wall, and we'd smashed face-first into it. Would every day be like this? Was this what the next forty-plus years of our lives would be? There seemed to be no way, even with God's grace, that we'd survive a week, let alone a month, year, or decades. "It has to get better. Easier," we promised each other.

Long past midnight, I stared at the ceiling over my bed.

"Lord, I don't want to be a statistic," I prayed. "Just get me through the first five years of priesthood."

The next morning, a man pushed into my office and badmouthed Father Frank, whom he claimed was bankrupting the parish and didn't care about the Catholic schools. A group had written the archbishop, demanding Father Frank's removal. Afterward, the staff's liturgist, who was in charge of music, training lectors, and all the trappings of Mass, cornered me in my office. Father Hunter, now back from Rome with his ABD (All But Dissertation), had warned me that she had a reputation and might try to seduce me. She told me the finance committee and business manager wanted Father Frank fired because he created the liturgist job and hired her. I felt myself getting angry at Father Frank. Why hadn't he prepped me for this?

~~*(16) Staff situation?*~~

My professors had warned against making major changes our first year in a new parish. A priest should discreetly seed new ideas through homilies, casual conversations, and allies so disgruntled parishioners would believe that they were the originators of change. If I couldn't learn from Father Frank's strengths, I'd learn from his weaknesses.

On Wednesday, his housekeeper did my laundry without asking. I'd washed and folded my own clothes since age fourteen, but I couldn't protest. Father Hunter warned, "The last person you want to piss off is the housekeeper." That night, I wondered if I already had. She'd bleached my new black clerical shirts and rearranged the contents of my dresser. Seminary formation had drilled the importance of maintaining appropriate professional boundaries, but even my underwear drawer, where I hid my lovesick journals and cum-rag, was no longer private.

On Thursday, minutes before my first funeral, the business manager stepped into my office, holding a box packed with pictures and knickknacks. "I'm sorry you landed in the middle of this. You're a nice guy. I hope you don't get hurt." She turned and walked out. Lizz, the liturgist, and youth minister stood dumbfounded in her wake, but I had a hearse rolling down the driveway. As I greeted grievers in the lobby, the woman who'd hit on me on Monday barged in and demanded a private meeting. When I explained I had a funeral and she needed to make an appointment, she shouted, "You're the worse priest in the world," before running out.

“Fantastic,” I said at the funeral dinner when folks asked how it felt to be a priest. “A true blessing.”

On Friday night, I returned to the rectory after a wedding rehearsal. Father Frank was sprawled out on his recliner, amber drink in hand, nose in the *New Yorker*.

“Welcome home,” I said.

“Thomas!” he shouted, offering a strong handshake. “What a week, hey? How ’bout a toddy?” His cottony hair and push-broom mustache popped against his crimson complexion. Thick glasses magnified his blue eyes, one of which wandered.

I sat on the couch, sipped my whiskey, and recounted the week from my first confession to my first funeral, from the sexual abuse victim to the woman who’d hit on me. When I admitted that I’d cried Monday night, his eyes rolled back and his belly bounced in laughter. I didn’t know whether he was reacting out of shock, discomfort, or vindictiveness. Perhaps he didn’t know how to handle my emotion. I did know that I wouldn’t share anything personal with him again. And that I wanted the hell out of St. Jude’s.

THE WOUNDED HEALER

Pat snored off a late night of Guinness toasts, so I left the curtains of our hotel room closed while I cleaned up. I was leaving Felix's tour of Ireland early for St. Jude's annual festival. Pat and I had roomed together for the week. He'd called it "a test" to see if we could remain celibate. The morning before, he'd pretended to sleep as I jacked him off. The entire trip had been pretend. After each time we'd made love, he acted like he didn't want it, and I, like I believed we could quit.

When I finished my shower, he was still in bed but not snoring, his back to me. I slunk between the sheets and curled around him into a spoon. When I reached into his briefs and stroked, he didn't protest, but he was as unresponsive as I had been in Lauz's office. He didn't want me. He wanted to get off. And I didn't want him. I wanted him to love loving me. I released him, got dressed, and dragged my baggage to the bus station.

As the bus squeezed through Galway's colorful storefronts, diesel fumes churned my stomach. The nausea felt good, a reminder that I was alone, as God intended, betrothed to Iowa whose black dirt and barren gray winters were my landscape. The bus approached my hotel, a final pass of the funeral procession before burial at celibacy.

I scanned for the third-floor window, the last place I would know Pat's flesh. Framed by the pane, he sat at the window with his breviary in hand, praying for the salvation of the world. He'd make a fine priest. Then he saw me. One last moment of longing. I pressed my palm against the streaked window. He looked bereaved. "I love you, Pat," I said, as he vanished into the passing façades.

Two parishioners begged me to put on the prescribed costume. I pulled the green bodysuit over my clerics. Over my head, they lowered a cylindrical mask shaped like a cob of corn with two upward-turned parentheses for eyes and a broad, almost deranged green smile. Crowned with an emerald top hat, I became an eight-foot-tall walking cornstalk, the star of the St. Jude's Sweet Corn Festival. When word got out that Father Tom was in the suit, parishioners swarmed. Parents asked me to hold their babies for pictures, even to offer a few blessings. The Jolly Green Giant had nothing on me. When I took off the costume, I retained the ever-smiling mask.

That's what Number Ten had told me to do when I called him after my first month in the parish: "You're a caring, loving, gifted, and ordained person, Tom. If you posit the behavior of a happy priest, if you change your behavior, your psyche will eventually follow."

At the weekend Masses, I ditched my preaching notes and stepped out from the ambo. Figuring I had nothing to lose by further pissing off those angry with Father Frank, I preached about loving and praying for one's enemies and persecutors, how Osama Bin Laden needed prayers more than anyone in the world did. If we followed Jesus's command by trying to love and pray for Bin Laden, could we not do the same for our neighbors, parishioners, and family members with whom we disagreed? An elderly fellow nicknamed me "Father Fulton" after the renowned twentieth-century preacher Father Fulton Sheen. Parents told me that their teenagers looked forward to my homilies. Some kids said so in person. One young dad asked me to be in a commercial he was shooting for the archdiocese that promoted vocations to the priesthood. Among the other featured clerics was Father Scott. Smiling, I accepted the part.

"You sound conflicted," Counselor Number Eleven said. He was a lanky, bespectacled fellow whose office was in a Victorian home with 1960s décor. I chose him for a fresh perspective beyond the closeted gay, supposedly celibate clerics who'd advised me in seminary. Eleven was married, straight, and Lutheran. "You see the positive results of your work, and—"

"How can I deny that?" I said.

"You're doing great work as a priest," he said. "I'm not discounting that. And I want you to know you still have options."

Options. Not a word that I'd heard in seminary. Eleven was wrong.

I'd squandered my options at deaconate ordination. I'd gambled them away in the archdiocese's $150,000 seminary tuition. I was an investment obliged to produce a return. Besides, gay men having lasting intimate relationships was just a fantasy. Pat proved that.

"I chose this," I said. "I need to make it work. To focus on the positives, my ministry."

"And if that doesn't work?"

"It has to."

If only my faith were as great as a mustard seed, I thought, *God would answer my prayers.* But my prayer was desolation. In the Liturgy of the Hours, the phrase that spoke most to me was "my tears have become my bread." I wasn't alone. My contented mom, the emotional rock of the family, was clinically depressed: staying up all night, sleeping all day, losing weight, crying uncontrollably one moment, and emotionally void the next. My sisters called from the West Coast and begged me to help Mom, but when I spoke to her on the phone, I cried with her. So I did as had the psalmist with a diet of tears: through my pain, "I led the crowds rejoicing."

In the hospitals and nursing homes, I anointed the foreheads and palms of the sick and dying with holy oil. They vented their dread and pain; I listened. When mothers gave birth, I blessed and baptized their babies. When an infant was stillborn, I stood confounded with the grieving family, staring into the miniature coffin at the round face whose eyes it seemed would open at any moment. When a two-year-old fell down the stairs and died, I absorbed her family's anger with God. I gave it voice in my funeral homily, hoping they might be heard and find peace. When divorced individuals sought annulments, fearing the hurt from old failures, I understood their shame. When homosexual men and women confessed feeling that they belonged in hell, I guided them toward embracing their sexuality as a divine gift; chastity was an ideal to be sought, not necessarily achieved. It didn't matter how much loneliness I suffered in my personal life. God was working through my wounds to heal others.

But at night, when I took off the mask, I had to face my lesions. When the phone rang, my heart raced. Would it be a death, a car accident, or another angry parishioner? Would it be Pat? I wondered which bishop or priest would go down next. Throughout the presbyterate, rumors pulsed like back pain. The Vatican had leaked an unpublished document containing Cardinal Ratzinger's homophobic theology; it deemed homosexuals' ordinations invalid. In the Catholic media, the conservative narrative dominated, blaming gay priests and "liberal" seminaries like St. Mary's for the sexual abuse scandal. It seemed a matter of time until the pope and Ratzinger banned gay men from seminary or invalidated known homosexuals' ordinations. If they acted, my conscience wouldn't allow me to remain a priest. But I didn't want to abandon my parishioners.

I just needed support. After my two-year placement at St. Jude's, I would likely be shipped to a cluster of three to six rural parishes, the lone celibate in a thirty-mile radius. The archdiocese's handbook for priestly formation strongly encouraged all newly ordained priests to join a "priest support group"—three to seven priests who met monthly to discuss their struggles—but none of the existing groups had openings. I sought to start one with other young priests, but we were forbidden. Each group needed a senior priest who had survived the first five years. The only one I knew who was looking to join a group was Father Scott.

On Thursdays, I met with a group of local priests for supper. On Friday mornings, I met with two recently ordained guys for Morning Prayer. We developed our own informal groups, but when I shared a hellish situation I'd encountered, my brothers didn't comfort me. They clobbered me with tales of something worse. After ordination, everyone unloaded their horror stories. I joked, "The real ontological change from ordination is that priests start telling you the truth about ministry, how miserable everyone is."

The most joyful priests I knew were retired. They didn't live in rectories but had apartments or modest homes. They were relaxed, jolly, and unmedicated, at least psychotropically.

My favorite moment of the week was behind the wheel of my truck, speeding across golden cornfields to spend my day off with my friends, parents, or grandparents. The most harrowing moment was driving back the next day as my chest, shoulders, and jaw tightened.

Throughout the autumn nights, I curled up in bed like a poisoned earwig. (Father Frank had given in to my requests for an exterminator.) A good celibate was supposed to undress his wounds so God could enter them. Ten had said, "Keep turning the pain over to God. Accept the pain. Moving through it is how we grow. Eventually, the pain will end."

I needed Pat but didn't call him. After Ireland, he'd "made boundaries" and forbade me from calling more than once a week. I was on day six. My fantasies wandered. Father Foley was only half an hour east. I could call him and feel someone's flesh. He would tell me he loved me. Father Scott was an hour away. He'd been calling and wanted to pick up where things had left off. I needed to preach about vocations at St. Stephen's. I owed the community. They'd thrown me the Mass of Thanksgiving. "It's the least you could do, Pastrone." He had no shame; he was worse than the Knights of Columbus. During seminary, they'd given me five hundred dollars per year, their standard "gift" to seminarians. In return, I now suffered through the meetings of their homophobic boys' club as chaplain. Nothing was free in the Church.

I called Mom and Dad instead. No change. Dad was at wit's end, worried Mom might hurt herself. She sounded like a breeze rustling through a hollowed tree after a lightning strike. The move to Des Moines and Dad's job loss had broken her.

"You have to get counseling," I said.

I wrote a funeral homily, read a chapter from *The Lord of the Rings* about Samwise carrying Frodo up Mount Doom, and went to bed.

Father Scott kept calling. On a day off between Halloween and the first winter storm, I gave in. We met for lunch at the new Panera in Cedar Falls.

"Pastrone!" He leapt from what looked like the tiniest table in the joint and gave me a bear hug before twisting my nipple. Just like old times. If I didn't resist, it would end sooner.

Over soup and salad, he filled me in on the happenings at St. Stephen's. I nodded and smiled. He'd aged, but he looked younger. His mustache and most of his belly weight were history. He'd quit biting his nails. His hair was silver; his skin, bronze. He still apologized that when he was tan, people believed he was getting out of the office and didn't badger him to take his day off. I thought it screamed, "I'm gay."

He pushed his empty plate aside. "So how are you?"

His brown eyes looked sincere. I couldn't tell my friends at seminary how priesthood sucked. My family was overwhelmed with Mom. Pat was stonewalling. I needed someone. I vented. The basement rectory was killing me; Father Frank was jovial but distant; and the abuse scandal and debate over the validity of gay men's ordinations had zapped my trust in the institution. I didn't tell him about Pat. He listened as he never had in our old meetings.

"I think I'm depressed," I said.

"Have you considered antidepressants?"

"I don't wanna be dependent on drugs to be happy."

His nose and eyebrows lifted into lecture mode. "Well, in my old priest support group, most guys were. Even the archbishop says that everyone's on medication." He waved his hands. I hated when he told me what to do. He must have sensed it, because he flared his nostrils and clicked into his nasal ghostlike voice: "Pastrooooone, Pastrooooone! Jesus loves you!" Other customers were staring. I laughed to shut him up.

The following Sunday, my phone started ringing. Folks from Cedar Falls called "just to check in." During the fourth conversation, I got angry and demanded to know why. At the Masses, Father Scott had announced that I was struggling in my priesthood and needed prayers. He'd used the information he'd gleaned during our lunch to show the community that we were best buds. He was an inspirational, holy pastor, not someone who would assault a penitent or blow a boy in a broom closet, and I was Father Tom Rastrelli, a product of Father Scott Bell, Vocation Seeder.

I shot him an email, castigating him for breaking a confidence and telling him to stay out of my life. He wrote back, begging forgiveness. He wanted to come to Cedar Rapids on Thursday for dinner, to "make it up" to me and to talk to me in person about something that he couldn't put in writing. He offered to get a hotel so as "not to disrupt things at the rectory."

"I told him that I'd hear him out one last time," I explained to Number Eleven.

"Why?" he said from his mossy chair.

"Because he'd hound me and guilt me until I gave in. I don't have the energy to fight him." I met Eleven's glaring lenses and admitted, "He's coming to have sex with me. I don't know if I can resist."

"Then you probably won't," he said without judgment.

"Will you be disappointed in me?"

"No. But is this what you want? To go back to where you were five, six years ago?"

I'd never known loneliness of the kind I experienced in my basement. No brother seminarians dropped in to chat or watch television. No spouse greeted me with a kiss. I held the grief of the family whose father died of a sudden heart attack. I felt the anguish of the woman with cancer who'd been starving to death for a month since coming off her feeding tube, a dignified death according to Vatican moralists. I had celibacy, the reality that I would never again know love and share my nightly burdens with the man I loved. My old life with Father Scott, no matter how abusive and wrong, seemed a dream by comparison.

"I don't know."

I put on the priest, went about my week, and focused on the positives. In the social concerns committee, we were making a difference at our sister parish in Haiti. I was planning a metro-wide Mass of healing for the victims of sexual abuse by clergy. An eighth-grade boy stopped in my office to tell me I'd inspired him to be a priest.

On Thursday, Father Frank and I celebrated reconciliation with the third graders. They were my favorites, fearless in their inquiry. "How does it work living forever in heaven?" one had asked during my weekly class. "Yeah. Wouldn't that get boring?" another rang in. "If God can do anything, then why do people get cancer?" "It's dumb that the pope won't let you get married. You'd be a great dad." One by one, the children stepped forward in the gymnasium and trusted Father Frank and me with their sins, just as I had trusted Father Scott on the Antioch retreat. After the last child had finished and Father Frank offered a final blessing, the class swarmed around us in a group hug.

I held on to that hug. It had to be enough. Having briefly known Pat's love had to be enough. The affirmation of my ordination weekend had to be enough. Father Scott would arrive after dark to test whether they were.

Then the rain turned to ice. The state patrol closed the interstate. For the first time since arriving at St. Jude's, I returned to my dungeon suite relieved.

QUICKENING THE FIRE IN OUR MIDST

I sloshed through the mud. In the darkness, I could barely distinguish the unpaved trail from the spiny bushes lining it. Down the ridge from the abbey where I was on retreat, the lights of Oceanside illuminated the low clouds. When I'd scheduled my trip, I thought I'd be trading February's subzero wind chills for California's sun. All week, El Niño torrents had pounded the blue metal roof of my guestroom in the cloister.

Since arriving, I'd written seventy-five pages in my journal. I'd read *The First Five Years of Priesthood*, a study of why priests leave ministry, hoping that it would encourage me to see how I could survive, but I had more in common with the guys who'd left ministry than those who remained. Seeking clarity, I ventured down the dark trail and dared the rains to return.

Distant voices grew louder. While I couldn't make out their words, I recognized their singsongy cadence, interrupted by beats of laughter. I'd heard that sound one continent away and seven months before, the sound of men in love. Two hooded monks emerged from a shadowed gazebo less than thirty feet away. Against the distant light of the city, the monks' silhouettes looked like small walking poplars. My mind wandered to fantasies of what they'd been doing. As they walked away, I castigated myself and begged Christ to clarify my vision. I pulled my soles from the sludge and stepped onto a dry patch. I stumbled and caught myself on one of the wooden shrines of the Stations of the Cross that dotted the trail. My eyes adjusted enough to read the station's title: *Jesus falls the third time.*

I had done the same in my celibacy: Father Scott, Father Foley, and Pat. My three falls. I should have quit seminary, but I'd trusted the lead of my counselors and spiritual directors. I'd remained silent in a system that rewarded me for hiding the truth of my being. Had I been honest, the seminary board never would have accepted me, but the affirmation had lured and assured me: "God's too present in your ministry for you not to be a priest." "God worked through your shame and your wounds to get you into the priesthood." "You are just a priest, who happens to be gay." "Your orientation is ancillary. It doesn't define you." I'd believed them. I'd needed to save myself by becoming a priest. The priests who'd formed me needed me to remain in the closet to justify their own vocations. The system had played me, and I'd let it.

A deluge burst from the clouds. The pair of monks darted for the cloister. I continued on to the tenth station, *Jesus is stripped of his garments.* Karl Rahner's theology flooded my mind: grace builds on nature. Underneath the trappings of Father Tom Rastrelli, I needed to love and be loved. It was not in my nature to be celibate. My three falls proved that. But maybe I could find the strength to be celibate if I knew that others loved me in spite of my being gay. Maybe if I exposed my nature, if the secret were out, it might lose its power. I had been so frightened of being rejected that whenever I confided in someone and they accepted me, I was bound to fall in love with them. Something had to change.

"I might come out of the closet to the archbishop," I said to Pat and Abdel as we walked the beach a week later. After my retreat concluded, they'd joined me in San Diego for their February break and my vacation.

"That's career suicide." Pat's voice was panicked; his skin, magma red. He halted. So did Abdel. The waves lapped their feet, stringing their toes with sand. "You're joking right?"

"I'm sick of living a lie. It's draining me," I said. Pat shook his head. Abdel squinted over the blinding surface of the water. "Haggis is supposed to be my shepherd. What's he gonna do? Throw me out?"

"Yes!" Pat extended his hands like he might strangle me. "Are you trying to throw your life away?"

"No. Jesus Christ. I'm just thinking about it." I'd done everything he'd demanded since Ireland. We'd spoken on the phone only once a week, when we prayed Night Prayer together. I hadn't come on to him. Still, he was paranoid I'd out him. "It's not like I'm gonna say, 'I'm here and I'm queer,' and confess all my sexual sins."

Pat admonished me with his eyes, as if I'd outed him to Abdel, as if Abdel would care. When I'd come out to Abdel months earlier, and he to me, the tension between us evaporated. I trusted his judgment more than Pat's, but Pat had forbidden me to talk to anyone about what had happened between us, especially Abdel. "What do you think, Abdel?"

He slid the ball of his foot over the water and flicked a splash out to sea. "Tommy, I understand your desire to be honest. I know the theology of a bishop's 'special relationship of mutuality' with his priests, but it doesn't work that way. You were just bitching about how you've only had one private meeting with him. A half hour."

"Twenty minutes."

Twenty minutes with the man to whom I'd sworn obedience.

We walked. Pat and Abdel's warnings blended with the churning of the waves. Maybe they were right. I'd only seen Archbishop Haggis once since ordination, at his Christmas party for the priests ordained in the past five years. He held the mandatory annual dinner as a way to show he cared about us. As in seminary, he'd granted each of us one question to ask. He still hadn't answered my years-old inquiry about his calling to the priesthood. After my ordination, he had smiled while handing me a card with his private number: "Use it anytime, *Father* Rastrelli." A few days later, I rang to thank him for the ordination reception and his moving homily. He said he was in the middle of a meeting and hung up.

On my retreat, I'd read *Quickening the Fire in Our Midst: The Challenge of Diocesan Priestly Spirituality.* Its author claimed: "Radiating from this special relationship with his bishop is the opportunity for a priest to put a personal face and presence on the institutional and hierarchical dimensions of the Church, which often seem very distant and coldly impersonal to people." The archbishop hadn't sent a single note in the months following the advent of the sexual abuse scandal. No "Are you OK?" No "I know you were a victim of sexual abuse. I'm here for you." Since the ordination, he'd emailed the priests to thank us for doing a great job in the shadow of the scandal. Once. But I was supposed to give him and the bishops exposed in the headlines a "personal face." I was supposed to trust him with my darkest secrets in the spirit of "mutuality."

He was supposed to be a brother and shepherd to me, just as priests were supposed to be a brother to their parishioners. But we were called "Father." We were supposed to be a spouse to the Church, which was also the Body of Christ. But the folks in the pews were also called the Church and the Body of Christ. That made me my parishioners' brother, father, and husband. Furthermore, at the altar, when I consecrated the bread and wine, the Body and Blood of Christ, I stood *in persona Christi capitis*—in the person of Christ the head—but the bishops were the head of the diocese, the pope was the head of the bishops, Christ was the head of the pope, and Christ was one of a triune Godhead. How many heads were on this beast called the Church? How could I be head one moment and foot the next? Wasn't it contradictory that we, the Body of Christ, were eating the Body of Christ at Mass? We were consuming ourselves. No wonder the archbishop had trouble being head-shepherd-brother-father to his priests. When put into practice, the ecclesiology that defined our roles was theological incest.

When I got home, I got a new haircut. The barber sheered the sides and back of my head to within a quarter inch of my scalp. Then he tapered the length to just over an inch and a half on top. I gelled my hair forward into a spiked, upward wave of the bangs. If I couldn't use words to come out, I'd use style.

"That's just Jacob being Jacob," Father Hunter said, when I vented about the archbishop's lack of response to the abuse scandal. He'd invited a few priests to his vacation home in the Galena Territory for an overnight. Over cocktails, I unloaded my struggles at St. Jude's and how Father Frank had laughed at me after my hellacious first week.

"If you were to be transferred to my parish, I would never laugh at you," Father Hunter said, sipping his Dewar's. He hadn't been the same since returning from his studies in Rome. He'd always had somewhat melancholy features, but now his cheeks had settled into jowls. His lips drooped in a constant frown. "My associate's term is up in July. I wouldn't protest were you to," he raised his tumbler, "come my way." After a swallow, he grinned. "By the way, I like the new haircut."

The following week, I spoke to the archbishop's intermediary for those in the first five years of priesthood, Father Dixon. Maybe I'd never recovered from my first week at St. Jude's. I couldn't judge the priesthood and my incapacity for happiness in Iowa by just one placement. I requested the transfer. Father Hunter assured me of his connections on the Priests' Advisory Board, the archbishop's select group of clerics that counseled him on parish assignments.

Back at St. Jude's, parishioners continued to praise my work and express gratitude for my presence. I felt like a hypocrite. Some still hounded Father Frank, hoping they'd get him to transfer. I was sympathetic to his plight. Because of the expenses of its school, the parish was more than two hundred thousand dollars in debt. The neighboring public schools were fantastic. It seemed wasteful to dump the majority of the parish's resources into a few hundred students while there were homeless folks coming to our door, people starving in our Haitian sister parish, and senior citizens in the pews who still had a third-grade understanding of sin and God.

Things outside the parish weren't better. More priests and bishops were removed from ministry for abuse. Mom and Dad started counseling. We waited for her meds to kick in. The United States became a first-strike nation by attacking Iraq and deposing Saddam Hussein. Our nation's leaders had violated the Church's just-war theory. I hoped Archbishop Haggis and the bishops would speak out against our invasion. As with the abuse scandal, I heard nothing.

When I received word in late March confirming my transfer, I felt hope for the first time since ordination. God (and Father Hunter) had given me a second chance at priesthood. Blindsided, Father Frank was apoplectic; the staff, devastated. We had a week to tell the parishioners before the news hit the archdiocesan paper.

After distributing Communion at the Saturday evening Mass, I sat in the presider's chair, flanked by child acolytes. In pews that wedged out from the sanctuary like a fan, St. Jude's congregation awaited the announcements. I closed my eyes. This was my favorite moment of Mass: five hundred men, women, and children joined in silence, basking in the afterglow of God's presence. I looked at them. When I stood for the post-Communion prayer, they would follow. There was no need for stage directions in this ancient dance.

"Please remain seated for the Communion prayer," I said. They obeyed, albeit with confused glances and mumbles. I stood, offered the prayer, and moved to the ambo. Some parishioners' faces filled with annoyance, fearing a second homily. I read: "It's with mixed emotions that I tell you this news. Effective July, I am being transferred—"

They gasped.

Over the next few months, they inundated me with cards, compliments, and Father Tom stories. It was like being at my own wake.

My guilt deepened. I self-medicated with fantasies of Pat. I lived from call to call, our weekly chat, my closing "I love you," and his hesitant "you too." I did my best not to appear needy or burden him with my problems. He spoke of possibly ending his friendship with Abdel because they didn't have enough in common and would be living so far apart after seminary. I was twice as distant from him as Abdel. I countered that the three of us were friends for life, that we'd invested too much time in our friendships to cast them away. Pat said, "Some people just won't let me cut them off."

In May, I took vacation and flew to Baltimore to assist Pat the week of his ordination, my way of thanking him for helping at mine. I wanted to recreate the hope we'd had when we'd promised to stick by each other come what may. He refused to put me to work. I read books in the rectory waiting for other guests to arrive.

Two weeks later, I rose with the sun and my first hangover. I'd been buzzed before, maybe even legally drunk at Father Hunter's parties, but I'd never woken up the next morning feeling like there was rubber cement in my joints and a sandbag in my skull. Limoncello was to be sipped, not tossed back, but the night before I would have done anything to dull the pain.

The old St. Mary's crowd was in upstate New York for Ryan's priesthood ordination, except for Abdel, who was being ordained a deacon in Massachusetts. He was irate that I'd chosen Ryan over him. I didn't blame him. I'd abandoned Abdel to be with Pat, but Pat had avoided me for two days, hanging instead with two young and handsome newbies with the same first name. To get into Pat's good graces, I'd done as he asked and chauffeured his parents around. When I asked whether we could talk, he'd say, "Stop being so clingy."

As I rolled out of bed in the unair-conditioned retreat house, I regretted everything. I should have gone to Abdel's. I should have stopped after the second shot. I smelled fresh coffee. Pat was likely the only one up. I ambled to the kitchenette, poured a cup, and found him outside on a bench next to the door, mug in hand, closed breviary in his lap.

"Good morning," I said.

He rolled his eyes, set down his mug, and opened his breviary. "You can't even let me pray in peace."

The dew glistened on the barbed-wire fence lining the neighboring field. Didn't he realize that his life was about to change, that the parish would rob him of all autonomy, that parishioners would spy him grocery shopping and comment on his choice of toilet paper, and that last-minute funerals would supersede long-planned vacations? Why couldn't he just be with me, like at the beach, when we'd snuggled on the back porch in the thunderstorm? We didn't have to talk.

I said, "We could pray together."

He slammed his breviary shut. "You need to stop."

"What?"

"Suffocating me."

Fuck. I needed a clearer head for this conversation. I tasted my coffee. "I just wanted to talk."

"Haven't we *talked* enough?" He tossed his book on the bench. "Normal people go weeks or months without talking to friends, but with you it's constant. Exhausting."

The dew dripped from the fence onto the grass. A mourning dove cooed. I wanted to gaze in his eyes, to tell him I loved him. But he'd be repulsed and leave. "I'm sorry. It's just you're all out here on the coast while I'm stuck in Iowa."

"Then bug your friends there."

"Normal friends don't schedule monthly conversations. They just call." He looked away. Shit. I hadn't come to hurt him. "I'm sorry, Pat, but we're more than just friends."

He stared at the ground and said, "I never loved you differently than my other friends. You were physically attracted to me. I wanted to see what it would be like. It was just an experiment, a sin that I regret."

The fence and the field twirled. I felt like I was spinning from the planet. I wanted to wrap myself in the barbed wire so I wouldn't float away.

He'd said that I'd kissed his soul. He'd lied.

I returned to St. Jude's a hopeless cause. Pat had ordered me not to call; he'd email when he was ready to talk. I slogged through the days cracking jokes, making others laugh. In the evenings, I attended goodbye suppers. When I returned to the basement, I emptied the dehumidifier and stewed in my rejected love. I "imitated the mystery," letting the pain consume me as it had Christ on the cross.

I emerged a week and half later with a sense of peace. Pat was calling. Next to the bed, I waited on the floor in my prayer space. Scribbling nightly in my leather-bound journal, I'd hashed out our relationship, every bad choice I'd made. In the pain, I found clarity, a way to rebuild our friendship. Knowing his love for a moment, even though he now denied its reality, was enough. Its memory had to sustain me for the remainder of my celibate life. The rest was for God. I could move on and be chaste. I could respect and care for Pat as a friend. I'd rewritten these realizations into a letter that would heal everything.

My new cellphone rang. Eleven had advised me to purchase it to sustain connections with my seminary friends. "Hello."

"Hi, Tom. It's Pat." As if I didn't know the sound of his voice.

We exchanged news of our families and friends. The muscles in my chest became so tight that I thought my ribs would implode. Clutching my journal, I read him the letter. He listened without interruption. I asked for another chance at friendship in whatever capacity he could offer. Hanging over my prayer space, the icon of Christ sending the disciples forth two by two soothed me. "We aren't meant to serve God alone, Pat. We're in this together."

"Are you done?" he said.

"Yeah."

"Thanks for sharing that, but I called tonight to tell you I'm cutting you off." The icon blurred. "I have to protect my priesthood, my celibacy." He spoke mechanically, as if he'd been coached. "I can't do that with you in my life. Don't call or write. You can be better than this, Tom. I want you to be the priest God called you to be. Goodbye."

My final weekend at St. Jude's, I preached about our common wound: the inability to love purely, and thus we hurt those we cherish most. In spite of our imperfect love, God worked through us. Our fear of being unlovable was our greatest weakness; self-loathing, our greatest sin. God loved us in our brokenness and would use it to renew the earth.

In the vestibule after Mass, an elderly man grasped my biceps and locked onto my eyes. He was crying. "Thank you, Father. For the first time in my life, I finally understand what it means to be Catholic."

When I returned to the sacristy to prepare for the next Mass, I looked in the mirror. The green vestments, the rimless glasses, the tired blue eyes, the smile and dimpled chin: a priest people loved stared back at me. But I saw a lustful faggot with a trashed heart. I'd come to respect myself as holy, good, and a gift from God. That was bullshit. Pat didn't love me. God didn't love me. The hypocrite in the mirror deserved to be alone.

PART V

RESURRECTION

2003–4

Thomas, called Didymus, one of the
Twelve, was not with them when
Jesus came.—John 20:24

SACRED SILENCE

Father Hunter promenaded through the furniture warehouse like an aristocratic museum docent. He showcased options for my sitting room chair. "This one looks comfortable. After all, we want Resurrection to feel like your home," he said. "Unlike Father Frank, I don't keep my associates chained in a dungeon." He ran his fingers over a taupe recliner. "How do you feel about leather?"

"Is it more expensive?"

He swallowed a laugh. "Just pick what you like."

I'd never been furniture shopping. I just wanted something that matched the cream couch with burgundy dots I'd inherited from the previous associate.

When I'd arrived in the morning, Hunter greeted me with a hug before ushering me through the office as if I were a war hero. He gave my movers, some folks from St. Stephen's, a tour. A pragmatic post–Vatican II edifice, Resurrection crowned one of the large hills on the west side of Dubuque. Locals likened the landscape to the Seven Hills of Rome. Created in the 1970s to accommodate the suburban expansion of baby boomers, Resurrection had grown to more than two thousand families. The chapel was a cheap precursor to St. Jude's. From a drab sanctuary that lacked statues the raked pews fanned out through the nave to brown brick walls. A hallway led from the back corner to the rectory. The offices were below the priests' bedroom suites. After I'd spent the afternoon unpacking, Hunter feted me with a homemade Italian feast. He'd joshed that the reason he'd brought me to Resurrection was the cutlery discount he could get from my dad. We'd split a bottle of wine and chatted like old times, but after I tested the eighteenth recliner, his joviality waned.

We still had to get new linens at K-Mart. "I don't want you sleeping in sweat-soaked sheets feeling unappreciated," he said, furrowing his thin, black eyebrows. As I tested the top three candidates, I realized he was observing me, using the furniture as a Rorschach test. I chose the least expensive La-Z-Boy with burgundy upholstery, something my grandpa would pick. I didn't want Hunter thinking I put my comfort before parish finances.

He sighed, "Are you absolutely sure?"

"If I say no, you'll slap me." I hopped up. "This is the one."

"Thank God. We can still make the Second Coming."

This banter, this camaraderie, was exactly what I needed to resurrect my priesthood. Later, I knelt at my bedside, rested my elbows on my starchy new bedding, and thanked God for a fresh start.

I unpacked boxes in my office, one of seven that stretched the length of the rectory's underbelly. It had been the previous pastor's office, but Father Hunter didn't want it, for it housed the parish's closet-sized, fireproof safe. To retrieve checks, cash, sacramental records, and other valuables, the secretary and business manager constantly entered. The computer faced away from the door, protecting its onscreen information. My seminary professors would have commended the previous associate, Father Lessing, for creating "a pastoral space with appropriate boundaries."

Jumbled icons crowded the computer's desktop—Hunter had warned that Lessing was unorganized. I opened Internet Explorer to reset the homepage and insert my links. A list dropped down with folders entitled *Adult Sites* and *Free Adult Content*. Below these were fifteen or so websites named things like *Hot Boys*, *Teen 69*, and *Young, Hung and Full of Cum*.

I buzzed Hunter. After closing my door, he joined me at the computer.

"You need to see this." I scrolled down the Favorites.

"Dear Lord." He pointed at the questionable folders. "What do these open into?"

I clicked one. It opened an alphabetized list of subfolders ranging from *Anal*, *Animals*, and *Asians* to *Watersports* and *Young*.

"Holy shit," I said. "I don't even know what half of these mean." I wondered what *Watersports*, *Felching*, and *Rimming* were. Other folders, such as *Groups*, *Jack Off*, and *Cumshots*, were more obvious. Folders like *Teen Hardcore* frightened me. I didn't care if priests jacked off to adult porn, but child porn was another issue.

Hunter scanned the subfolders, which opened into lists of links to what appeared to be porn sites and chat rooms. I refused to click on them, afraid something illegal might pop up. Investigating the properties of the Favorites file, we found 159 websites in thirty-one folders and subfolders. Four shortcut icons graced the computer's "Start Menu" with naked graphics: *Live Boys*, *Live Girls*, *Cashgold*, and *Naughty Strip Player*. The dates the questionable materials were created fell within Lessing's stint at Resurrection.

"What should we do?" Hunter said.

I couldn't believe he was asking me. Before failing to finish his dissertation, Hunter had been on the way up. He worked in the chancery for a decade. His office had been two doors from Haggis. More than anyone, he should have known what to do.

"We call the police," I said. "Give them the hard drive. Let them deal with it." In response to the sexual abuse scandal, the American bishops had promulgated the Dallas Charter. It prescribed that information about priests breaking child-sex laws must be relinquished to secular authorities. The days of cover-up in the name of the good-old-boys' club were over.

"It's too soon for that," Hunter said. He dialed the archbishop's chancellor, but she didn't know what to do. He slammed the phone, "Worthless bitch."

"What the hell, Jim? I mean, they're supposed to handle shit like this. We need to call the police."

"It's too soon. I'll handle it," he said with a wave of his hand. He called in the office manager. She had cropped gray hair, a smoker's growl, and a glare that could silence a giggly altar boy. She confessed. Father Lessing had asked her to remove pornographic icons from his desktop. He'd claimed computer incompetence, porno ex nihilo.

"Shut it down," Hunter said. "I'll speak to Father Lessing tonight."

He withdrew to his quarters for a smoke. I recorded what had occurred. When the police finally got involved, I wanted them to know we weren't hiding anything.

After a committee meeting and another Hunter-cooked meal, I leaned against the rectory kitchen's celadon countertop, sipping Irish whiskey, Hunter's welcome gift. He paced, tethered to the wall by the phone cord, scotch neat in hand. Lessing's mumbling emanated from the phone.

"You can tell me the truth, Bob," Hunter said. "My concern is your welfare. You've been under stress. You lost a toe to diabetes. We make mistakes when we're not well." As Lessing responded, Hunter rolled his dark eyes, before mouthing *blah, blah, blah.* I wondered how he could sound sincere while looking so sinister. "The fetishes and paraphiliae on your computer indicate a tortured soul. I only want you to figure out who you are. To be at peace."

Lessing admitted nothing.

In the days that followed, the liturgist, a boyish fellow in his midtwenties, admitted he'd walked into Lessing's office and seen him looking at a pornographic picture. Lessing claimed middle-aged computer illiteracy and asked the liturgist to remove the image. I found this strange, because the computer now refused to display any images, showing instead a blank window containing a small red X. Lessing asserted that one of the teenaged phone sitters, who worked the front office during the evening, must have trespassed, or that an outsider had hacked the machine. The archbishop's staff dispatched two computer experts to investigate. Both failed to determine a cause, but they did show me that right-clicking on a red X and selecting "Show Picture" did exactly that. It seemed Lessing knew more about adjusting computer settings than he claimed. Hunter's sources at Lessing's new parish reported that he'd purchased a private computer for his rectory the morning after Hunter confronted him on the phone. We needed to call the police, but I obediently held my tongue, waiting for the archbishop to decide Lessing's fate.

I turned on the computer only to check email. Windows and websites popped up like Marian apparitions: *Gay Cam Tour*, *Find a Gay Lover in Your Area*, *Wanna Get Laid Tonight*, *Enlarge Now*, *Gay Super Cocks.* One pop-up contained previously entered information: "User name: Mondale. Password: w977j." LilAngel424 had been begging Mondale to meet. I recorded the time, title, and text of each intrusion before closing it down. The office manager signed each update as a witness.

After nine days, the archbishop's second-in-command phoned. He commanded me to disconnect the hard drive and lock it in the safe. I followed his orders, assuming we were securing it for the police. A few weeks later, the chancery's computer expert arrived and erased the drive.

"I can't believe they just wiped it," I said to Hunter.

He paused from his cooking at the stove and poured me another drink. "Let it go."

He'd invited Father Scott, now head of campus ministry at nearby Loras College, for supper. Even though we hadn't spoken in months, Father Scott and I played our parts in Hunter's drama, razzing each other like old buddies.

Throughout the night, Hunter refilled my tumbler. House rule dictated that he prepare the spirits. Mixers were scorned; ice, tolerated. Whenever I said I was done drinking because I had the seven o'clock Mass in the morning, he offered to preside over it if I had another. He felt alienated from the archbishop, maybe because of the computer incident, more likely because he'd been passed over for monsignor—an apparent punishment for not completing his dissertation. He needed the support, and I'd do anything to avoid waking at five-thirty to prepare for Mass.

Father Scott nagged me to preach about vocations at Loras and visit his new house, a Craftsman across the street from the campus. "Why wouldn't you?" Hunter asked. Father Scott smiled; he knew that Hunter suspected our sordid bond. To avoid looking guilty, I had to accept.

When I visited the campus, a fair-haired freshman boy trailed Father Scott like an acolyte. I was furious. My spiritual director said this was "another layer of forgiveness" I had to offer Father Scott. "It's all about letting go." Over the years, Father Scott, Father Hunter, Father Quinn, Number Ten, various spiritual directors, and Pat had told me that coming out of the closet was hubris. After the computer incident and Pat's rejection, I was done silencing my integrity.

"Before you go, I have to tell you something. In private," I said to my younger sister, Maria. Our extended family mingled about the rectory, enjoying Dad's homemade ravioli and tomato sauce. Hunter sauntered about cracking jokes and refreshing drinks. We had gathered in Dubuque for my nephew Timothy's baptism. My siblings had all moved to the West Coast. We hadn't been together since my ordination and might not be for another year. The weekend had rushed by, a blur of toasts, homilies, meals, and sacramental rites.

I closed the door to my sitting room. Maria and I sat on the dotted couch. Framed by long brown hair, her hazel eyes widened with concern. I inhaled and said, "I have a primarily homosexual orientation."

I hadn't wanted to ruin the gathering by coming out, but I needed to tell my siblings in person and before my parents. During my teens, at the height of the AIDS epidemic, Dad had made comments at the dinner table about "immoral gays" stopping by the restaurant to lobby for condom machines in the bathrooms. In the nineties, Jenny had commented how Dad's new sales friends were homophobic. If he freaked out when I told him, Mom would need my sisters' support. Maria looked confused by the awkward seminaryspeak of my proclamation. I clarified: "I'm gay."

She smiled, "I've known for years."

I said, "I've known since preschool."

We laughed and hugged. Everything was changing, and for the better. She and her husband, Gabe, were expecting their first child. Jenny and Mike had two beautiful sons. Jeff had landed his first job out in San Diego. Mom was healthy again. She and Dad were making things work in Des Moines. And I was being honest.

Later, after Mom and Dad had left with Maria, I sat around a coffee table with Jenny, Mike, and Jeff reminiscing. Despite two C-sections, Jenny still had a figure from when she was crowned America's Homecoming Queen. Mike's quarterback build had morphed into an electrical engineer's potbelly. Jeff had transformed from a frumpy video game fanatic into a chiseled surfer. After I said, "I'm homosexual," they took turns hugging me, as if I'd won a beauty pageant. Smiling through tears, Jenny said, "Thanks for trusting us. I love you. I'm proud of you." Jeff, stoic as always, patted my back saying, "You're my brother. This changes nothing." After giving me a quick hug, Mike said, "You're celibate. So really, it's a nonissue."

It wasn't a nonissue when Hunter invited a redheaded former seminarian from my time at Loras to dinner. The ex-sem was visiting from Chicago—"the Lakeview area," Hunter had informed me, as if that was supposed to mean something. Hunter presided over the festivities from the head of the rectory's stretched dining room table, the spot closest to the kitchen. And the bar. Toddies and wine ranneth over, but I couldn't relax. I sat to his left across from the ex-sem and his boyfriend.

Outside a brilliant thunderstorm flashed over the low-pitched silhouette of the chapel. The chandelier flickered.

"If this keeps up," Hunter said, "the two of you will have to spend the night."

"I don't know, Jim," the ex-sem said. "Does the guestroom have a deadbolt?"

Hunter guffawed. "Touché."

They clanked their glasses and drank. My face warmed with the alcohol. The jokes grew funnier. We recalled the crazy priests that we'd survived at Loras. The ex-sem's hair was the color of fire; his skin, the purest snow. Why wasn't I attracted to him? He lamented having a crush on the Columbian soccer player who'd lived a few doors down from us in the dorm. Why hadn't I been hot for guys like them instead of Father Scott and Father Foley?

The ex-sem chewed the last of his filet. "Tom, you should come visit us." He swallowed. "You'd love Boystown. Right Jim?"

Hunter swirled the crimson wine in his glass. "I'm sure Father Rastrelli would appreciate . . . the architecture."

They chuckled. Hunter smirked at me. I wanted to throw my drink on him but joined the laughter instead, hoping to deflect attention. I felt like I was back in Ocean City with Father Stout and the two Bens. Why did I always feel like such a doofus around gay men? I drained my wine. Hunter opened another bottle.

"Is it weird being among priests?" I asked the ex-sem's boyfriend, trying to include him.

"Not really," he said. "I mean, we're all, like, human and all."

They babbled about Chicago's restaurants and bars. Hunter seemed to know the area quite well and repeatedly promised to take them out when he visited. Hail smacked the windows. I got up to look outside. The room spun. I grabbed the back of my chair.

"Jesus, Tom," the ex-sem snickered. "How can you still be a lightweight after living with Jim?"

Hunter paraded to the bar. "He handles his celibacy better than his alcohol."

"Damn right," I said. "I'm celibate. And I need to go to bed. I have Mass at seven."

"In the morning?" the boyfriend asked.

"Yeah."

"Shit, man," he said. "Early mornings, no sex, I could never be a priest."

"Come on, Tom," the ex-sem leaned over the table, "stay. When do we ever get to hang out?"

Hunter returned with the after dinner liqueurs. "I'll take the Mass for you." He poured me a sambuca, some brand he'd brought back from Italy especially for me.

I wobbled back to my seat. "I'll stay. But I'm taking the Mass, Jim."

"Your choice." He slid me the snifter.

I rolled out of bed at one-thirty in the afternoon, threw on my flannel sleep pants and made my way into the kitchen. Hunter tromped in, "Well, good afternoon, Father. You were sure lit last night. Hilarious. I don't think I've ever seen you so animated."

I set the milk on the counter. "I'm disgusted with myself. This morning, I had Mass with a hangover."

His soft hand patted my shoulder. He sounded like a mother cooing to a child after a nightmare as he said, "Don't worry. You'll get used to it."

HOMOSEXUALITY IN THE CHURCH

In the months that followed, those words lingered like Hunter's second-hand smoke. Ten had long ago advised me to behave like a happy priest and happiness would follow; I would get used to the pain of losing Pat. Perhaps Hunter's celibacy by anesthesia was the true way.

I stopped drinking with him. Over the dinner hour, I scheduled pre-marriage counseling appointments, accepted meal invitations, puttered around town after visiting the hospitals, worked out at the gym, and walked along the river rehearsing my homilies. Anything to avoid the rectory.

A mother of four sat in my office. She had the pristine makeup of a Mary Kay consultant, but her eyes were like weathered stone. She said, "Father, after hearing you preach, I don't think you'll judge me. Can I go to confession?" She confessed unquenchable anger. "I'm even mad at you. With what you preached on Sunday. God doesn't answer prayers."

She was right. How long had I been praying to be straight, get over Pat, and find peace in celibacy?

"You sound like you've lost hope," I said.

"I have lung cancer." She laughed. "I never smoked. But it's terminal."

Hunter's secondhand smoke clung to the air like bad incense.

"That's terrible news," I said. "So unfair."

She crossed her arms and stared out the window. I wasn't surprised that she'd requested confession. The most common "sin" I'd heard people confess was anger.

"It's not a sin to be mad, Janice. Your anger is justified. It's a healthy response to this god-awful situation. Does that make sense?" She nodded, still staring out the window. "How's your family?"

She described how her husband had abused her since their wedding night. This was why she'd requested the sacrament; she wanted the seal of the confessional so I couldn't report him. "I haven't told him. One more reason for him to yell at me." Tears spotted her rose blouse. "What's going to happen to my kids?"

I searched my files for counseling referrals and pamphlets on cancer, dying, and spousal abuse. It was my job to offer some semblance of peace or hope, but with each suggestion, she became quieter. The more I tried, the more her face contorted with fury.

"Do you want me to stop?"

She nodded.

I absolved her and asked if she wanted to be anointed. She sobbed. I chastised myself. "I apologize. We don't have to talk about that now."

She blotted her eyes with a tissue. "Thank you, Father." She stood and straightened the wrinkles from her blouse. "I have to get back to work now."

"Can I call in a few days to check in?"

"Not at home, please. Only at work." She pulled a business card from her red leather purse. "Don't leave a message. That'll just make things worse."

I extended my hand. "Call or stop by anytime."

Her arms remained crossed.

"Janice, I know you feel alone. Please know that I'm here for you."

She shook her head and walked into the sun's afternoon glare.

I wandered up to the rectory in a daze. Hunter stood at the kitchen counter, flipping through mail. "Taking another break?" he said.

"Tough confession." I poured a glass of water.

"That's ministry," he said. His glasses flashed under the fluorescent lighting as he passed me a long, crinkled receipt. "I'm not paying for these."

The stains of discarded coffee grounds peppered the receipt. He'd pulled it from the trash. We paid for groceries with gift cards purchased by the business manager. I hadn't been instructed to save receipts. He'd outlined tissue, soap, all of the toiletries.

"I thought the parish paid for our room and board."

"Not your inedible personal items." His voice was velvety, as it had been when he'd spoken to Lessing on the phone. "We don't want Father taking advantage of the parishioners' good will. Do we?"

"Of course not, Jim." I wondered if his Dewar's was on the parish's tab. I set the soiled list on the counter. "I'm just surprised. This wasn't an issue at St. Jude's."

He whipped his mail on the counter and clenched his fists. "If I were Frank, this parish would be bankrupt." My heart raced as he brushed past me into his quarters and slammed the door.

That night, when I called my St. Mary's friends seeking support, no one answered. I stared at the ceiling over my bed, wondering how easily the lock to my suite could be picked.

"He's searching the trash," I said to Father Dixon in our "early formation" check-up. As director of the newly ordained, he served as the archbishop's go-between. Since becoming my superior at Loras, he'd been climbing the ecclesial ladder. He now held two of Hunter's former positions.

"He's just testing you. That's what Jim does," he said. "Do you have to turn in your receipts to the business manager?"

"No."

"Then trash them on the way out of the store."

Days later, I sat at my desk writing a homily for a nursing home Mass. Hunter charged in. Brandishing a piece of paper, he towered over me like the Grand Inquisitor. "I'm not paying for you to commiserate with your friends in Maryland!" He smacked the phone bill on my desk. He'd circled seven of my calls in red. Three were to Ellicott City, a suburb of Baltimore. "Isn't that what your precious cell phone is for? How do you explain this?"

After I ceased drinking with him, he seemed to loathe anything about me that he couldn't control. I paid for the cell phone so he couldn't monitor my private calls or interrupt my day off. Following my meeting with Dixon, Hunter had mentioned that his contacts had seen me at the chancery. He'd pretended to know more than he did in an attempt to wring information from me. Each day was a hunt to catch me in a hypocritical lie. "Explain this," he commanded of the phone calls.

I surged with adrenaline and concentrated on my breathing, what Father Dixon had told me to do: *When he makes outrageous statements, be very direct with him. Confront him in the moment.* I retrieved a marriage preparation file from my desk, opened it and pointed at the number to a couple's parish in Ellicott City. "I've been calling their priest to discuss premarriage requirements."

He tore the bill from my hand and pointed at four Iowa numbers. "Account for these."

My damn face blushed. "I'm trying to join a priest support group. Come on, Jim, you know the archbishop requires this. Those were business calls."

He tossed the bill in my face. "I won't pay for your personal bullshit." He stomped upstairs into the rectory. The ceiling shook with the crash of his door.

I wrote the apologetic business manager a check for the calls: $1.78.

"I feel like Jim pulled the bait and switch," I said to Dixon on my phone. "He manipulated me to get here, and now he's punishing me for not drinking with him. I think he's an alcoholic."

"The alcohol is Jim's issue. Not yours," he said. "You have to focus on your own needs. Take your days off. How's your prayer life?"

The archdiocese guaranteed priests one evening and the following calendar day off each week, but Hunter claimed I could only be away for a single twenty-four-hour block. He always demanded to know where I was going. I refused: "The secretary has my cell phone number. Unless there's a fire or you're in the ER, it can wait until I'm back."

On workdays, I retreated to my quarters after the 7 a.m. Mass for an hour of prayer. Hunter chided that this was self-centered. One day, he chewed me out after discovering that I'd answered my cell during this time. I'd taken a call from a friend with whom I was trying to start a priest support group. Hunter was combing our mutual friends for information. I began censoring what I shared with those friends.

After spiritual direction and mentor appointments—things I was required to do—he'd say things like "With all the time you spend away, one would never know that Res was your community." In front of parishioners, he'd say: "Father Rastrelli is always gone." "You know Father

Rastrelli needs his prayer time." "Does anyone know his cell phone number?" "He puts his friends first." And "You'd think I worked here alone."

"Am I a bad priest?" I asked Father Dixon.

"No. You're doing well," he said. "Keep your guard up."

Hunter took September to finish his dissertation at his vacation home in the Galina Territory. The funerals, weddings, confessions, anointings, homilies, committee meetings, school Masses, and so on fell to me.

But he never left.

During the day, he scoured storage closets and rearranged furniture. He scrubbed the kitchen cabinets and alphabetized the spices. Whenever he had an idea, he barged into the office, assigning employees more projects. Then he disappeared into his quarters for days. When we passed in the kitchen, I smelled alcohol. The next week, he didn't sleep and poked around the office all night. When I returned from a movie or a pastoral emergency, he assigned more chores. If anyone inquired about his departure date or the paper, he became petulant.

One weekend, I had a wake and wedding rehearsal on Friday night. On Saturday, I presided at a morning Mass, funeral, and wedding before hearing confessions and preaching the two Saturday evening Masses. On Sunday, I had three Masses, baptisms, and an evening wake. Monday morning, the regular Mass was followed by a funeral. In seminary, I'd been instructed to spend one hour of preparation for each minute of preaching. Therefore, the weekend's eight homilies should have taken an estimated fifty-five hours to write and rehearse. It became clear that seminary was bullshit, especially its prescriptions about professional boundaries and conflict management with one's pastor.

Toward the end of the month, Hunter wandered barefoot into the kitchen, dressed in an undershirt and boxers. His pupils were glassy. I looked up from my scripture commentary and sandwich. "Hey, Jim."

He rubbed his eyes, poured some coffee, and said, "Why did you move the living room's furniture around last night?"

"I didn't."

"Well neither did I," he sneered. "Shouldn't you be working?" He withdrew to his room with the usual slam.

A few weeks later, the wheeled cart in the utility room began migrating around the rectory at night. He blamed me: "You're a prolific night wanderer."

One afternoon, when I took out the trash, a gallon-sized Dewar's bottle bulged against the bottom of garbage bag. September passed. He failed to finish the dissertation.

I didn't fail in my mission to come out to my parents. On the cool leather couch of their family room, I told them. They weren't angry or sad, as I'd expected, but asked: "How long have you known?" and "Can you still be a priest?" I quoted my notes from seminary and explained that my orientation was only one facet of my larger sexual-relational being. They assured me that they loved me.

In the weeks that followed, Mom had discovered a pair of rainbow-vision goggles. Every single man was suspect. She said, "He's never been married. Do you think," she fell into a whisper, "he's gay?" Dad and I went to a bookstore and rummaged through the gay and lesbian section until we found him a book to explain everything: *Straight Parents, Gay Children*. I searched for titles about the coming-out process. It was time to learn what noncelibate homosexuals had to say.

As we walked across the parking lot, I said, "That was a historic Rastrelli moment."

Dad put his arm around me and said, "A proud Rastrelli moment."

Back in priesthood-land, I held on to that moment. Gene Robinson had been appointed the first openly gay bishop of the Episcopal Church. In Vermont, civil unions granted legal recognition to gay couples. In Canada, same-sex couples had won their equal marriage rights. In Massachusetts, a case that could declare marriage equality for gays and lesbians worked its way through the courts. In response, the Vatican and Cardinal Ratzinger issued a new document, condemning all political actions to legitimize any sort of committed homosexual "marriage." Even civil unions and domestic partnerships were damned. Maybe they were worried we'd all couple off and leave the priesthood. Being gay was so utterly "disordered" that the Church even condemned homosexuals' right to adopt children.

On Mondays, I taught in Resurrection's school. A fourth grader asked, "Why does the Church hate my gay uncle?" Eighth graders challenged the Church for "picking on gay couples." I responded with what I was ordained to teach: the Church didn't hate gay people and wasn't discriminating against them. The Church was upholding its moral teaching that all sex must be open to procreation and within the confines of marriage. Since homosexual couples were incapable of producing children, they couldn't get married. That didn't mean the Church hated them. Then I tried to change the subject.

Parents asked me to council their freckled son because he was being bullied for "being different." Adults and teens tearfully confessed being gay. Men confessed "self-abuse," "touching the naughty place," "physically pleasuring myself to emission," or whatever euphemisms they conjured. I responded, "So you masturbated." I spoke about sex as if it wasn't something to be feared. Instead of worrying about hell, the octogenarian who weekly confessed jacking off to late night movies on cable should have been praising God that everything still worked. But that wasn't Church teaching.

I helped straight couples to get annulments so they could be remarried in the Church. I tried to convince a divorcee that the Church didn't classify her children as bastards. One husband and father of eight confessed that he was going to lie to his children about an upcoming business trip; he was really traveling to have a reverse vasectomy. According to the Church, he and his wife were living in a state of sin. Their union was no longer "life giving" because they'd closed the marriage bed to "the possibility of procreation." I explained the primacy of conscience in Catholic moral theology. In his case, raising his children on a menial salary while giving money to charities and volunteering as a family for social outreach opportunities, revealed his marriage was significantly life giving. If he took his marriage and the pending surgery to prayer and found peace in his conscience that his marriage was already life giving, then he didn't need to reverse the vasectomy. He had the surgery. His wife was in her forties.

No matter how hard I tried to be a pastoral voice of reason, my hands were bound by the Church's medieval sexual teachings. I fell into depression.

Hunter's jabs bruised more deeply. He made "dyke" comments about the kindergarten teacher. He speculated on the orientation of married male parishioners. When I asked him to stop, he'd said things like, "Well, I figured you were interested in your own kind."

Each weekend, he pointed out how a certain woman enjoyed pushing "her perky breasts" against him when hugging after Mass. When an overweight mother and grandmother came for help because their (grand) daughter needed a risky lifesaving surgery, he dumped them on me claiming they were "white trash." He referred to one parishioner as "that old-maid bitch." Her picture was on our refrigerator. During my Masses, he stood in the vestibule and toyed with those who left after Communion, forcing them to shake his hand and wishing them a joyous premature exit. He joked about this among the staff and council members.

"He says that I don't care, that I'm deceiving the parish, when he's the guilty one," I said to Father Dixon.

"Focus on yourself, Tom," he said. "On your ministry. On what feeds you."

Nothing did.

Hunter finally left to work on the dissertation in November. He left me the duty of preaching a series of homilies about the revised *General Instruction for the Roman Missal*—the roadmap to Catholic calisthenics: when we sat, stood, and knelt at Mass. In the midst of the continuing sexual abuse headlines, the American bishops deemed these liturgical adjustments our national focus.

The weekend Hunter returned, I preached about reverence, venerating one another as Christ did us. I worked in the new prescriptions for genuflecting. To lighten the mood, I manically genuflected before each of the dozen folks in the front pew. During the announcements, Hunter quipped: "I'm shocked Father Rastrelli graduated from seminary. Even nursery school children know to genuflect on the right knee." Everyone laughed. Some joshed me on their way out. I smiled along. No need to "scandalize the faithful" by airing my aggravation with Hunter.

After Sunday's Masses, I sped across the frozen cornfields, needing to feel warmth. Pat wouldn't take my call, but Father Foley did. He welcomed me with a hug. After a drink, we migrated to his bedroom and thrust against each other's bellies. I imagined Pat. I kissed his neck. I felt his chest hair. The ecstasy erupted and passed. As I drove back to the parish, guilt and repulsion consumed me. I was no better than Hunter and the duplicitous clerics ruining the Church.

I didn't tell Father Dixon about Foley. I called the lead that he'd given me for a priest support group.

My sleep became restless. My appetite waned. My eyes twitched. Jenny and Mike invited everyone to San Diego for Christmas. I couldn't go. During my first week in the parish, Hunter required me to schedule my coming year's vacations; I hadn't known to list the week after Christmas. I was stuck in Iowa. With him.

Depressed, I sat at the rectory's breakfast table, trying to eat despite my lack of appetite. Each bite triggered my gag reflex, but I forced myself to chew and swallow. Hunter swept in with an empty tumbler. We hadn't spoken privately in a week, not since he'd railed about my improper genuflection.

"You look like hell," he said. He reached below the counter for the Dewar's.

I slammed my spoon on the table. My face burned. This was it.

His dark eyes were soft, his posture relaxed. He looked like the Hunter of my college days. "Are you OK?" he asked tenderly. "You know you can talk to me."

Great. If I confronted him now, he'd play the martyr.

"My parents might move west. Everyone's going to California for Christmas."

At the next staff meeting during "New Business," he announced, "Father Rastrelli's family is abandoning him for Christmas."

After the meeting, I smacked on his door. "We need to talk," I said, trying not to yell.

He looked up and smiled. "Indeed we do. In gratitude for your work while I was away writing, why don't you take the days after Christmas to be with your family?"

There had to be a catch. I didn't care. I stuffed my anger and sold my soul for the vacation.

As I turned to leave, he said, "Schedule your return before New Year's Eve. I'll be off to Chicago for a few days."

The priest support group invited me to join. At my first meeting around Thanksgiving, I told the five of them about Hunter. "It's like he can smell my rage festering. Every time I'm about to confront him, he does something kind. That way, he's the one being wronged. A few weeks later, he berates me again. I feel like a battered wife."

"How's his drinking?" the eldest member, with a thick, graying beard, asked.

I sat in Hunter's office with a legal pad covered with commands he'd dictated in our weekly scheduling meeting. As we concluded, he let it drop that we were having two daily Masses each weekday during Advent, the four-week season of anticipation and preparation for Christmas. This meant we'd have to take a 7 a.m. Mass before leaving on our days off. No overnights.

"But we need to pace ourselves for the frenetic pace of the season," I said.

Because folks wanted their souls to be as clean as Christmas morning snow, the number of confessions a priest heard during Advent increased a hundredfold. Priests survived this penitential onslaught by banding together for communal reconciliation services. In addition, the music and liturgy planning meetings multiplied. Holidays brought out people's depression. Family conflicts exploded. More people seemed to die. And everyone wanted Father at every party.

"Jim, we're going to need our time away."

He scribbled the additional Masses into his datebook and said, "Any decent priest would support an increase in daily Mass attendance during Advent." On one of my December days off, he also scheduled a communal reconciliation service, and on another, three hours of private reconciliations in the evening. When I protested, he said, "Don't you want the faithful to experience God's forgiveness before the birth of our Savior?" He informed me that we were hosting a pre-Christmas open house. Parishioners would be touring my bedroom.

"That's my private space," I said. "You have no right to open it up."

"This is my parish. You will do as I say."

The next morning, I wandered into the kitchen to make coffee. The cutlery was arranged on the counter like a crop circle.

Hunter stumbled in, wearing yesterday's pants. "Why are you up so early?" he said.

"I have Mass."

"I thought I did." As he turned back for the doorway, he did a double take when he noticed the bizarre, cutlery crop circle. "Now, Tom, what possessed you to do that?"

Two days before Christmas, on my day off, I rolled into the rectory fifteen minutes before the marathon confessions. I'd spent the past week in bed with a fever, bronchitis, and a violent cough. During my three-hour sentence, I sat in the damp confessional, hacking up my lungs. Two penitents came. When I exited, Hunter's confessional was already dark.

I returned to the kitchen and nuked some soup. My back and chest ached from coughing. My throat burned. I felt clammy, as if my fever were returning. My family was already in San Diego. I just needed to stay healthy enough to fly out after the Christmas Masses.

Hunter entered. "Well that was a waste. How many did you have?"

"Two." The bowl was hot. I grabbed a dishtowel to insulate it. "You?"

"Just one," he moved to the alcohol cabinet. I lifted my bowl and inhaled the chicken-noodle vapors. He refilled his cup and said, "I left a couple hours ago. We didn't both need to be there."

"What?" I set the soup on the counter. "I'm barely over bronchitis. It's my day off. If we didn't both need to be there, I should have been in bed."

He kicked the cupboard door closed. "Oh boohoo. That didn't keep you from seeing your friends today. In frigid weather, at that."

"What I do on my day off is none of your business." He rushed me. I held my ground, "Stay out of my private life."

"Your precious life. I care about my parishioners." His enraged face was so close to mine that his coffee, ash, and alcohol breath smothered me. "All day people dropped off gifts for us. You abandoned me to do this alone. You abandoned them."

"They're adults. I'm sure they're fine. You could learn from them."

He lifted his scotch like he might smash it into my head. "Fuck you." He shoved past me toward his quarters.

"Run away like you always do. Slam your door so you don't have to listen to me."

He turned and peered. His voice was low, almost a hiss, "I'm listening."

I felt my hands shaking and put them in my pockets. "Look, I don't wanna fight."

"I didn't know we were. Jesus. You're so antagonistic." His eyes flooded with sincerity. "Maybe it's time to return to therapy."

"Let's face it, Jim. This isn't working."

He swirled his drink. "I had no idea."

"We need to sit down and discuss this when we're not exhausted. Right now, we should rest for the holiday."

"Whatever you prescribe," he bowed his head slightly. "Can I leave now, or would that constitute running away?"

"Do whatever you want."

He left. I dumped the soup in the sink, returned to my quarters, downed a double dose of NyQuil, stripped, and passed out in bed.

When the alarm roused me in the morning, the air was glacial. I tried to shake the cough syrup's residual stupor. The thermometer on my dresser read: *Outside Temp 16.4°F, Inside Temp 44.6°F.*

I tore the comforter from the bed and wrapped myself. I touched the heating vents. Cold. I hurried through the open bedroom door into my sitting room. Over the television, the blinds flapped before the wide-open window.

Was it possible that I didn't remember opening the window? Or moving the knives, the cart, and the furniture?

"Good morning, Jim," I entered the kitchen. He ignored me and poured a coffee. Thumbing through the newspaper on the counter, I recalled what my acting professor had said: *You get more with honey than vinegar.*

I channeled my scorn into my need to sound pleasant, "So the weirdest thing happened. When I woke up, it was only forty-four degrees in my room. The window over my TV was open."

His face remained unchanged. He stirred a packet of stevia extract into his cup. "The housekeeper must have left it open. She cleaned yesterday, while you were away."

"I watched TV for a few hours before falling asleep. With the wind gusting like it was, I don't know how I could have missed it."

Without making eye contact, he said, "You must be sleepwalking again," and strolled back to his room.

After midnight Mass, I locked the door to my quarters and wedged the desk chair under the doorknob.

The San Diego sun shot through the living room window and warmed my face. In addition to my eyelids, now my right cheek twitched. Cheers echoed from the hallway. In the next room, my nephew Titus, now two, showboated his Nerf basketball skills. Between hoots, I heard Mom chatting with Maria and Gabe about the 3-D ultrasound of their unborn daughter. Dad prattled with eight-month-old Timothy. I stared out the window.

"Tommy, what's wrong?" I heard Jenny's voice in the foyer.

I shook my head. She sat next to me and hugged me. I closed my eyes and wept.

A small, warm hand touched my knee. Titus stared up at me. His golden curls and aquamarine eyes shimmered in the morning light.

"Uncle Tommy?" His developing voice stressed each syllable. "No cry." He climbed onto my lap and patted my cheeks. "I love you, Uncle Tommy."

Absolute fear overwhelmed me as I realized I didn't believe him. I didn't believe anyone could love me.

I stared at the bumpy texture of the ceiling over my bed. I rolled onto my side. The alarm clock read 11:55 p.m. I'd taken the redeye from San Diego to Chicago before driving to Dubuque, arriving in time for the vigil Mass for the Solemnity of Mary, Mother of God—a holy day of obligation that all Catholics are required to attend. When I was kid, it had been called the Feast of the Circumcision. What a way to bring in the New Year! No wonder so few attended. 11:56.

Somewhere along the highway, Hunter had sped past in the other direction. My body shuddered with the thought of him entering my room to open the window as I'd slept. Even though he was gone, I still couldn't relax. 11:57.

I recalled my previous New Year's Eve at St. Jude's annual dance. As elderly couples twirled and stared into their beloved's eyes, I drank Two-Buck Chuck and stuffed myself with sour-cream-and-cheddar chips. "Who's going to kiss Father Tom at midnight?" a lady had said. A few minutes before midnight, I decamped to the rectory.

A year later, I still missed Pat. The clock's digits didn't care. They rolled onward. 11:58. 11:59. 12:00. My tears blotted the pillow. "Happy fucking New Year," I said.

Three hours later, my self-scrutinizing continued. How could I be so far gone that I couldn't believe my nephew loved me? Something had to change. I didn't want to be crying myself to sleep in another year.

I made a resolution: to seek joy and stop living in fear.

My spiritual director, a twiggy, bald Trappist, had a plan to rekindle my hope. There was more to the priesthood than Jim Hunter, the Dubuque Archdiocese, the isolation of the rectory, and my depression. We brainstormed a list of five options, which I recorded in my journal:

1. *Change nothing. Stay at Resurrection for the remainder of my two-year term.*
2. *Continue to work at Res, but move out of the rectory.*
3. *Apply for a transfer within the archdiocese & move to another parish in July.*
4. *Apply for a temporary pastoral assignment in the archdiocese as I prepare for a leave of absence.*
5. *Take a leave of absence now, in order to face my divided heart & to look into options other than priesthood in Dubuque; perhaps religious orders, San Diego, who knows?*

Each night before bed, I was supposed to put a checkmark under the option that felt best. After a month or two, I would know what to do.

I contemplated the list for the rest of the day. A cheery grandfather, who was in the hospital recovering from a hip replacement, gushed, saying I'd brought vigor to the parish. As he spoke, I chastised myself for considering the possibility of leaving. I couldn't hurt the folks at Resurrection as I had the people at St. Jude's. How could I take a leave of absence? That would raise questions. Everyone would know something was wrong. As I sat in the kitchen eating a carrot cake made for me by a parishioner who volunteered more than anyone and never complained, I told myself to tough it out. I could survive Hunter. I returned to my room and put a checkmark under *1. Change nothing.*

Father Scott sat across from me at a square table in a Chinese restaurant. He'd covered the two Saturday Masses for Hunter. According to canon law, a priest was supposed to celebrate at most three weekend Masses, four with special permission from his bishop. Since Resurrection had two Masses on Saturday evening and three Sunday morning, whenever one of us was absent, we booked a replacement, preferably for the two Saturday liturgies. In gratitude, the nonvacationing priest took the substitute to dinner. Hunter always asked Father Scott. "The two of you are so close," he'd said. "I thought you'd be happy."

Father Scott had insisted on driving to the restaurant to showcase his new black SUV. Along the way, he'd said that he needed to fetch a guest. "Don't worry, it'll be like the old days," he'd said. I'd figured one of our mutual nun acquaintances would join us.

A young man sat between us, struggling to use his chopsticks. We'd picked him up from a dormitory at Loras. He was a new student, who'd arrived a few days early to settle in before orientation. Father had run into him on campus: "I found him wandering like a lost puppy." As I sipped my hot and sour soup, they blabbed about retreats, liturgical music, and spiritual direction. Tall and skinny, the freshman had brown hair, blue eyes, a strong chin, dark red lips, and alabaster skin that blushed when he laughed at Father's jokes. He was barely eighteen.

"You're still holding them wrong," Father said of the chopsticks.

"Then teach me, Padre." The boy smiled. He extended his hand and the utensils. "I'm here to learn."

"And I'm here to serve."

"Of course you are," the kid said sarcastically.

Father flared his nostrils and tickled the boy's side. "If you don't watch it, I might have to use excessive force." He leaned into the kid like a golf pro correcting an amateur's stroke.

He reached out and pinched the boy's nipple.

"Ouch," the kid dropped his chopsticks. "You dork. What was that for?"

"Forgetting to thank me, you ungrateful turd."

Giggling, the boy jabbed Father's love handle but was blocked. Father gave him the Vulcan neck grip. "Say uncle."

The kid squirmed but was unable to pull away. "Padre. Father. Uncle."

Father released him.

"So what was Padre like before he went completely gray?" the kid asked.

"Watch it," Father said, threatening with pincer-like fingers.

I had no interest in going down memory lane, but the two had already parked there. I recognized that kid. Naïve, confused, curious, needy, and vulnerable. Me. Ten years earlier. Father had promised to "get help." He'd "learned from our mistakes" and "grown." But he was playing the same old game.

"He hasn't changed much," I said. "He's still dangerous." Father Scott glared at me and forced a bleached grin. It felt good to fuck with him. "Did Father tell you that when he was in seminary he stabbed a seminarian with a fork?"

"Shut up!" The boy turned to Father.

"Just in the thigh," Father said. "He was drunk and he wouldn't quiet down. So you better behave." He glared at me. "You too, Pastrone."

I wanted to tell him off and call a cab, but I couldn't leave the kid. I had to make sure he got home safely.

Around ten, we zoomed up Loras Boulevard. Father passed the kid's dormitory. Three miles later, he dropped me off at Resurrection. "Thanks for dinner, Pastrone." The freshman hopped into the front seat to replace me.

I thought about following them. The boy needed to be saved. But maybe he didn't want to be. I rushed to the bathroom and threw up.

To distract myself, I turned on the television. Archbishop Timothy Dolan of Milwaukee pontificated on the news. He blamed gay priests for the sexual abuse crisis, saying that homosexuals were predisposed to molest. From all that I'd studied about sexual abuse and homosexuality, I knew that science proved him wrong. Father Scott and the others like him gave all gay priests a bad name. Still, Dolan spoke with such surety.

What if Archbishop Haggis believed the same thing? Maybe he had an arrangement with Father Scott. I needed to know. But if I admitted everything, I'd lose everything and scandalize the faithful.

I opened my journal and put a checkmark under 5. *Take a leave of absence now . . .*

The next morning at the seven o'clock Mass celebrating the Solemnity of the Epiphany, I stood before the congregation. We confessed the Nicene Creed, "We believe in one God . . ." As usual, their voices were flat. I overcompensated, injecting thought and energy into each phrase, as if I were confessing my beliefs for the first time. ". . . the Father Almighty, maker of heaven and earth, of all that is seen and unseen . . ." I thought of the sexual abuse and cover up, Lessing's computer, Haggis's inaction, Dolan's gay scapegoats, and Father Scott's new boy. The Church was infected, not in its extremities, but at its core. The nature of the ecclesial hierarchy was to preserve power at the expense of truth. When the congregation and I reached "We believe in one, holy, catholic and apostolic Church," I mouthed the word "holy."

Throughout the remainder of the Mass and the two that followed, a quotation from the Gospel of John spun through my consciousness: *The truth will set you free.*

Pat called that evening. He wanted to rebuild our friendship. I could visit him when in Baltimore for my retreat in a few weeks. Relieved that he still cared about me, I felt complete again. Maybe that was the truth.

After Night Prayer, I put a checkmark under 5. *Take a leave of absence now in order to face my divided heart & to look into options other than priesthood in Dubuque; perhaps religious orders, San Diego, who knows?* After *San Diego*, I added the word *Baltimore.*

I entered the oncology ward dressed in my clerical attire. My wingtips clicked against the tile. As always, the sound summoned memories of Lauz approaching my examination table. Years of therapy and practice had enabled me to treat each intrusive flashback like an annoying friend who was easier to acknowledge and ignore than to fight.

Janice was on my list of patients. I hadn't seen her since the summer afternoon she'd disclosed her terminal cancer and husband's abuse. I'd called her workplace a few times but failed to connect. I'd listed her in my personal prayer book, prayed for her daily, and moved on as my spiritual director had prescribed: "She's out of your control." Now, that seemed a shameful cop-out.

Alone, she lay under white sheets. Machines chirped. Her chest billowed. The outlines of tubes and wires bulged from the linens like gopher trails. Others sprouted from her nose, mouth, and arms. The skin hung from her skull like withered rose petals.

"Hello, Janice. It's Father Tom from Resurrection."

Her glassy eyes held the same fear as when she'd stared out of my office at verdant branches. She turned toward the window. Snowy skies pelted the room with a garish brilliance.

"Is it OK if I sit and talk?"

Unable to speak, she nodded. I asked yes or no questions. She silently answered.

"Would you like me to hold your hand?"

She opened it.

We prayed. I anointed her. She cried.

Afterward, I retreated to a bathroom and slunk into a stall. Before leaving, I'd asked whether she'd been able to find any sort of resolution with her husband. She'd violently shaken her head. When I asked whether she'd found any peace with God, she'd done the same.

"I don't want to die alone," I said to Counselor Number Twelve at our next session.

She was petite, brunette, and professionally dressed. I'd chosen her for an unsullied perspective: a woman's. She wrote on her notepad and said, "Don't get me wrong, but isn't that the nature of celibacy?"

---

5. *Take of leave of absence now . . .*
✓ ✓ ✓ ✓ ✓

I stood on the icy stoop of Pat's rectory in Baltimore. Although near his bedtime, the lights two stories above in his bedroom beamed. I'd ditched the Trinitarian monastery where I was on retreat with Father Quinn. I rang the doorbell.

Three nights earlier, Pat had picked me up from the airport, not inside at the security line, but curbside. He remained in the car as I tossed my bag in the trunk. We stayed up late, chatting in his sitting room. He spoke of discovering peace in the parish and how celibacy was his calling. When I went to bed, he followed me into the guestroom to be sure I had fresh towels. We said goodnight and hugged. We said, "I love you." His erection bulged against me. I nearly reached down but had been too frightened. I didn't want to risk losing him again. After a bit, he released me, returned to his quarters and bolted the door.

After three days of silent retreat, I'd had it. When he answered the door, I would demand an answer. He either loved me and wanted to be with me or he didn't. I'd been reading Henri Nouwen, who wrote that God loved us no matter what we did. I didn't have to be celibate for God to love me; I just had to be me. I'd also read the biography of Father Mychal Judge, a Franciscan chaplain for the New York Fire Department and the first listed casualty at Ground Zero. He was openly gay and said, "Is there so much love in the world that we can afford to discriminate against any kind of love?" No more fear. Pat would hear the truth. I tightened my scarf, the evergreen one I'd purchased with him at Blarney Woolen Mills in Ireland, and rang again.

After ten minutes and a third ring, his room went black. My nose and toes were frozen. I drove to Little Italy and stuffed myself with hot chocolate and gelato.

When I was back in bed at the monastery, I checked *3. Apply for a transfer within the archdiocese & move to another parish in July 2004.* God had called me to be a priest. Like Pat, I needed to throw myself into my ministry until all other options dissolved in grace.

Father Quinn listened from a chair across a coffee table as I recounted everything that had happened with Pat and since I'd quit drinking with Hunter. By the time I finished, I had curled up into a ball on the couch.

Quinn's eyes became grave. He leaned forward. "Tom, is Jim Hunter abusing you?"

My chest went hollow. I felt like I was back where I'd been in my sophomore year at UNI, when I couldn't deal with the reality of being abused by Doctor Lauz. Just as I had then, I blamed myself. I didn't deserve love. My heart was petrified in fear.

"Jim Hunter is abusing me," my voice sounded lifeless. "And Scott Bell, what he did. He abused me, too."

"They did," Quinn said. "I'm sorry."

As I wandered into the woods that encircled the monastery, I ran my palms over the moist trees. The bark scraped my skin. It felt good, like being alive. My body needed to molt. I needed to get out of my head. I hurled fallen branches. I ran and stomped through icy puddles. The wet, grimy earth spattered my legs and face. The mud oozed into my boots, between my toes. I sang as loudly as I could. Birds flapped away. Rabbits and squirrels scurried. I belted, "I don't know where I'm going, but I know where I've been." Pat had quoted the anthem from *Hairspray* on the night of my arrival. He'd said that he didn't want to go down the path of "acting out" on his gayness again. That was depraved and would only bring "spiritual death." But who was he to condemn my need for love?

Fuck Pat. He didn't know shit about the real world of homosexuals, how Father Mychal Judge had cared for those dying of AIDS when the majority of Christians judged them worthy of God's wrath. Fuck Jim Hunter and his alcoholic parties. Fuck his mind games. Fuck Scott Bell. Fuck his titty twisters and guilt trips. Fuck Lauz. Fuck his lawyers and the Church that gave him Communion. Fuck God. And fuck myself for conspiring with them all.

I stopped between two trees that stood no more than three and half feet apart. With one hand on each of them, I pressed as hard as I could. My temples throbbed and my arms shook. I felt like Samson in the book of Judges. Blinded and betrayed, he stood in the temple, pressed against its columns, and brought it crumbling down. I bore down on the trees, welcoming the same fate.

I would tell the archbishop everything.

BECOMING A MAN

Father Dixon led me down the chancery's main hallway. It didn't have the dizzying length of St. Mary's but was long enough to intimidate. The recessed fluorescent lights flickered like pulsars. We passed pairs of opposing doors. Over the years, I'd come to know their occupants. So had Hunter. Which one of his insiders would report that they'd seen Dixon escorting pale-faced me to Haggis's office?

Minutes earlier, I'd told Dixon everything. I'd exposed Father Scott, our sordid history and that I'd seen him grooming students. I'd listed Father Hunter's past and present abuses: everything from his telling me to lie about being gay on my intake interview, getting me and other seminarians drunk before asking us about our sexual fantasies, to his increased drinking and night wandering. Dixon had promised assistance, "You have nothing to worry about."

During the 7 a.m. Mass, I'd nearly passed out at the altar. As I extended the paten and hosts, saying, "Take this all of you and eat it, this is my body which will be given up for you," my arms became dumbbells. They tingled as if they were being jabbed by thousands of needles. The words of the *Sacramentary* blurred. I couldn't catch my breath and thought I was having a heart attack. Just as I was about to tell the truth, my body or God had decided to silence me. I willed myself to remain conscious and made it through the Mass. I went to the emergency room. The doctor diagnosed it: a panic attack. As I followed Dixon through the archbishop's door, my body felt like a separate entity. It was trying to break me, but the newly prescribed Xanax was on my side.

The archbishop's office was a large rectangle with windows lining the breadth. On one side, his cluttered desk backed up to the windows. On the other, a shiny wooden table stretched from wall to wall. Before us, upholstered furniture, a coffee table, and a Persian rug formed a small living room. I sat on the edge of the couch. Archbishop Haggis and Dixon listened from armchairs. The archbishop's strong hands, which milked cows in his youth and anointed me during my ordination, scribbled on a notepad. When I finished, he said, "I commend you for your courage. Thank you for coming forward."

I relaxed.

He would not remove me from ministry. He needed time to contact Father Scott and to figure out what to do about my situation with Hunter. Dixon would get back to me in a day or two concerning the next step. I should fulfill my duties at Resurrection and turn to my priest support group, spiritual director, and counselor for support. When I rose to leave, Haggis shook my hand and said, "I will pray for you. Please do the same for me."

Back at the rectory, the kitchen smelled like an ashtray. Hunter had again broken our agreement to smoke only in his private spaces. My hands quivered as I poured a glass of orange juice. Had Haggis already called him? If Hunter knew I'd reported his alcoholism, would he harm me? I decided to retrieve the bear mace from the camping equipment in my truck. As I turned for the hallway, Hunter pounced from his quarters.

"I hurried back from Galina as soon as I heard."

"Heard what?" I scanned the cutlery block. The knives were all present.

"Your heart attack scare." His dark eyes conveyed more compassion than Christ on the cross. "Are you OK?"

"It was just stress. I'm fine."

"Thank God. I've been worried sick." He leaned against the counter. "Where have you been all afternoon?"

I grabbed my juice and stepped toward the hallway. "Hospital rounds."

"So you didn't have business at the chancery?"

The rest of the week, I heard nothing. I remained in bed, too frightened to sleep and too exhausted to remain awake. Leaving only in the mornings, I pulled myself together enough to get through the daily Masses. I went to the office and checked my messages. I canceled my appointments for the day and returned to bed. Midweek, I couldn't cancel being on a panel about vocations for the freshman confirmation class, so I mused about the satisfaction of being a celibate diocesan priest. At night, I adjusted the chair under my doorknob and called my family and friends. My sister Jenny feared Hunter would kill me. I thought he'd rape me. I worried that I'd lost my mind.

On Friday evening, I confided everything to my priest support group. A few said my news "filled in the gaps" about Father Scott. They'd observed him "grooming" me and other male students but had hoped it was only friendship. They all knew Hunter was a verbally abusive drunk. They assured me that I wasn't crazy to be concerned for my safety. They advised me to take a leave of absence from Resurrection. Two offered me refuge at their rectories.

The patriarch of our group, Father Ev Hemann, who looked like an elfin Santa Claus and had the jolly disposition to boot, was unusually somber. He said, "The archbishop has the well-being of numerous people to consider. Who's going to be your advocate? Someone in the coming meetings needs to be sure he does what's best for you." They all lived on the other side of the diocese and suggested I ask Dixon, who had been in the group before me.

On Saturday morning, I phoned Dixon. He didn't answer. I left a message, called Archbishop Haggis, and demanded a meeting.

An hour later, the archbishop and I sat in the dual recliners of his den, where at my first seminarian gathering he'd offered me a mint julep. A semester later, he'd reclined barefoot, dressed in pants and an undershirt, while visiting with Father Scott and me. This morning, he wore black leather shoes, his collar and episcopal ring, and a black sports jacket.

"You told them *what*?" he said of my priest support group.

"Everything. And they think I should leave Res and go on leave immediately. I need treatment for depression."

"You can't be talking about Father Scott. I haven't spoken to him yet. He hasn't returned my calls."

Typical Scott. I surged with anger. Why hadn't Haggis driven over to Loras and confronted him in person?

I told Haggis how a bearded parishioner had cornered me in the sacristy after Mass. He'd asked how I was and offered me a hug. In that moment, I'd wanted him to undress me, caress me, and make me forget my pain. "I'm too weak to maintain my boundaries, Archbishop." I cried. "I don't want to hurt anyone."

He leaned forward in his chair, "When we're weak, Christ's grace is most abundant. Right now, you can do your best ministry. Open your weakness in prayer. Trust Christ.

"You need to make things work with Father Hunter. If you don't, you'll just be running away like you did at St. Jude's. You'll be playing the victim again. It's time to be a man. To live up to the promises you made at ordination."

He promised to meet when he returned on Monday from a confirmation ceremony in a distant parish. "That is, if the blizzard they're forecasting doesn't leave me stranded."

I smiled through the weekend's Masses and sobbed through the nights. On Sunday night, I spoke to Father Quinn, who invited me to stay with him in Baltimore while I figured out a long-term plan. I phoned my old counselor, Number Ten. He advised me to follow my gut: "Tell Hunter to 'fuck off' and then get out of the rectory." But the archbishop had ordered me to wait. God's will for my life was supposed to be revealed through the archbishop's commands and my obedience. Maybe Haggis was right; I had to grow up and quit playing the victim. I emailed Father Dixon, inquiring again whether he was my advocate. Though the blizzard hadn't materialized Monday morning, there was still no news from the archbishop.

On my way to the hospital to make rounds, I stopped to see Number Twelve. Her office was in the Loras College student union on the floor directly over campus ministry and Father Scott's office. Twelve gave me Al-Anon pamphlets and prescribed local meetings to cope with Hunter's "toxicity." "It's illegal, what Scott Bell did to you," she said. "He used his authority over you to gain sexual favors. He exploited you. I'm furious the archbishop hasn't removed him from Loras yet." She concluded the stress alone of what I'd told the archbishop was reason enough to take a leave. "You're raw right now, Tom. And that's dangerous for you." We scheduled a meeting for the next morning.

When I exited the stairwell on my way out, Father Scott stood twenty feet away. Under the vestibule's glass ceiling, a group of boys circled him as though he were Socrates. Before I could turn, he spotted me, "Pastrone!"

I froze. He darted at me. I wanted to retreat, but the archbishop had said to stop running. He extended his arms and hugged me. "Thanks again for dinner the other weekend. It was great being with you."

"You're welcome." I gave him a couple pats on the back and pulled away.

"You OK, Pastrone? You look piqued."

I scanned the crowded space for anyone I knew. "I'm fine."

"You don't look it. You can use my house anytime. You know," he poked my side, "if you need to escape the clutches of Herr Hunter."

"Thanks for the offer." A campus minister from my Loras days entered. She waved. "Excuse me."

He returned to his entourage of *epheboi*. Over his colleague's shoulder, I watched him. He jabbed the boys, pinched their chests, and rested his hand on their shoulders and biceps.

When I got to the hospital, a parishioner whom I'd referred to counseling for depression was in the psych wing. As I entered her room, she burst into wails. I sat in a simple chair at the foot of her bed. The walls were barren. Anything that could maim, slash, or strangle had been removed. "I'm such a failure," she repeated. "Just look at me." She gestured to her dangerously obese body. "Just let me die." I tried to let her know that I understood her feelings while challenging her to see that there were reasons to live: God loved her, her grandchildren and children loved her, and I loved her. We'd help her. She dismantled every one of my arguments.

Back at the office, I shot emails to the archbishop and Dixon. It was unacceptable that Father Scott still didn't know. I explained how Twelve's advice matched that of my priest support group, my family, my spiritual director, Father Quinn, and Ten: I needed to get out of Resurrection as soon as possible.

Late in the afternoon, the archbishop replied. He addressed the email, *Dear Fr. Rastrelli.* Father Scott had returned his call. They would meet in the morning. After that, the archbishop needed time to confer with Father Dixon. He might be able to have an evening meeting. He signed: *Fraternally, Archbishop Haggis.*

Darkness had settled by the time Father Dixon retrieved me from the waiting room at the opposite end of the hallway from the archbishop's office. The chancery workers were itching to leave for the night. A new blizzard loomed. Dixon hadn't responded to my inquiries about being my advocate. No matter. I was armed with a proposal that I'd prepared with Twelve. When I'd told her how the Archbishop had ordered me to toughen up, be a man, and quit running, she'd become indignant: "You can't be intimidated by the archbishop. If he bullies you again, you must say 'No, that is not acceptable. What I need is . . . ,' and then read your proposal."

Dixon closed the door. The archbishop sat at the center of the wooden table with his back to the wall and hands folded. A file stuffed with papers lay before him. He extended his hand to the spot directly across from him. "Please sit down, Father Rastrelli." At his right, his second-in-command, Monsignor Boyle, made eye contact with me and nodded. He was pushing seventy, but thanks to his full mane, he looked younger. The archbishop had nearly gone bald since I'd first met him and sported a wiry comb-over. "Thank you, Father Dixon," he said.

Dixon smiled, his retainer flashing in the light. I wondered if he made more than the parish priest's salary of $13,900 by working in the chancery. He slid around the table and sat to the archbishop's left. They wore clerical attire. Since it was my day off, I was in a sweatshirt, jeans, and tennis shoes. The truth will set you free, I silently repeated. I set my proposal on the table, pulled a pen from my pocket, and took my seat.

"I hope you don't mind, but I asked Monsignor Boyle to sit in with us," the archbishop said. This made sense. Boyle had a doctorate in psychology and had worked at Loras for years. He was responsible for handling all accusations of sexual abuse and knew Twelve.

"I spoke to Father Bell," the archbishop said. "He confirmed your relationship."

For the first time in a week, I felt like I could fully inhale. "Good," I said, "I mean, I'm just relieved that Scott admitted it. So he can get help." They remained stoic as jurors. "Did you ask him if there were others?"

Haggis focused on the contents of the file. His voice remained calm, "That doesn't concern you. What should concern you is your inappropriate relationship with Father Bell and your celibate commitment."

I wondered which file he was fingering: my public file or the private one that bishops were rumored to maintain for their eyes only. I tried not to sound confrontational. "I'm sorry, archbishop, but I have issues with the word 'relationship.' What Scott did to me was an abuse of power. Illegal even."

"Let's just settle down," Monsignor Boyle said with open palms. "We're handling Father Scott. You need to focus on yourself."

They explained how they would send Scott to the St. Louis Institute—a place where priests who committed sexual indiscretions with parishioners and children were sent. He'd be there over spring break for a psychological assessment. For the next month, he'd remain at Loras in his current position. I was to compile and submit to them an outline with the dates of our "relationship." I should include as many details as possible about our "relationship," including patterns in Scott's behavior. Each time Haggis said "relationship," something that sounded like satisfaction undergirded his tone. He reminded me of Lauz's lawyers when they threatened to expose my gayness.

"Do I have a choice?" I said.

"Tom," Dixon said, "we need your help to help him. Please."

"I don't understand." I jotted their demands on the back of my proposal. "Scott's staying at Loras?"

Haggis crossed his arms. "How do you feel about that?"

"Confused. I mean, with all the sexual abuse headlines. If other victims come forward, they'll find me. They'll know that you left Scott in ministry after I spoke up. There'd be a scandal." The archbishop's face flushed. "But I don't have to live with that, archbishop. You do."

"Yes, I do," he snapped. One of his hands balled into a fist. He pointed at me with the other, his episcopal ring flashing in the light. "Be careful about how widely you talk about Jim and Scott with people. Your sister sent me an email. That's inappropriate. I will not visit with your family about this. I suggest you do the same. This doesn't concern them."

"She asked for your help. How are we supposed to heal if we can't talk?"

Boyle extended his hands slowly and set them on the table, "It would benefit your healing not to hash through this stuff over and over. Share it with a smaller group of people: your counselor and spiritual director. Reputations are at stake."

The archbishop spoke again, sounding exhausted, "Hasn't the Church already seen enough scandal?"

A great void opened inside me. Twelve was right. They wanted me to be their coconspirator.

I lifted my proposal. The paper shook in my hand. "Can I read this?"

The archbishop looked annoyed, but he nodded.

"This is what I need and why. I need to leave Resurrection. I need a space where I can face the deeper vocational and identity issues that I've been unable to address in my current living conditions. I need a temporary place, a neutral place, while I figure out a long-term plan of action." I listed the options that my priest support group and old seminary professors had offered. I paraphrased spiritual guru John Main: in spring, one needed to scrape away the dead layer of autumn's remains to find the blossoms of new life. My plan had the blessing of my counselor, spiritual director, and priest support group. "Please grant me a leave of absence for medical reasons. I need to escape Hunter's toxicity."

The archbishop interrupted. "But the buzz around town is that you and Jim have revived the parish. You're doing great work. Why would you want to ruin that?"

"But you work with him," I said. "You've seen him drink. He's abusive. An alcoholic."

"It's not your place to diagnose him," Boyle said. "His drinking never affected his work here at the chancery."

"What about his dissertation?" I said. "He drank away the months he took off to finish it. He doesn't remember moving things around at night." Dixon stared at the table. "Rich, you've been to Jim's parties. I've been up front with you about his drinking all year. You know I'm not making this up."

His gaze could have burned a hole in the tabletop.

"No one has accused you of lying," the archbishop said. "You're going to return to Resurrection and confront Father Hunter. You will remain there until your term ends next year. You're a public leader in this community. Your disappearance would raise questions."

"Good," I said, as I flipped over the proposal and wrote down what he'd said. Again, Twelve's words came to mind. I quoted her, "People need to ask, 'Why can't Jim get his life in shape?' "

"But this is about you," Haggis said, "and your pattern of running away, playing victim."

"I'm not running away! I confronted the doctor. I confronted Scott and Jim many times. They didn't change. I'm depressed. I can't sleep. I can't stay awake. Each bite of food makes me gag. My face and neck won't stop twitching. A week ago, I had a panic attack during Mass. I thought I was dying of a heart attack. I need help."

Their voices overlapped like a barrage of gut checks:

"You need to prove to yourself that you can do this."

"This is an opportunity for growth, for professionalism."

"We want you to find your voice."

"You need to stand up for yourself."

"We want you to fight and succeed."

"You have to stop running from confrontation."

Everything that Twelve, Quinn, my priest support group, and family had said was the same as Haggis, only they'd meant it in the opposite context. I felt disconnected from reality, as if I'd ventured into an alternate universe.

"Can I finish my proposal? Please? I prepared it with my counselor." My vision blurred with moisture. Haggis acquiesced. "I don't think I'm running away. I've again been the victim of an abuse of power, and now I'm going to be assertive to get myself into a healthy environment. I've been living in a harassing environment and I refuse to stay in it any longer. There are—"

The archbishop smacked the table. "Look, Tom. We understand that you feel this way, but you need to—"

"Can I finish reading this, please?" I said, nearly yelling. If I had to obey him, he could at least give me the respect of hearing me out.

He nodded. I read about the deeper issues that I needed to address. My depression was larger than Father Scott and Father Hunter. I'd been miserable since leaving St. Mary's. Life in rural Iowa had drained me. A leave of absence would enable me to heal, to overcome my depression, and to discern whether I should switch to an urban diocese or a religious order.

"You need to show some stability in your life." Haggis swallowed a sardonic laugh. "With your history, no religious order would accept you."

Dixon's face registered surprise. He'd seen Haggis's sneer. Haggis was tightening my ecclesial balls in a vice. He'd ruin me before he'd allow me to go to another diocese or an order.

I continued reading. "A leave will help me to address my homosexuality. Can I live as a homosexual and be celibate? Can I live an integrated life within a Church that considers my sexuality a gift from God but at the same time says that using this gift is intrinsically depraved? To be fulfilled, do I need a partner with whom I can share my life?" My questions went on, but I knew they'd stopped listening long before the meeting began.

"For reasons of mental health, my counselor says I should leave Res immediately."

"Really, Tom," Haggis said. "What does she know? You've only seen her a few times." Boyle followed suit, "She's just telling you what you want to hear."

They ordered me to return to Resurrection. I was to compose a list of my "issues" with Father Hunter, using phrases like "This is what I need and why"; "these are the behaviors that have a negative effect on me"; and "this is what I perceive as mentally harassing." I was to propose changes and state that if he didn't change, I would leave the parish. But I was *not* to confront him about his drinking or use the word "alcoholic." "That's not your place," Boyle, the archdiocese's foremost expert in psychology, said. "You need to be careful about assessing Jim's motivations." Finally, under no circumstance was I to confront Hunter. First, I was to send my list of grievances to Dixon for editing and approval.

"Tom, how're you doing with all this?" Dixon asked.

I felt like I'd been browbeaten with the archbishop's crozier. Hunter's bait-and-switch was nothing; I'd fallen for Haggis and the Church. Before my family, friends, and God, he'd ordained me a priest forever. There was no divorce from the priesthood, no recanting of vows. I'd wanted to help people. Across the table, Haggis smiled benignly, looking no different from when I'd placed my hands within his and promised obedience. After the ordination, he'd flashed that same grin in photos with family, and he would sacrifice my mental and physical well-being to spare a sexual perpetrator and a drunk. He would sacrifice his "flock" to Hunter's abusive rants and violent mind games. He would sacrifice the truth so Father Scott could continue to hit on boys. Haggis was no different than the bishops who'd repressed women, sacrificed children, and burned martyrs for two millennia. Because I'd sworn to obey him, neither was I.

An uncontrollable urge to escape the pain bored through me. I could drive off the bluffs lining the river or jump off the Julian Dubuque Bridge.

"Tom," Dixon said, stiff as a marionette, "Are you OK?"

"I'm afraid I'm having a breakdown."

"I don't think you'll have a breakdown," Boyle said. "You're stronger than you think."

"I'm afraid I might hurt myself."

The archbishop rubbed his temples. "Don't be so melodramatic, Tom."

They summarized their orders. I wanted to cry, but fuck if I was going to give them that satisfaction. I knew what I had to do. I stopped protesting and agreed to every demand.

When they finished, I stood, gathered up my notes, and put on my coat. They remained seated. The archbishop's bloodless lips continued, "We believe in you. We're praying for you. Please pray for us."

I turned my back and walked away.

NOW THAT I'M OUT, WHAT DO I DO?

I hurried from the archbishop's office. My senses heightened, veins pulsing. I focused on the glass door at the end of the hallway.

"Tom, wait up," Dixon called. "Please!"

I increased my pace to a near jog. The floor creaked. Dixon's footsteps closed. I pressed through the door into the waiting room. He grabbed my shoulder. "Do you need to talk?"

I tore away and turned to him. "I have nothing to say to you." He looked like he'd just stepped in front of a bus. I zipped my coat and stepped outside.

The single-digit air seared my sinuses. In a shadowed corner of the parking lot, my compact pickup waited. I drove toward the bluffs. The blocks of Catholic homes were warm with butterscotch light. Would the people inside, who trusted the archbishop with their souls and their tithes, hear the truth? Or would they rather remain in deluded bliss? The archbishop's words drained my resolve: *Hasn't the Church already seen enough scandal?* He was right. Thousands of victims had spoken, yet the faithful continued to pack the pews. They would do so long after I'd exposed Father Scott.

But what about the boys at Loras and those who'd followed me at St. Stephen's? Were they also to be sacrificed, made victims like Christ, in the name of saving the faithful? At my ordination, Haggis had charged, "Imitate the mystery you celebrate: model your life on the mystery of the Lord's cross." For days after, the bittersweet scent of chrism had emanated from my consecrated hands. I pounded them against the steering wheel and dashboard.

I needed a place to go. The rectory wasn't an option with Hunter monitoring me. If he'd heard I'd been at the chancery again, he'd pump me for information. My friends out East didn't need my drama. My parents and siblings had enough to deal with: Grandpa's dementia, Maria's pregnancy, and their own job problems. What would I tell them? I'd failed again? Would they accept me if I weren't a priest? If I were just gay Uncle Tommy?

I decided against the bluffs. Driving off was too risky. The truck might smash into a house or roll into traffic. I didn't want to kill anyone else. I, alone, had to pay for my sin. I should have finished myself off the night Jonathan called me a pedophile. I never would have returned to the Church and heard Father Scott preach about the deaf-mute: *Ephphatha*. "Be opened." Bullshit. The people in the pews weren't the deaf-mutes; we, the victims of abuse, were. Now that we could speak, the Church deprived us of our voices.

I turned down a dim back road that split the limestone cliffs where the chancery lorded over the Mississippi. Skirting the foot of the bluffs that edged the river flats, I approached the Cathedral of St. Raphael, "God's remedy." The Julian Dubuque Bridge arched upward from behind a grocery store. I'd have to walk halfway across the bridge before jumping; someone might stop me. I decided on the ice. It would be Tom's remedy, a bitter baptism, a return to the unfeeling womb.

Don't be so melodramatic, Tom. Maybe the archbishop was right. Histrionic. Needy. Seductive. Sexually disordered. The words he used to describe me behind closed doors clashed with what the Church publicly professed me to be. Fulfilled. Loved. Holy. The poster boy for vocation recruitment.

On the north end of town, before bottlenecking bluffs choked off the flats, there was a bike path. During warmer months, I'd walked there while reciting my homilies. I'd noticed but never paid much attention to a boat ramp. It would be my access to the river. I'd drive until the ice buckled under the weight of the truck.

The closer I got to the shore, the more my thoughts collided in an unstoppable cascade, like a psychological game of *Asteroids*. No matter what course of action I took—silently complying, going to the press, hiring a lawyer, leaving Resurrection, abandoning the priesthood, or committing suicide—someone would be scandalized, harmed, and disappointed. I thought of my parishioner in the hospital psych ward. What if the ice broke before the channel was deep enough to submerge the truck?

I pulled over, four blocks from the shore. I screamed. My breath clung to the rearview mirror and windshield. I caved into the steering wheel and sobbed with my forehead resting at twelve o'clock. I could drive into the countryside, steer into a tree or an oncoming semi, make it look like an accident in case I failed. Or I could park on a remote dirt road and walk into the night until my body went numb. I'd feel nothing. My nose and eyes dripped over the horn. "Help me, Lord," I begged. The desolate hopelessness and shame that I'd felt after Lauz's lawyers had forced me to admit my "relationship" with Father Scott was nothing compared to this. Where was God? Working through the Church? In the voice of the archbishop? Working through my wounds? Punishing me for my sins, for having loved Pat? Judging me for having loved Father Scott? Was God taking pleasure in my pain? Teaching me a lesson? Loving me in spite of myself? Or was God standing idly by, the unmoved mover?

I was alone.

Through the frosty passenger's window, I noticed a pay phone outside a gas station. A metal binder hanging from the phone encased a phonebook. I left the truck and skidded across the slick parking lot. Cars zoomed past. As I thumbed through the pages, my hands shivered. I found Twelve's home number, entered it into my cell, returned to the truck, and called.

I spoke through sobs: "It's Tom Rastrelli. I'm sorry to bug you at home. You were right. They covered it all up." I wanted to tell her that I was four blocks from the Mississippi and an icy demise, but she was a mandatory reporter. She'd call 911. They'd "rescue" me and check me into the Catholic hospital five blocks from the chancery. The archbishop would be at my bedside, controlling the story and assuring me that Christ was working through my wounds. When she asked how I was, I pulled it together as best I could and lied. "I'm fine."

She reminded me of our meeting in the morning. We could talk then. Even in these circumstances, it was inappropriate that I'd called her at home. She told me to call Father Ev from my priest support group and said goodnight.

I turned the ignition and started for the river but after two blocks was again consumed by sobs. I opened my phone and dialed. Ev answered.

"Ev, I think I'm going crazy."

Minutes later, as I recounted the meeting with Haggis, he interrupted. "Hold on, Tom. It sounds like you're reading. Are those quotes? Did the archbishop actually say that?"

"Yes. I took notes."

"And Dixon didn't stand up for you?"

"No."

"I should have been there with you. I'm so sorry." Hearing the shock and pain in his voice, I realized that I wasn't crazy. He offered to call my parents. He told me to call Father Quinn. I needed to get out of the archdiocese. If I took refuge at Ev's rectory, he worried that Haggis would order him to return me to Dubuque. I couldn't think, so Ev remained on the phone, leading me step by step away from the river. He told me to eat; I went to McDonald's and bought a burger and fries. I drove back to the rectory. Hunter's sitting room lights were on. I pulled into the garage. If Hunter intercepted me on the way up to my room, I was to hand him my phone. Ev would deal with him. I sprinted up the back stairway into my quarters, locked the door, and slid a chair under the knob. Ev stayed on the phone until I sat in my recliner with Father Quinn's number in hand.

Quinn was asleep, but I got his housemate, Fin. He was the newly appointed spiritual director at St. Luke's Institute in Maryland, where bishops sent the worst of the pedophiles for treatment. We spoke for two hours. He advised me to find a canon lawyer outside Dubuque. "The archbishop isn't taking care of you. And he's not going to," he said. "You have to take care of yourself, Tom. You're depressed because you believe you don't have options. You have to create them. A new plan. You can leave Dubuque. You can even leave the priesthood. Reach into your anger and tell Hunter, 'Fuck you,' and then leave."

I called my parents, who'd been on the phone with Ev. They would arrive midmorning to pack. I had a new plan: write up my grievances with Hunter, say Mass in the morning, call a canon lawyer to find out my rights, confront Hunter, and leave.

After the morning Mass, I hid in my quarters. I called a priest friend in Cedar Rapids, who'd asked me to inform him if I decided to move out. I phoned Quinn to get the names of some canon lawyers in Baltimore, but he didn't answer. I couldn't talk to Fin because he'd already broken protocol by talking to me. He was Pat's counselor. Since I'd been suicidal, he'd made an exception. But I was no longer despondent. Even though I hadn't slept, I felt focused. I'd spent the night amassing a three-page, single-spaced list of grievances with Hunter. I'd added and put a check under a new option to the list in my journal: *6. Leave everything, Dubuque and the priesthood.* I needed to protect myself before doing so. I needed the consultation of a canon lawyer. There were only two other people who knew everything about my situation and had contacts outside the archdiocese. Ten didn't answer. That left Pat. He didn't want me calling him more than once a month. If he loved me at all, he'd make an exception.

He picked up. I briefly explained the events of the past week, including that Fin had helped.

"He's my counselor," Pat said. "You didn't talk about what happened between us?"

"No. Wait . . . I don't remember. Quinn was already asleep. I was suicidal. He helped me. It was a one-time thing. I'm sorry."

"OK. Just settle down."

He gave me a few numbers. The canon lawyer from Baltimore advised me not to leave the parish. According to Church law, nothing had happened that violated my rights. Father Scott hadn't done anything "canonically inappropriate" by assaulting and exploiting me, because I was "not a cleric at the time." If I'd been a deacon or his associate pastor, then he would have violated my rights. But it was okay to bed a layperson. By Church law, Haggis had done nothing wrong by leaving Scott at Loras. Hunter could be as verbally abusive as he wanted. The lawyer confirmed what Ev had said. If I left, the archbishop could require me to return. He said, "You have to play ball with them a little bit. You need to do everything they ordered you to do. After that, if they don't listen or help, you can leave."

I protested. What they'd done had to be against the law.

"It was canonical," he said. "Civil law is irrelevant."

My office printer churned out my gripes with Hunter. I'd cancelled my appointments for the day. Hunter barged in and closed the door. I quickly turned off my monitor.

"What the hell is going on?"

He looked somber, but his voice was impatient. I didn't know if he was angry, concerned, or both. Out of the corner of my eyes, I noticed that my grievances had emerged from the printer, face up. "I'm sorry, but

I can't talk now." I snatched the pages from the tray and set them face down on my desk.

"What's that? Why'd you turn off your monitor?"

If he knew, he might hurt me. "It's nothing. Private"

He plopped into one of the guest chairs and spoke like a teacher working detention hall. "Well, I'm not leaving until you explain what's going on. You've been reclusive. The staff says you've been canceling all your appointments. We're concerned. This is my parish. My associate is AWOL. I demand to know why."

"Please, Jim. I will explain, but I can't right now."

He ran his finger along the windowsill. "What? Are you under orders from Jacob?" He flicked the dust from his fingers and pointed at my freshly printed pages. "Why don't you show me that?"

He'd been tipped off. Perhaps Boyle or Haggis. They'd invested decades in his career. They'd groomed him for Rome. Maybe they wanted him to chase me away. I couldn't decide what to say. Suppressed tears burned in the bridge of my nose. I said nothing.

Hunter grinned, wide and yellow. His voice was a lemon drop, "I know things haven't been ideal here. Do you need to live somewhere else? I realize that I've been passive-aggressive. I've had some unfair expectations of you. You can talk to me. I'm here for you."

He was going to smother me with honey until I choked.

"Fine. But you have to promise you'll listen. You won't interrupt or yell. If you do, I'll stop. And when I'm done, you won't contradict me. I'm too exhausted to discuss this now. We'll do that another time. And when we do, we'll converse cordially, like adults."

He looked surprised by my directness. Or was he amused? He bowed his furrowed forehead. "As you wish. Whatever I can do to help."

Clutching my unapproved list, I read my grievances, supporting each with specific examples of how he'd intruded on my personal boundaries, belittled me or parishioners, played mind games, and deceived me. It felt good to watch him squirm, swallowing his rebuttals. With each complaint, I pushed harder. He'd recruited me away from St. Jude's with a bait and switch. His sexual comments and innuendos were inappropriate. He'd misused privileged information about my sexuality that he'd gained when he was director of seminarians. This harassment had to stop. Obeying the archbishop, I didn't call Hunter an alcoholic. Instead, I recalled how he'd said, "Don't worry, you'll get used to it" after I'd had Mass with a hangover. "If I ever got used to it," I said, "I'd be an alcoholic." After three pages, I concluded: "Your behaviors and this series of events have left me feeling manipulated, used, and abused by you. Things need to change because I can't and I refuse to go on living and working like this."

With cinched lips, he sat with arms and legs crossed. Again, I couldn't tell whether he was angry, concerned, or amused.

"That's it, Jim. I'm finished."

He exhaled and threw up his arms. "Well, I feel ambushed." His lips slid into a frown. "I didn't know you thought I was such a monster."

He expressed disagreement with some of what I'd said but would respect my request not to discuss it immediately. If we wanted that conversation to be fruitful, he suggested that I rest first.

"I want to help you," Hunter said. "That's all I've ever wanted. But if you really hate me this much, why would you want to stay?"

"I didn't say I hated you. And I'm not going to have this conversation now."

He ascended to his quarters. My ceiling shook with his trademark door slam. I needed sleep. The secretary buzzed. Father Dixon had phoned. I was to call him at once.

During the course of our conversation, I explained how Hunter cornered me and refused to leave until I explained things. The confrontation had taken place uncensored. Dixon wasn't pleased. He apologized for what he called "the inquisition-like feel" of the meeting with the archbishop and for not getting back to me to explain that he was the archbishop's advocate, not mine. "There are one hundred things I could have done better," he said. "I failed. I'm sorry."

I didn't respond. After a sustained silence, he informed me that my friend in Cedar Rapids had called and told him that my parents were moving me out. Dixon begged me not to go.

"I told him that in confidence," I yelled, unconcerned whether the staff could hear me. "Why are you even talking to my friends?"

"We just want what's best for you."

"You're lucky that I didn't kill myself last night." I dug through my desk, pocketing my personal items: Grandma's engraved letter opener, my backup floppies, and photos. "I don't trust you. You don't know what's best for me."

"I'm sorry you feel that way. Just please don't go. I'm sure you regret some of the things you said last night, as well."

"I don't."

"Let's take a day to cool off. Get some rest. We can meet again tomorrow."

My parents kept guard in my sitting room the remainder of the day. Thanks to a double dose of Xanax, I slept soundly for the first time in months. When I woke, they brought me food and made sure I ate. They spent the night on my couch and recliner, keeping Hunter at bay.

In the morning, my head felt clearer. I had to move out, but again the canon lawyer advised me to meet with Dixon to hear his terms. "Play ball." Even though I needed to leave, I couldn't afford to violate canon law and have the archbishop cut me loose without health insurance and a paycheck. I had to meet Haggis halfway.

A blizzard barreled toward Iowa. I told my parents to get on the road. If Hunter got violent, I'd get a hotel. After they left, I drove to Loras and met again with Twelve, who said, "You need space to find clarity, to figure out what is best for you" and "keep a record of everything they say." She wrote and equipped me with an official letter prescribing a medical leave of absence. I drove to the chancery and delivered it to Dixon, who scoffed, saying "the archbishop takes her opinion with a grain of salt." He continued, "You are in this place at this time to be a vessel of grace"; "you don't want to make any rash decisions in your state of mind"; and "the question is how much pain can you tolerate for the sake of God?"

As I drove back to Resurrection, I called Abdel and told him everything. He struggled to find words of consolation, eventually settling on, "Hang in there, Tommy."

I said, "That's easy to say when you're not the one on the cross."

When I entered the rectory, Hunter tailed me into my office and closed the door. He looked like he'd spent the day drinking. I gripped my chair and waited for him to slice into me.

His eyes softened. "I want you to leave," he said gently. "I don't want you in my parish in this state. You're obviously depressed and in no condition to be caring for my parishioners."

"That's what I've been saying to the archbishop, but he isn't listening. He could force me to come back, Jim."

"He isn't your pastor. I am. I have the canonical right to manage my staff. Go to your parents for a few days, a week, whatever it takes."

He looked sincere but had to be working an angle or setting me up. It didn't matter. I needed to go.

"Thank you, Jim."

"Just get yourself better."

Flurries wisped over the windshield as the hills of Dubuque County stretched into the open expanse of central Iowa. In three and a half hours, I'd be in Des Moines with the two people in the world I knew I could trust. When I reached Cedar Falls, darkness had fallen. The blizzard engulfed me, but I continued westward. I'd faced Haggis and Hunter. No storm would stop me. Twenty miles later, I lost visibility and phone reception. The taillights of the truck I was following disappeared onto an off-ramp. The exit ramps were less plowed than the highway. If I took one, I'd risk sliding into a ditch or getting on a county road that was in worse shape. Not a single town dotted the highway for the next forty miles. I was alone in the black whiteness.

Unable to distinguish between the road and the shoulder, I pressed on at a glacial pace. I no longer wanted to die, to drown in an icy river, or to freeze to death in a cornfield.

The trip took seven hours, but I finally made it home.

THE END OF THE AFFAIR

I sat in a pew between my parents. The blizzard had passed. I'd spent the rest of the week in bed. They'd forced me to come with them to Mass, hoping it would cheer me. Their church was eerily reminiscent of St. Stephen's. A reproduction of the San Damiano cross hung suspended over the altar. For the past decade, this crucifix, its stoic Jesus, oversized iconic eyes, and phallic abs had comforted me as a reminder of God's sacrificial love. All I saw now were torture, betrayal, abandonment, and blood. A warning: this is what happens to people who challenge the religious establishment.

From the ambo, a woman invited everyone to stand and greet one another. Ten years earlier, at St. Stephen's, I'd silently cursed Dad as he hugged me and kissed me on the cheek. I hadn't wanted anyone to think I was gay. Now I didn't care. The Church claimed: "All are welcome" and "No matter where you're from, we're glad you're here." But the "revealed truth" as I'd experienced it was this: I was lovable and had a place at the Communion table as long as I sacrificed the very authenticity that I was ordained to preach to others. In exchange, my parishioners coddled me, the seminary awarded me, and the archbishop affirmed me. The Church thrived on the fear of its gay priests. It was safer to remain silent and omit our truth than to be open and get rejected. Because we played into their straight delusions, we got no credit for the sacrifice of our celibacy. *No more fear*, I'd promised myself at New Year's. I threw my arms around my Italian father and gave him a peck on the cheek.

During the eucharistic prayer, I knelt, not with the assured posture with which I'd knelt before the archbishop and promised obedience, but wilted like a parched palm frond. The Church promised salvation, but Haggis and so many of the bishops lacked the virtues their teachings demanded. At the altar, the celebrant prayed the "words of institution"—*Take this all of you and eat it, this is my body which will be given up for you—*

and elevated the host. The bishops catechized that in this moment a priest stood "in the person of Christ" and transformed the bread into Jesus's body. This was the centerpiece of our faith: the Real Presence of Jesus in the Church. For months during this moment, I had silently quoted Mark 9:24, "I believe, help my unbelief." But now I no longer believed Christ was present and prayed only, "Help my unbelief."

After I'd had been home for five days, Father Dixon informed me it was time to return to "discuss options."

I'd spoken to my seminary pastoral counseling professor. He'd recommended a place called the Southdown Institute, a house of healing for priests, nuns, and pastors who'd been crushed by the demands of ministry. When I returned to Resurrection, Hunter also suggested Southdown. A nun he knew had gone there. Who knew that the Church chewed up and spit out enough of its dedicated servants to warrant an asylum?

I popped a Xanax and curled up in my recliner with my laptop. Thanks to Hunter's smoke, my head filled with congestion. I googled the damaged vocations' sanctuary. A slideshow of lush trails and pristine ponds promised peace and restoration. The website welcomed religious and clergy suffering from addictions and mental illness. Twelve thought my depression was situational. Would it heal once I escaped?

My email inbox dinged with a message from Pat. He'd been an incredible support during the days I was at home; we'd spoken daily. My elation vanished with the first line of his letter. He wrote to tell me that the second chance he'd offered our friendship had expired. My numerous calls, depression, and drama were too much. He said I was clinging to him and expecting him to fix everything. I was endangering his resolve and his priesthood. He was frightened that I would tell people about what had occurred between us. He couldn't even use the words "we fell in love" or "we had sex." He didn't know that while I was home, I'd told my parents. They still loved me. They would have loved him too. He felt "betrayed" because I'd called his counselor on the night I nearly drowned myself. I was never to contact him again.

The suicidal ideations returned. Pat would be better off without me. After six restless hours in bed, I remained awake, but the direction of my anger changed. A book Abdel had given me said that depression and shame were anger turned inward. It now made sense. I was done punishing myself for Pat. Someone capable of loving me wouldn't abandon me when I needed him most. I deserved better and had to get over him. The next morning, I said to Twelve, "I'm clinically depressed. Let's beat this."

Twelve prescribed an antidepressant to help me get through the coming weeks or months in the parish with Hunter. Since we didn't know how long I'd have to "play ball" with the archbishop to get my leave approved, Twelve advised me to refocus from the uncertainty of the future onto things that affirmed me in the present: my parishioners and ministry.

The ambulance had already pulled away when I opened the door of the single-wide trailer. The scent of soiled kitty litter and vomit whooshed out. I wanted to wrap my scarf over my mouth and nose, but that would send the wrong message. I needed to be the strong one.

On the couch, a middle-aged man dressed in an oil-streaked jumpsuit hugged his despondent daughter, who was my age. The other daughter stood at a distance, behind the cluttered kitchen counter, smoking a cigarette. She stroked a long-haired calico. In the center of the living room's mustard carpeting, the parishioner from the psych wing lay flat on her back with outstretched arms. The floral pattern of her terrycloth nightgown was wet with urine; her mouth, agape and discolored with vomit. Perched near her shoulder, another cat emitted quizzical meows. My counselor had said, *Depression, if left untreated, is a terminal illness.* This time, the pills had worked.

The husband and sobbing daughter collapsed into me. They squeezed me, cursed God, and begged me to anoint her. I wasn't supposed to anoint the dead. "The sacraments are for the living," my canon law professor had taught. I pulled my oil stock, a quarter-sized, golden cylinder, from my pocket. It contained a cotton ball saturated with the oil of the sick that Haggis had blessed at the annual chrism Mass. The husband and daughter sat on the couch.

"What good will that do?" the other daughter screamed and ran outside. I would chase after her later.

Kneeling at my parishioner's side, I recited the prayers, knowing that they couldn't save her. I smeared oily crosses on her forehead and palms. She'd been on antidepressants. After two weeks, my Lexapro had yet to kick in.

I woke and the psychological game of *Asteroids* that had cluttered my mind had been replaced by a vacuum of pure space. The week-old pain and guilt surrounding the death of my suicidal parishioner were gone. The voices of fear, paranoia, anger, loathing, and anxiety had been exorcised. My head felt so light that it might float off my shoulders. I walked through my appointments and Masses a priestly zombie. I no longer cared whether I disappointed or offended people. My interactions with Hunter and Dixon felt like social experiments; contradicting them and saying what I actually thought brought me mild amusement. When I met with Dixon, my logic was no longer muddled with agony. I brokered a compromise: if my pastoral counseling professor from St. Mary's—a top expert in his field—recommended to Boyle and Haggis that I go to Southdown for a psychological assessment, they would sign off on the plan. They didn't know I'd already spoken to the professor and earned his blessing. Within days, my preliminary assessment was scheduled for April, the week after my newborn niece Isabella's baptism in Washington.

Isabella slept on my chest. My brother and I had spent the morning hiking to waterfalls in the lush canyons of the Columbia River Gorge. The exercise and the Lexapro demanded that I snooze too. Her hand gripped my pinky. I relaxed into the couch and inhaled the pure scent of her dark hair. I was grateful I hadn't killed myself. Another life awaited me beyond the priesthood. Perhaps in the Northwest I could find a man, fall in love, and have children of my own. Or I could focus on my nephews and niece. I could live near them, take them camping, and be sure that they understood that no matter how hopeless certain moments seemed, life could get better.

Besides my niece and nephews, the only thing that had been giving me energy was my reading. I devoured gay-themed books about coming out, same-sex relationships, civil rights, history, and theology. These texts became my sacred canon; their gay authors, my psalmists. These men gave voice to my struggle. They called religions to account for their abuse of LGBTQ persons and challenged political institutions to legislate equality. My gay brothers and sisters existed in history. We would be heard in the present. When I poured the holy water over Isabella's head, I knew she would be the last niece or nephew I'd baptize a Catholic.

My five-day assessment at Southdown was a barrage of psychological tests, interviews, questionnaires, and essays. Psychologists, psychiatrists, nurses, and spiritual directors dissected my emotions, thoughts, and experiences. When asked to write a brief autobiography, I wrote in one sitting until forty pages explained my history of sexual abuse. When the topic of orientation came up, I was honest. In the Rorschach blots, I didn't see any female genitalia, just a number of He-Man guys and Maryland blue crabs.

In the parish hall–like dining room, I shared meals with the sixty or so residents. They were completing four- to six-month stints. Some joked about whether I'd receive "a scholarship," a prescription to move in. Hearing their tales of addiction, mental illness, and abuse in the Church, I realized that we weren't crazy. We'd just been stressed beyond the breaking point. The staff psychiatrist summarized my situation: "It's tragic, the disaster priesthood has been for you."

At the end of the week, the psychologist-assessor concluded that I suffered from dysthymia—chronic, low-grade depression. I told him that Father Scott had returned to campus ministry after his assessment in St. Louis and that I wanted to take legal action against the archdiocese to protect others from Father Scott and the archbishop. He said, "They should be the ones coming here, but the Church doesn't always work that way."

He offered me the scholarship.

Archbishop Haggis summoned me on my return. We met almost three months to the day from when I'd last seen him. Since then, he'd communicated through the medium of Father Dixon. I felt no affinity with them now. This was business. I needed health insurance and money to pay for Southdown—the cost would be in the tens of thousands. Haggis needed my silence.

We sat in the living-room portion of his office. His eyes were tired. He called me Father Rastrelli; I called him archbishop. His black clerical attire seemed faded. I sported blue jeans and a burnt orange shirt. I was done wearing his collar.

Armed with legal pads, we engaged in pleasantries.

He smiled, "How's your family?"

Now he cared about them. I clenched my pen and silently recited Number Ten's old mantra: *That was then. This is now.* The last thing I needed was to blow up or break down. My canon lawyer had prepped me: *The bishop won't admit he did anything wrong. That's not how the game is played.*

"They're well, Archbishop. Thank you."

"You have my permission to call Southdown and tell them you're coming."

"Thank you, archbishop."

He presented my options. Did I want to take a leave of absence while remaining assigned to Resurrection or resign from my post as associate pastor? If I did the latter, my leave would be announced in the archdiocesan newspaper.

"I'm resigning."

"What shall the wording be? A medical leave of absence or a leave for vocational discernment?"

"Both," I said firmly.

He looked displeased. "Well, I have no canonical reason to remove your faculties. Unless you want that." "Faculties" was canonical lingo, meaning allowance to perform sacraments. He explained that a "priest in good standing" retained his "faculties." He prescribed the wording for my letter of resignation and his promulgation in the newspaper: *Father Tom Rastrelli from associate pastor of Resurrection Parish in Dubuque to medical leave of absence at his request. He remains a priest in good standing.* He omitted vocational discernment. He stipulated that I stay in the parish three more weeks "to facilitate a smooth transition." The archdiocese would pay for Southdown and leave me on their health insurance. I would receive a stipend for travel expenses to Southdown but would not receive a salary. My canon lawyer had explained that health insurance was the least bishops were canonically required to provide priests who left ministry. Some bishops had been exposed for paying priest-pedophiles' salaries after they were accused and removed from their parishes. I just wanted the depression to end. I accepted his terms.

Haggis informed me that he wouldn't keep a file on my stint at Southdown. He would read the reports that my primary psychologist would send. I was to sign a waiver permitting Haggis to share my medical records with Boyle and Dixon. After they were finished, Haggis would return all documents to Southdown. "It's best for your safety and confidentiality," he said, with generous grin and pastoral nod. "Do you have any questions?"

"Yes." I finished scribbling his instructions on my notepad. "What did St. Louis conclude about Father Scott?"

"That's not your concern."

"I deserve to know."

"You don't." His voice was as hard as an unpadded kneeler. "I will not discuss Father Bell with you. That would be violation of professional boundaries."

"Then I have no other questions." I set down my pen. "Everything's pretty clear."

He assured me of his prayers, offered a lukewarm handshake, asked me to pray for him, and directed me to the door. Most of the staff had already left for the weekend. Again, there were no witnesses. If I sued, it was my word versus theirs.

I stood at the ambo before the people of Resurrection. Hunter loomed behind me in the presider's chair. I readied myself for the parishioners' reactions. The staff already knew; a few had confided that Hunter should have been the one seeking treatment. The parishioners' heads shook as I read, "It's with mixed emotions that I announce I am taking a leave of absence for medical reasons and vocational discernment." I explained I had dysthymia, was in counseling, and encouraged those who suffered depression to seek help. I'd committed no crimes and would remain a priest in good standing. I wanted to tell them the whole truth: that I was gay, Hunter was a drunk, Scott was an abuser, and Haggis was as bad as the bishops in the papers. I wanted to reveal my secret fantasy, how all gay priests should come out of the closet on Transfiguration Sunday, because we were the ones with the power. The bishops couldn't fire us all.

Instead, I said, "Finally, I want to make it clear that I am not leaving for any *person*. If only life were really that romantic." They applauded. Hunter had no choice but to join them.

As I greeted folks outside after the Masses, they inundated me with their experiences of depression, near suicide attempts, fights to recover, and the names, dosages, and side effects of their medications. Some said my sincerity had given them hope, inspired them to call a psychologist, or to see beyond the false stigma surrounding psychotropic medication. In my honesty, I seemed to be making a difference, but I still felt a phony. How many had been sexually abused or exploited by priests? Their struggles deserved validation too.

Hunter said nothing. We wore lilacs in public and garlic in the rectory.

"That's for the better," Twelve said. "Deal with him as little as possible. As for not telling the parish about Scott, don't be so hard on yourself. You're doing the best you can under the circumstances. Right now, you need to focus on packing and getting yourself healthy. Deal with that other stuff later."

After our session, I walked across the Loras campus. The priests of the archdiocese were gathering in the chapel for a Holy Hour followed by a banquet. The college grounds had changed since pretheology. A new library and bookstore filled what was once a field. Mom had asked me to get a sweatshirt for my cousin, who would attend Loras in the fall on a wrestling scholarship. Nine years earlier, I'd asked my parents to tell my aunt and uncle that he and his brother were at risk of being abused by Lauz. Now, I worried about the same with Father Scott.

I set the shopping bag under the pew and opened my worship aid. A dozen rows of priests buffered me from the sanctuary and archbishop. An old fellow, who'd helped me with my first wedding when I was a deacon, whispered: "I'm sorry to hear you're going. You were one of the good guys." I offered a weak smile.

A nasal voice boomed through the speakers, "Please join in our opening hymn, 'God of Day and God of Darkness.'" Father Scott sat at the piano, speaking into the mic. His eyes scanned the congregation. He grinned at me. I flashed back to Dr. Lauz's leering at me at the country club. I dropped my head and stared at the distressed grain of the pew. Priests blocked me in on both sides. They rose and sang. Panic burned in my chest. I stood but couldn't inhale to sing. Strobes of black and white fluttered in my field of vision like an old movie. I clutched the pew and dropped into my seat. A hand gently squeezed my shoulder. Ev stood behind me. I concentrated on his support and slowly regained my breath.

Ev and the rest of our group sat with me at the banquet that followed. I hadn't retreated, because I knew this would be our last supper. Plus, I wanted to show Scott and Haggis that I wasn't intimidated. The men in black encircling the round tables of the reception hall were my brother priests too. Even though I was leaving, I still had a place at their table.

Sometime between the main course and dessert, before the antsy guys started leaving, Archbishop Haggis stepped onto a small stage and took the microphone. He thanked us for coming and said something about the signs of the times making it more important to gather in support of our shared vocation. Across the table, a few guys from my group exchanged incensed glances. Haggis expounded the need for all Catholics to claim and sustain our heritage and identity. More than ever, we needed to empower educators to witness the faith and pass it on to our children. He announced that he'd entrusted this duty to a new archdiocesan committee on "Catholic identity." He smiled and said, "I'm proud to announce the new Director of Catholic Identity, Father Scott Bell."

The priests applauded. A few tables away, Father Scott hopped up. His smile stretched wide. Archbishop Haggis shook his overtanned hand and hugged him. Throughout the banquet hall, the black mass of clerics rose in ovation.

Baffled, Ev and my support group refused to stand. They remained with me until I could leave.

I received an email two mornings later.

Dear Tom,

It was good to see you (even if at a distance) at Monday's gathering. I would really be pleased if we could chat at least a litle [*sic*] before you leave. I realize you don't owe me anything, and do not want to cause you any more stress, but maybe I could ease some pain. Either way, I am praying for you daily.

God's peace, Scott

I responded:

Scott,

I don't have time to get together and chat, but if you have something to say, you can use email. I hope you are getting help.

Thank you for the prayers, Tom

He didn't reply.

The weekend of my final Masses at Resurrection, there wasn't a banquet. Not even coffee and donuts. The regular crowds attended. The standard songs were sung. Beforehand, the usual sins were confessed. Out of the hundreds that celebrated my ordination and first Mass, only four attended my last: Mom, Dad, Uncle Jim, and Aunt Karen—the four who kept vigil during my first deposition. They sat in the fifth pew of the center right choir.

When I stepped to the altar to pray my final eucharistic prayer, I noticed Mom and Dad crying. I would mourn with them eventually, but in that moment I felt elation. For I no longer feared the future. I no longer feared myself. Outside, charcoal fields sprouted. The Mississippi flowed. An entire world existed beyond the walls of the Church. I focused on the words I'd known since childhood and the gestures my body performed without thought. I extended the paten. I stood *in persona Christi* and consecrated the bread. When I genuflected behind the altar, I no longer prayed, "Help my unbelief."

PART VI

BEAUTIFUL CHILD

2019

And when they finally fall
These wailing walls and burdened
  crosses
God's twilight and all

How I'll feel like a beautiful child
Such a beautiful child again.
—Rufus Wainwright

EPILOGUE

WE ARE THE CHAMPIONS

Freddie's mustache nicks the microphone as he plays the piano and belts the opening lines, "I've paid my dues, time after time . . ." I watch from my chair as YouTube transports me and the anthem I've associated with straight men at sporting events for the past thirty years back into Wembley Stadium, 1985. Surrounded by a sea of swaying arms and voices, Freddie Mercury, outed and HIV-positive, sings, "We are the champions, my friends," and I begin to sob.

I'm forty-five, the same age as Freddie when AIDS claimed him in 1991. I don't recall the day he died. I remember little of him from my Iowa youth other than he was a punchline. But the man on my television transcends life. He channels an unbridled energy, a spirit I recognize. Strutting around in his tight white pants and fingering his phallic microphone, he is unabashedly alive, sexy, powerful, honest, beautiful, masculine, and gay. And I feel proud. To be alive. To be like him. And to be me.

I needed that tonight. There's a letter from Father Dixon on my desk with a deadline: May 23, 2019, fifteen years to the day since my final Masses at Resurrection. The certified letters from Dubuque and the Vatican that have found my Oregon mailbox over the past two years have come to fruition. In March, the Congregation for Clerics laicized me, effectively nullifying my ordination. To get a copy of the Vatican-issued "Document of the loss of the clerical state, together with the related dispensation from priestly obligations, including celibacy," I had to meet a local monsignor by the deadline and sign the Latin document after he read the English translation. Until now I'd refused to respond to the letters and cede the Church power over me. But I wanted that document for posterity.

Three weeks ago, I dressed in my fuchsia wingtips, matching polo shirt, and pink glasses. Over my lunchbreak, I walked from the university where I work to the monsignor's parish four blocks away. When I entered his drab office, I flashed back to the twenty-year-old boy sitting in Father Scott's rocking chair. That kid oozed potential, creativity, and energy. He'd wanted to help people, to love and be loved. He'd been eager to ask difficult questions about Catholicism and to make sense of his spirituality, sexuality, and vocation. Unwittingly, he'd walked into the Church's crowded closet.

The oppressiveness of that closet immediately returned when the monsignor shook my hand. He read the letter's litany of rights that I'd lost, such as teaching, preaching, holding leadership positions in Catholic institutions, and celebrating the sacraments. As he read that I could now be married in the Church, I thought of my husband of eight years, Bruce. The Church would never recognize the love of our union. I asked for a clarification about the canons that allowed me to still hear confessions for those in danger of death, in case my parents or the few Catholics still in my life were ever in need. I signed the letter with my married name, "Mayhall Rastrelli." I waited by the door as he made copies. He didn't wish me well or offer any pastoral assistance but stood silently as I took the facsimiles, turned, and departed the rectory.

As I walked back to campus, paragraph 6 of the document, which called for the archbishop to take care that my "new condition" didn't "cause scandal to the faithful," strummed my anger. And a sudden, deep grief overwhelmed me. I mourned for that naïve kid who had trusted his life and heart to Father Scott and the Church. They scandalized him, but the Church still doesn't care.

After all the years, the trauma still cuts deep. Counselor Number Something, a cisgender, straight Native American Jew who uses she/her pronouns, continues the work of the twelve and more that preceded her. Stories like mine of young men being sexually exploited and abused by their ecclesial superiors have only recently garnered the outrage and sympathy of front-page headlines. After many years of relative inner tranquility, I again find myself full of wrath. My counselor calls it chronic trauma. The abuses of power I experienced—the power plays and exchanges, gaslighting, and mindfucking—feed it when triggered by current events.

But tonight, Queen rocks my walls, and Freddie flamboyantly blows kisses to the 1.5 billion people cheering in the stadium and on the other side of the Live Aid broadcast. His presence, love, defiance, and joy lift my aggrieved souls: the wounded 45-year-old man and the shame-filled gay boy unite with the queen who is leading the frightened, AIDS-ridden world of my youth in proclaiming, "We are the champions of the world."

Through the picture window to the east, Mount Hood's snowcapped triangular peak reflects lavender in the last light of day. Queen sings on as the high clouds fade from pink to blue. I am safe in a house of love as I look eastward to the setting sun.

ACKNOWLEDGMENTS

When I decided to become a writer in 2005, I wrote everything I could remember about my life. If I couldn't figure out how to illustrate my own story, how could I tell others'? The resulting manuscript was the first of many drafts that ultimately became this memoir. I am indebted to many people and communities for their support, encouragement, and generosity during these years.

My husband, Bruce Mayhall Rastrelli, thank you for listening to me read my drafts, helping me cut tens of thousands of words, and encouraging me when I'd given up. My parents, Tom and Jill Rastrelli, thank you for believing in me and growing with me. My sister Maria and the extended Spencer family, thanks for supporting me from the beginning of this endeavor. Cousins Tamara Rood and Abigail Bowman, thanks for your feedback. My grandparents, Rita and Dale Figgins, thanks for being my biggest fans; I wish you were alive to celebrate.

Thank you, University of Southern California Master of Professional Writing program faculty and classmates, especially my mentor M. G. Lord, Janet Fitch, Tim Kirkman, Orly Minazad, and Sara Lowe. Thank you, Amanda Fletcher. Thank you, Mary Roach, Garrard Conley, Michelangelo Signorile, Dr. Richard Wagner, Paul Dinas, and Patrick Merla. Thank you, Grunewald Guild, Musical Theatre Wenatchee, Clergy Project, Nicole Criona and LA Writers Group, and the New York Summer Writers Institute.

Thanks to my Salem writing community and readers: Jennifer Hillman-Magnuson, Isabel Choi, Carlee Wright, Victor Panichkul, Peter and Kathleen Vanderwall, Ricardo De Mambro Santos, B. J. Toewe and John Goodyear, Heather Toller, Jillian Sternke, the *Statesman Journal* news team, and my Willamette University colleagues. Thank you, Frank Miller, for the headshot. A special thanks to my friends—the poker crew, the gays, my neighbors, and Pentacle Theatre—for keeping me grounded in the joy and laughter of the present.

Thank you, James McCoy and University of Iowa Press, for giving my story a chance.

Finally, I extend my deepest gratitude to Abdel Sepulveda, Matt Grey, Geoff Farrow, Mark Zangrando, and my brothers who survived the seminary and priesthood. This story is as much yours as it is mine.